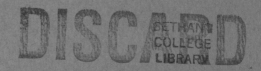

The World After Keynes

The World After Keynes

AN EXAMINATION
OF THE ECONOMIC ORDER

Eric Roll

FREDERICK A. PRAEGER, *Publishers*
New York · Washington · London

FREDERICK A. PRAEGER, PUBLISHERS
111 Fourth Avenue, New York, N.Y. 10003, U.S.A.
77-79 Charlotte Street, London W.1, England

Published in the United States of America in 1968
by Frederick A. Praeger, Inc., Publishers

© 1968 by Encyclopædia Britannica, Inc.

Library of Congress Catalog Card Number: 67-22295

THE WORLD AFTER KEYNES: AN EXAMINATION OF
THE ECONOMIC ORDER is a *Britannica Perspective*
prepared to commemorate the 200th anniversary of
Encyclopædia Britannica.

Printed in the United States of America

Introduction

"Everything flows," said the Greek philosopher Heraclitus. You cannot step into the same river twice: the second time it is a different river. So with economics or, indeed, with any branch of knowledge; as you try to say what it is about, it is in fact undergoing a change, both in the material with which it deals and in the way in which it deals with it. However, the attempt must be made, and it is to some extent eased by the fact that economic life and economic thinking, separately and in their interrelation with each other, do not progress in a vacuum. Something already exists; something has already happened in the past; and what is to happen in the future—however much of a change it may, in retrospect, be thought to have brought about—must link up with what already exists and can be seen to have done so. Briefly, therefore, what is attempted here is to show what economics has been about in the past, what it is about now, and what it is likely to be about in the next few decades.

Historians of economic thought, as in other branches of knowledge, all too easily fall into one or another extreme manner of approach. Some are so impressed by the continuous nature of the evolution of their subject that they tend to seek in the distant past rudimentary expressions of the highly developed theories of today, claiming that fragmentary references of older writers can be construed as foretelling the more sophisticated developments of a later age. Others, impressed with the significance of what in retrospect are clearly discernible as great watersheds in the history of their chosen discipline, tend to think of evolution as a discontinuous process: as something that takes place by discrete leaps from one age to another, each marked by some great revolutionary development.

v

The dilemma implicit in the choice of one or the other of these approaches is perhaps especially acute in a subject so relatively new as economics. As a systematic, scientific study the discipline is barely 200 years old. True, elements of present day economic thinking can be found in the specific writings and the handed-down traditions of thought of the last 2,000 years or more. In this respect, the Middle Ages, for one example, have undergone a steady process of revaluation, and research is constantly uncovering neglected treasures. Modern historiography has been responsible for a blurring of the chronological limits of that epoch; and it is now accepted that what was at one time regarded as a relatively barren period of several hundred years—barren both in material development and in the concomitant evolution of economic thought—was in fact a fertile epoch in which progress did not cease. In fact, it was quite considerable between the fall of Rome and the discovery of the New World. But when all is said and done, the fragments of economic thought to be found in the Bible, in the Greek philosophers, in the practical doctrines of Roman lawyers, and in those often interesting and ingenious analyses of medieval writings amount in total to very little when measured against the tremendous outpourings of doctrine and analysis that marked the fifty years or so on each side of the year 1800.

Economics, therefore, still must be seen as the child of the modern age, born of philosophic radicalism, of the consolidation of the nation-state, of industrial capitalism, and of world commerce. It was not until these aspects of modern society, reflected both in the material arrangements of life and in the field of thought, had become predominant that economics as a scientific discipline made its appearance. The body of economic doctrine we possess today is intimately linked with the other advances in thought rooted in historical developments of the last 200 years—the age of enlightenment and revolution, the industrial revolution of the 18th and 19th centuries, the uninterrupted and ever accelerating technological advance of the last 150 years. Economics is imbued with the spirit of enterprise that is responsible for the exploitation of these technological developments and discoveries—the same spirit that is giving rise to the development of a worldwide economic system based on world trade and a world monetary system.

It would not, therefore, be surprising if the issues currently preoccupying economists, and those that are likely to preoccupy them in the future, are found to bear a strong family resemblance to those identified in other branches of the social sciences. For these, too, are the children of the scientific technological epoch that has evolved in the last 200 years.

I consider it wrong to limit one's study of the history of economics to either of the extreme doctrines mentioned above. I do not believe there is an inevitable contradiction between acceptance of a subject's continuous process of evolution, and the recognition of occasional "leaps" which in retrospect can be seen to mark revolutionary change. Both explanations of the process of change have their part to play. Sir William Petty certainly built on earlier thinkers; and Adam Smith certainly built on Sir William Petty. Nevertheless, the writings of Petty, rightly regarded as the first example of economics as a scientific body of analysis, mark a significant advance over anything that had gone before. And Smith's *Wealth of Nations* (1776), written about 100 years after Petty and containing much of what he had already given the world, is so utterly different in its self-confidence and self-consciousness, and in the extent to which a systematic and comprehensive body of doctrine is evolved and expounded, as to be rightly regarded as marking the beginning of the great new era of political economy we have come to call the classical.

If one were dealing only with the past, that is, with the way in which present day economics has evolved over the last 200 years, the problem of method would perhaps not matter greatly. Emphasis on one or the other method would be largely a matter of taste, and argument about it would be relatively barren. But the aim of this essay is to portray what a thoughtful reader would wish to know standing midstream and looking both backward and forward. Thus, the problem of deciding on the significance of continuity as against discontinuity cannot be dismissed.

Take, for example, the developments of the 30 years since Keynes's *General Theory of Employment, Interest and Money* was published (1936). This work undoubtedly marked a most important change in economic thinking, and was seen to do so at the time. The world was then halfway between the beginning of the great economic depression and the outbreak of World War II. Much has happened since—the agony and devastation of war, the miracle of economic rebirth, and the literally fabulous advances in science and technology that to some extent have affected most of the social sciences. Yet it can be argued with some reason that economics alone has hardly been touched by these great events. Advances there have been, as will be seen in later parts of this essay. But Keynes's work seems to stand as the last searching reexamination of the heart and core of economic theory.

There are still echoes of the debate, now well past its centenary, between Marxist and neoclassical economists, but not much of this is heard anywhere in professional circles, and there is certainly very little in it to exercise the general body of economic practitioners. Economics seems—miraculously—to have ceased to be the battleground of conflicting ideologies. As we shall see, there are many and sometimes very profound differences of view on particular issues, especially where specific points of economic policy are concerned. But, while it may be going too far (paraphrasing Sir William Harcourt) to say that "we are all Keynesians now," it seems that in our analytical moments most economists are prepared to take the innovations of Keynes and his disciples for granted.

A number of questions immediately arise. Does this appearance of theoretical peace and quiet correspond to reality? If it does, how is this extraordinary change to be interpreted and explained? Does it mean that the 1930s marked a great revolution in economic thinking akin to that of, say, the Smith-Ricardo epoch some 130 years earlier, or the somewhat less extensive change that occurred in the latter years of the 19th century, and the beginning of the 20th century, with the emergence of the neoclassical marginalist school? Or is it to be thought that it has taken all this time for economics to come of age and that, at last, with the emergence of Keynesian doctrines, economics can now take its rightful place among the sciences? Is it now to be regarded as forever free from the continual uprooting of its foundations which marked its early years and which is sometimes the distinguishing sign of an infant science? Can one assume that, by and large, economists are now united in a consensus as to the purpose of their subject, and, broadly, as to the character of the analytical tools at their disposal; and can one, therefore, be confident that from now on economics will march happily along, only adding to its tool box the latest mathematical techniques?

Even more difficult questions arise when one tries to relate the developments in the field of theory to those in the world of economic practice. One does not have to be a devotee of any narrow "economic interpretation" to accept the simple fact that some relation exists between the economic arrangements of society in any given epoch and man's theorizing about it. Clearly, the economic ideas, fragmentary though they were, of Aristotle were much affected by the kind of society he lived in. By the same token, the doctrines of the Austrian (marginalist) school on price or market values, let alone the sophisticated notions of the present-day national income analysis, would have been simply irrelevant to the society of Aristotle's day. True enough, a sophisticated body of doctrine can very often be applied—always assuming that adequate quantitative data are available—to more primitive societies than the one in which it originated. The reverse process too is possible, but both are of very doubtful relevance.

It is therefore pertinent to ask at some point whether the developments of the last thirty years—and, a fortiori, the developments one might forecast for the decades immediately ahead—have resulted, or are likely to result, from other major changes in the economic structure. Thus, one may ask whether the preponderance of the Keynesian type of analysis, with all that has been built upon it in the way of a national accounting approach to economic problems, is due to some profound change in the nature of our economic order. If so, will the next epoch of economic thinking (assuming the economic order continues to exhibit those features that distinguish it from earlier ones) run generally along the lines prevalent today?

It is as well to say early that broadly speaking I accept the proposition that, for the moment at least, major doctrinal disputes have been relegated to the background. Though economic reality differs in different parts of the globe, and is reflected in different systems of economic organization, there is remarkably little basic doctrinal disagreement among economists, however sharp may be the controversy over precise application of the available theoretical body of analysis in the field of policy.

I propose to deal with these and related problems broadly under two aspects. First I endeavour to describe the present body of economic thinking as it emerged from, and differs from, earlier economic theory. This I hope is neither an exercise in pure description nor an exposition of elementary economic principles. Nor will it be wholly historical. It is rather a critical analysis of present-day economic theory, with emphasis on those aspects which are specifically different from the pre-Keynesian body of economics, together with some attempt at interpretation of the relationship of theoretical development to the changes in economic reality.

Secondly, I propose to go over somewhat the same ground but with the emphasis on developing trends of evolution in the future.

Here I encounter a dilemma in regard to method somewhat similar to that encountered in respect to historical interpretation. In viewing future developments in economics two approaches are possible. The first is to look at the existing economic situation and try to identify individual elements that may have a dynamic character, *i.e.,* those which continue to constitute areas of tension in economic reality as well as in economic thinking. One could then safely make the assumption that these will be the sources of future evolution of economic problems, as well as of future attempts at solving them. From a large number of these individual "growth points" a comprehensive picture of the future could then perhaps be constructed.

A second method would be to find a broad pattern in past history and isolate within it those trends that have been most operative, extrapolating from these the broad pattern of future development—from which individual features could then be derived.

The difficulty of the first method is that there are so many possible dynamic points in the present situation that could be selected as areas of tension. Here one risks giving too free a rein to individual idiosyncrasies in assigning orders of importance to individual issues. Moreover, even if individual tastes and pre-conceptions are curbed, the multiplicity of individual issues can, at least, make for considerable confusion.

But the second method is, if anything, more hazardous still. It can easily lapse into an exercise in extreme historicism—the application of some highly simplified abstraction as the mainsprings of historical change. Historiography abounds in these all-embracing explanations, from Arnold Toynbee's challenge-response pattern to Marx's class struggle, and in these extreme forms it has, rightly, suffered a major decline in recent decades. Nevertheless, the hankering after simplification of complicated issues remains a most powerful tendency of human thinking: understandably, the desire for order as well as comprehension is always present. This corresponds, moreover, not only to ob-served regularities in the physical universe but also to very strict limitations imposed by man's own nature upon the variety of change and evolution he can undergo during a historically meaningful time span.

Neither of the two approaches can, therefore, serve in isolation. For the rea-son given, I would regard primary reliance on the second method as potentially too misleading to be safe. The attempt must therefore be made, in spite of the difficulty, to proceed in the first place from the known facts: the economic problems of today and the body of explanation and analysis now available. On this basis, when something like a reasonably comprehensive picture of possible future developments has been achieved, it can be subjected to certain tests, checking the emergent outline of the future against the pattern of past develop-ment. With due care against the excesses of historicism, it may be possible to avoid the abstractions of historical dynamism, and simply check the results to see whether they make sense as a whole in the light of what one knows about the past.

It is at this stage too that the economic universe and economic science be-come less capable of being viewed in isolation. Whether one's view of the fu-ture makes sense cannot be stated with any confidence on economic grounds alone; the whole range of the social sciences becomes relevant.

One final word of caution. The second aspect of this essay must not be thought of as an exercise in prophecy. I suppose that in the physical sciences, and perhaps even more so in the field of technology, it is possible to make meaningful forecasts by applying a high degree of imagination to certain possi-bilities that are already known to exist today, if only in embryo. Thus in med-icine or physics "unfinished business" can be readily defined, the elements of future solutions identified, and, on the basis of informed guesswork, a predic-tion made whose main (though not only) uncertainty in achievement may well be in timing.

In economics (as in many other social sciences) progress is, I believe, necessarily more sluggish and uncertain. The organization of society and people's thinking about social problems are not easily and quickly adapted even to what may appear to many as the inexorable demands of a changing situation.

Furthermore, agreement on what is "unfinished business" in economics is much more difficult, because the issues are much more contentious. Is the devising of new or easier forms of international liquidity to cope with balance-of-payments disruptions on the social (and political) agenda and, if so, how high up? Is the provision of greater individual economic security a proper and/or inevitable task of the next decade, particularly if it involves a choice between a higher and a lower rate of economic growth? These and hundreds of other economic questions as to the objectives of policy are clearly in quite a different category from, say, the continuing search for a cure for cancer; or, in expectations of realization, from that of the replacement of existing sources of energy by nuclear power. Nevertheless, it is possible to speculate meaningfully about the future on the basis both of past evolution and of existing situations, though some measure of daring is necessary. This I propose to supply.

Contents

PART ONE

PROBLEMS AND INSTITUTIONS

Chapter 1 Boundaries of the Economic Order

DEFINITION AND CLASSIFICATION are tedious: arguments about them can be time-consuming, arid, and in the last resort confusing. But a modicum of definition is an indispensable working tool.

Fortunately, since this is not an elementary introduction, either to the economic world or to the world of economics, we need not be unduly meticulous about these matters. Nor need we spend too much time on the changes the definition of the economic order has undergone over the centuries. For our purpose it is sufficient to think of as *economic* that activity which is directed to the satisfaction of man's material wants. (Whether these wants arise from biological, psychological, social, or other compulsions is not immediately important from our point of view.) The *process of economic activity* consists of the application of resources—material and human, directly or indirectly—to the desired end. *Economics* studies the problems that arise in this process. I propose to apply the label "the economic order" to the sum total of the arrangements existing at any one time by which economic activity is carried on, together with the sum total of human speculation about these arrangements.

Thus labeled, the scope is wide. We need more landmarks to find our way around in this large area. It is at once clear that even the simplest description of economic activities cannot be meaningful if it does not distinguish certain obvious differences in the way in which they are performed by different groups of people. First of all there are states—national entities with separate legal frameworks—which interpose barriers to many kinds of economic intercourse with other states. The character of the arrangements within one state may differ from those of another to such an extent as to raise the question whether the same economic order can be said to embrace both.

Is it possible to distinguish and classify states or groups of states in a manner that assists in arriving at an appreciation of the economic order as a whole? One way of doing so is on the basis of the level of material satisfaction permitted by their resources, and their arrangements for employing them. Of the more than 3 billion people in the world today, it is probable that no more than one-sixth enjoy to a significant degree and extent the full capabilities of today's

3

resources. These fortunate few eat between 2,000 and 3,000 calories per day and their diet is varied; they enjoy relatively high standards of housing, clothing, transport, education, and entertainment; and they benefit from arrangements designed to make these advantages secure in the face of the natural vicissitudes of life.

A substantial part of the remainder have risen little above the bare subsistence level. The largest number, those in between, are in varying stages of development, sometimes mirroring an earlier level through which the more advanced economies passed a long time ago, and sometimes exhibiting features for which no clear historical parallels exist. It is not surprising that these marked differences of development should be reflected in varying arrangements that affect the character of the economic order of these groups.

In addition—though not in any manner correlated with the level of their economic development—these groups differ from one another because of different political or politico-economic organizations. These differences range from the quite limited results of the relative provision made for defense or for social services, to much wider divergencies reflecting different doctrines about the proper organization of society, doctrines which derive from the different roles assigned to the individual and to individual decisions.

From the standpoint of ease of analysis and exposition it is unfortunate that these two methods of classification, *i.e.*, by level of economic development or by differences in politico-economic organization, do not coincide. The rich, the developing, and the primitive countries are not coterminous with the capitalist, socialist, and "mixed-economy" countries. We are thus faced with a bewildering range of combinations on the basis of these two distinguishing characteristics alone.

The Neoclassical Base

Is it then possible to talk about the economic order in any meaningful way? An affirmative answer is readily provided by the very foundation of neoclassical economic theory. This begins by contrasting the infinity of wants with the limitation of resources for satisfying them, goes on to say that the economic problem is therefore the problem of allocating scarce resources, and concludes that economics must be the study of the implications of the choice thus forced upon the individual. Thus conceived, neither economic activity nor theorizing about it can be fundamentally different, whatever the level of development or the political framework of a country.

A large part of the existing body of economic doctrine still consists of the theories constructed on the foundations laid by earlier scholars during the thirty or so years each side of 1900, say from 1870 to 1930. It consists essentially of an ever more elaborate working out of the implications of the basic *economic* situation as defined in terms of scarcity. There can be no doubt that this body of doctrine has made a vital contribution to our understanding of economic reality. Its exponents are probably not exaggerating when they argue that what distinguishes the approach of one trained in economics from that of an amateur is precisely this ability to see an economic problem as one of allocation, and thus to be able to formulate it in terms of alternative choices. In view of what follows, I think that I should emphasize this. Again and again the value of an economic training—even in the limited neoclassical sense alone—has been demonstrated by the fact that it leads to the asking of more important questions in regard to issues of public policy than would be produced by an approach based merely on technological or accounting considerations. The latest and most sophisticated application is to problems of defense, where it takes the form of so-called cost-effectiveness or cost-benefit studies.

The neoclassical approach by itself nevertheless has serious limitations. It can be applied to one problem at a time, but its relevance is quickly exhausted when a multiplicity of complex problems have to be tackled at once. There is a further, more fundamental difficulty. To apply the neoclassical method alone involves acceptance of the theory that the implications of choice are the same for the economy as a whole as they are for the individual. This point of view was most clearly expressed by Adam Smith when he said that "what is prudence in the conduct of every private family can scarce be folly in that of a great kingdom." This view was evolved in connection with the problems of foreign trade and was applied in Smith's devastating attack on protectionism in every form. But the same thought is thematic in his whole work and came to inspire the outlook of neoclassical economics on all questions of public policy. Economic analysis of the behaviour of the "economizing" individual, and the Victorian virtues of prudence that should inspire individual conduct, went hand-in-hand and were thought to provide also the correct maxims for the management of the economy as a whole.

It was the supreme achievement of Keynes to have shown, against the backdrop of the Great Depression, that considerations which apply to the combined effect of the actions of a large number of individuals (and to the actions of the collective authority, particularly the state) differ from those that apply to the conduct of a single individual. The Keynesian view was decisively confirmed in the process of solving the great allocation problems of a global war.

In one sense, Keynes's appreciation of the "aggregates" of the economic process, greatly elaborated later by economic, statistical, and econometric advances in the national accounting technique, was not entirely new. Smith and Ricardo too had dealt in aggregates, notably the factors of production and their shares in the national product, wages, rent, interest, and profits. Indeed it was their view of the "overall" movement of these categories that constituted the true emancipation of political economy from prescientific forms. And against this achievement it could be argued that the neoclassicists with their excessive concern for marginal price theory represented a regression, perhaps a lapse into an outmoded Aristotelian concern with the problems of a handicraft economy.

What is new is that in synthesizing, or at least making possible a synthesis, between the economics of the aggregates and the marginal analysis of price movements within a market economy, Keynes immeasurably enlarged our area of understanding of the total economic process. As a result of the work that has followed in the last twenty years we can now distinguish between those problems for which it is appropriate to rely on careful calculation of "a little more or a little less," and those for which we have to use analysis of the economic solar system with its individual constellations (government expenditure, private investment, private consumption, etc., etc.), moving in a grand procession, determinable and measurable as the result of the interaction of a process of mutual attraction and repulsion.

If economics now possesses separate tools of analysis for individual and for collective conduct, the question arises whether it is possible and useful to distinguish different types of economic order by reference to the area left for decision by the individual and that which must be the subject of collective decision in one form or another. Alternatively, regardless of the pattern of social and political organization established for achieving this distinction in practice, is it useful to distinguish between areas of theory on this basis? This is in fact the distinction traceable to Keynes, which has become accepted in the last twenty-five years or so, between *macroeconomics* and *microeconomics*. These, briefly defined, can be said to deal respectively with the manner in which national income is determined, and with that in which relative prices of particular goods and services are determined.

The great advantage of this new definition is, first, that it is as capable of universal application as the classical system of political economy, or the marginalism of the catallactic (or "choice" and behaviourism) schools of the first decades of this century. Like them, it is not bound in by social or political institutions. Where it could be argued that the ineluctable nature of choice in the allocation of scarce resources is unaffected by the political character of society, so it can now be said that macroeconomic and microeconomic problems exist in all societies regardless of their political organization. The distinction between them is as applicable to a Western democracy as it is to a Communist system or to a semidemocratic, semidictatorial system in an underdeveloped country where strong tribal features survive. What will differ is the range of problems to which the two branches of economics are relevant. The great additional virtue of the new economics is that through its macroeconomic approach it has acquired a relevance to the most important problems of economic reality that the older theories lacked.

Thus, although the new economics is at least as "universal" as the old, it enables us to approach the problems of different types of society with greater discrimination. The old economics would have told us that each of the three broad groups we distinguished earlier had the same problem: to organize (simply or in a complicated manner) the maintenance and improvement of its standard of living.

But today we can penetrate much more deeply and distinguish issues according to the level of the standard of living already achieved, and according to the type of social organization. These issues will thus be very different according to whether, say, the impact of defense expenditure is great or negligible, whether there is a balance-of-payments problem, whether there is much or little collective provision for welfare services, whether the "private" sector is virtually untrammeled or is severely limited by the operation of a substantial "public" sector.

The Common Tendencies

There are a number of major tendencies at work in the world today which are steadily leading to an increasing similarity in the economic problems to which all types of societies are subject.

There is the increasing pressure to remove gross inequalities in living standards within a nation and between nations. This tendency may not be continuously successful; indeed there is some evidence that it has suffered some reverses recently. But its existence and the fact that it is now almost universally acknowledged as beneficent, nay, virtuous, is extremely important.

As living standards rise consumers' wants are seen to be subject to relatively more frequent changes. There is thus an "explosive" tendency associated with the improvement of the standard of living (a fact already noted by earlier economists).

The application of energy (and of new forms of energy) and of science and new technological advances is constantly increasing in importance; and it is doing so at an accelerating rate.

These tendencies produce a continuously increasing need for the provision of capital, and this in turn produces a continually increasing use of and reliance upon large-scale organization of business enterprise.

Material progress is always and everywhere accompanied by reliance on the social or communal satisfaction of an increasing number of wants. Many of these—such as security in the economic and social sense—have historically developed as an effective political demand only after material standards had improved to a certain level.

Finally, higher living standards are always and everywhere associated with increasing pressure for social fluidity and economic mobility.

It is no exaggeration to say that in all countries that are touched at all by world trade and international social intercourse all these tendencies are at work. Their relative strength may vary from one country to another, although not necessarily in any discernible correlation with the existing standard of living or with the country's political structure. Taken together they are the distinguishing features of the dynamism of the modern economic order.

It is not surprising, therefore, that this similarity of the real forces at work should be matched by a similarity in the analysis adopted to understand the economic process and in the tools of policy chosen to master it. I have already described the theoretical changes which produced the macroeconomic approach of today. Associated with it—in a causal relationship, which it is by no means easy to disentangle—is a major change in dominant economic ideology.

Despite repeated and often successful attempts to displace it, or at least to limit it severely, the prevailing theory of the hundred years preceding the Great Depression of the Thirties held that the fruitfulness of government participation in economic affairs was strictly limited. Society was best served by allowing the individual to pursue his own advantage with only a minimum of restraint, the degree of which was determined by the minimum need to protect the weaker members of the community, notably the young. The average adult in striving for his own economic advancement would come up against spontaneous limits imposed by the competition of others similarly engaged; the maximum social good consistent with individual freedom would be the automatic result.

This was the basis of Adam Smith's theory of governance in economic affairs by an "invisible hand." It received its final blow when the Great Depression demonstrated that the system it produced was incapable of preventing mass unemployment of human and material resources while elementary human wants went unsatisfied even in communities that commanded a high degree of scientific and technological knowledge. The demands of common sense, no less than of common humanity, finally taught—first a few theorists and statesmen, later a larger and larger proportion of the business community—that the mainsprings of government economic action could not be the same as those that motivated the individual businessman. Once government ceased to act on the principles of private business, it ceased to be concerned exclusively with its own accounts and began to look at those of the economy as a whole, and to recognize the controlling part its own actions played in their ultimate determination. Thus came the enduring synthesis of the Keynesian theory of employment, of the newfound readiness for government intervention, and of the statistical techniques of national accounting.

As usually happens, each of these advances supported the other. Freedom from the trammels of a rigid conception of the proper sphere of government action greatly stimulated theoretical advances beyond Keynes. This in turn brought forth new statistical needs and directed attention to new methods of economic measurement. And as more statistical data and measurements became available more possibilities were opened up for analytical techniques and, once a possibly fruitful area for action had been identified, for the development of the necessary governmental techniques of stimulation and control.

Taken together these advances have greatly enhanced man's understanding of the complex economy of the second half of the 20th century, and have helped to enlarge his ability to deal with its problems. Moreover it is not only those who analyze the economy, or those who control it from the political centre, who are increasingly conscious of and influenced by these advances. More and more "economic men," *i.e.,* individual businessmen, tend to familiarize themselves with macroeconomic data and to be influenced by them in their own microeconomic decisions. This is in fact the most recent and most striking development in the advance of the new economics, and its full significance cannot yet be adequately assessed. I shall return to it later.

In describing these recent advances I may have given the impression that we are on the threshold of an era in which the regulation of economic process can be regarded as approaching that of a fully automated factory. Even a casual glance at the facts would quickly dispel any such illusion. The world is still plagued by grossly inadequate living standards for the vast bulk of its population, and even the few so-called affluent societies are far from having achieved their recognized social objectives. They still suffer from cyclical economic fluctuations, albeit less violent ones than in previous decades, from balance-of-payment difficulties, and from inadequate growth rates. No forward look at the next few decades is going to discern an absence of problems or the need for further advances in theory and in the techniques of formulating economic policy.

Chapter 2   The Sources of Change

ONE OF THE PRIMARY AREAS of tension likely to produce changes in the economic situation of mankind and in theorizing about it (the total forming the economic order as here defined) is that between the individual and society, always
changing in its content, as yet unresolved in its essentials. On the one hand we
have the traditional individual freedoms: free consumer choice, free choice of
occupation, untrammeled exercise of free enterprise, and unrestricted enjoyment of private property. But these freedoms are constantly at odds with social
restraints which are not only the inevitable consequence of men living together,
but alone can give content and reality to individual striving.

Modern methods of creating wants and directing consumers' choices have
long since been recognized as making nonsense of any extreme emphasis on the
"god-given" right of individual choice in the marketplace. The facts of large-
scale economic organization, with its growing bureaucratic management and
dependence of scientific, commercial, financial, and industrial specialists, have
long since changed the scope and character of traditional individual enterprise.

The constantly shifting frontier between public and private consumption
demonstrates another critical aspect of tension between the individual and society In the United States, for example, prosperous suburban communities in-
habited largely by those who might be thought most anxious to preserve free
private consumption often also provide outstanding examples of concern for
maintaining and enlarging the scope of public goods—be they national defense
expenditure or local spending on schools, parks, or churches. And the changing equipoise between individual and society is profoundly affected by the impact of the "authority" (not only, though predominantly, the state) on a vast
range of private activities, through the regulation of monopolies, the control of
urban development, the planning of roads, scientific research, and education.
and the exercise of control over monetary policy and international trade relations, to say nothing of channeling billions of dollars through government con-
tracts.

Another area of tension is that between the acknowledged demands of the
present and the anticipated demands of the future. The dilemma in the case of
the individual is plain enough. His life span, his working day, and his capacity

10

for enjoyment (in addition to that which he gets from the exercise of the "instinct of workmanship") are all limited. Each individual want—though the totality of these wants and the interrelationship of intensity among them is highly if not infinitely variable—is always satiable. Family feeling and civic responsibility, however, act in varying measure to moderate a man's concern for his individual and present satisfaction. They provide some incentive (sometimes powerfully) to make provision for the future. In a time of rapid technological change many see it as increasingly important to make some capital provision within an individual's own lifetime if present standards are to be maintained through time.

This urge to save, and the possibility of raising material standards in the future, affects both the individual and the community, and is frequently in conflict with the desire for present satisfaction. The process by which the dilemma is resolved has become highly complex. It has become increasingly difficult to trace back from the actual economic result a clear line to the individual's decision, whether taken in relation to his own "economy" or made in the social and political sphere on issues of public policy.

The third area of tension lies in the social or collective sphere, except to the extent that it influences the consciousness of individuals: the issues that arise between the nation and the world. Here again the problems do not stem from any hard-and-fast choice. It is precisely because the good of one is linked with the good of the other, because the choices appear at the margin of action, and because over a period of time the balance of advantage may shift radically from what it appears to be at any one moment, that this is an area in which tension arises. Vast changes in this regard have occurred and continue to occur. The political nexus which surrounds economic relations between countries, and the trade patterns and the monetary arrangements by which they are carried out, differ greatly from what they were only half a century ago. These changes are reflected in the theoretical body of doctrine, which no longer tries to explain international economic relations as little more than an extension of neoclassical price theory combined with the noninterventionist economic tradition. And, of course, the change carries over to prescriptions for, and the instruments of, international economic policy. All of this may be seen as a manifestation of the modern world's new combinations of independence and fierce nationalism on the one hand, and deep poverty on the other, and of the urge for wider economic groupings, partly to accelerate growth, partly in response to particular political aspirations.

The Keynesian revolution affected the international no less than the domestic economic process, and provided new tools of analysis and policy for tackling the problems of both advanced and less developed parts of the world. At the same time, the acceptance of certain desiderata of domestic economic policy, particularly full employment and growth, and the development of the means by which they might be realized, has put a considerable strain on the traditional international monetary mechanism and on the theory by which it was rationalized. Here then is a further large area of tension.

These three areas indicate where tensions have arisen in the last few decades and where they may confidently be expected to continue to arise, at any rate over the next quarter century or so. From them will flow the actual problems of economic reality; and they will provide the intellectual stimulus for further development in the economic theory we need to improve our understanding of these issues and our ability to resolve them.

The Sociopolitical Framework

These tension areas are too broad and philosophical to serve fully as a basis for a forecast of future economic developments. It is possible to define and isolate more specific factors that have been operating dynamically in the last two hundred years in all countries, either as socially integrating or socially disintegrating forces, and to see how they are likely to work in the immediate future. Here we are less concerned with tensions created solely within the economic sphere, more concerned with the broad sociopolitical framework within which are set the problems of the private and the public economy.

Nationalism ranks first and foremost among these forces. During the last two hundred years, and longer, the emergence and consolidation of nation-states must be reckoned as the most powerful background fact of economic development. This was the characteristic feature of Europe, and Europe dominated the world economy through its superior scientific and technological knowledge and rate of growth. These elements made possible a system founded partly on the ruins of more ancient empires.

For the older countries of Europe the emphasis on nationalism was a powerful progressive force; it provided an element of cohesion which made possible the encouragement of technical invention and the introduction of new forms of enterprise. It usually was also associated with more advanced political movements, and thus helped to infuse the whole of society with a new liberal spirit. If it also produced disintegrating features in international terms these were restrained by *Pax Britannica,* challenged but not finally ruptured by Napoleon, challenged again in World War I, and once again sustained—although the old British hegemony already was passing into eclipse because of the emergence of the United States as the strongest world power.

World War II completed the process, and established a much more complex pattern of international relationships in which the old nationalism was joined by new forces, some integrating, some disintegrating. The technological basis of national power is now utterly different; *Pax Britannica* was based on the domination of the seas, which has become almost incidental to a defense system based on highly complicated nuclear weapons with automated, airborne delivery systems. The United States and the Soviet Union emerged as the only nations initially possessing this capacity; and it is by no means clear yet how their control of the means of almost total destruction is to be "absorbed" into a new system of power relationships which will include nations that possess some significant fraction of this nuclear power and others perhaps never likely to possess any.

To some extent this technological revolution in the means of warfare has led to an attenuation of the overt forces of nationalism. The fresh impetus the older nationalism received in Europe after World War I, under the principle of "self-determination," can now be regarded as spent, except perhaps in the case of the rather special and surely anachronistic effort to revive it in France under General de Gaulle. The other nationalistic impetus—that which motivated the new countries that emerged from the destruction of colonialism after World War II—is, however, still very powerful. Even so, both in the older and in the newer countries, strong new integrating tendencies have begun to appear.

The facts of military power, the speed of communication, the range and intensity of cultural interchange—and, perhaps above all, economic necessity—have combined to impel old and new nations toward a search for regional groupings. Regionalism is, then, another major contemporary force. The historical parallels that are sometimes adduced—the federation of the German Reich, the Italian kingdom, and the United States—are not, in my view, valid, since the circumstances in which they appeared were quite different. Thus, no analogous tendency can be found in the last two hundred years for the trend toward regional integration, which I deem to be of great importance for the future, and which I will deal with at some length later on.

A third aspect of the transition away from the old nationalism deserves mention. Although the growth and consolidation of the nation-state was often thought to require, and certainly was often associated with, economic nationalism and protectionism, the process had gone far enough by the end of the 19th century to allow a reassertion of the doctrines of free trade evolved in the age of British industrial supremacy and directed primarily against the remnants of the old colonial and mercantile system. On the foundation of the classical theory of the international division of labour and the doctrine of comparative costs, a more elaborate body of theory was developed, designed to demonstrate the mutual benefits of unimpeded trade between nations. And in the period from the Seventies of the last century to the outbreak of World War I the theory was translated into practical arrangements, such as increasingly uniform customs nomenclatures, extension of the benefits of trade agreements through the principle of the most-favoured nation, and a variety of supporting treaties of commerce, navigation, and establishment.

This network of international economic intercourse was sustained by an international monetary mechanism which depended largely on automatic processes. At its core was the gold standard; and where that did not operate fully—within parts of the British Empire or in the Latin Monetary Union—arrangements existed which provided an almost equal spontaneity. Thus, taking it all in all, the disintegrating tendency of nationalism was balanced by the integrating effects of world trade and the monetary arrangements required to support it. These included a network of capital movements, primarily centred in London, which provided old and new countries with access to resources needed for economic development.

The two world wars disrupted this network; and what had been a relatively simple set of more or less automatic mechanisms had to be replaced by an institutionalized system which we may broadly call the "Bretton Woods" model. The analogy for the world trading and monetary system of the 19th and early 20th centuries therefore must be sought in the more deliberate and conscious arrangements, regional as well as truly international, that have been evolved in the last twenty years. Inevitably there is both similarity and difference; but as the present system is still in a state of flux—indeed it provides one of the most potent factors of tension in the present economic order—I shall return to this topic later.

Ideological Influence

To complete this account of significant movements in the recent past and their parallels today some further factors of a political/ideological nature must be mentioned. While the last century was on the whole marked by the steady progress of political democracy, the period since World War I has seen a much more uneven development.

Between the two great wars we experienced the emergence of the European dictatorships, and there was and is the Soviet system which, although it claims to be the logical culmination of the progress of 19th-century democracy, has, at the least, strong authoritarian features. Marxist ideology in the states newly allied with the Soviet Union, and having a similar political and economic system, has given rise to similar forms of "authoritarian democracy." These appear also, whatever the differences with the European predecessors, in the Chinese People's Republic.

In the newly independent countries, particularly of Africa, new political forms have arisen which, even where they have democratic features, can certainly not be likened to the systems existing in the economically more advanced countries. Indeed, their experience suggests that, unlike the European pattern, intense nationalism is often allied with a strong tendency toward political dictatorship.

The 19th century and the first part of the 20th also was a period in which the working-class movement came to full flower. In all the advanced countries trade unions grew more powerful as a force in industry, and in politics through the rise of labour and social-democratic parties. Today the situation in the most advanced countries is somewhat different. In many—notably in the United States, Britain, and Sweden—the unions' power in the economic sphere is, if anything, greater than it has ever been. This power is still exercised through individual union bargaining; and the traditional features of labour disputes—lockouts, strikes, arbitration machinery, and so on—are accepted aspects of the contemporary scene. But, in addition and perhaps more significant, organized labour is now, along with management and the state, one of the three recognized sources of authority for the determination of the broad pattern of the economy.

It is as if the macroeconomic categories of modern economics required actual embodiment in the world of reality to correspond to theoretical statistical measurements. Organized labour has become one of these; and as macroeconomic analysis and policy spread, so does labour's new role become more important. The search for an "incomes policy," so significant in the modern economy and surely a major dynamic factor for the future, is proof of this development.

At the same time, the unions' relation to the political parties is undergoing a change. In Europe they are usually still closely allied to socialist or labour parties; and in the developing countries the link is even closer. But both the parties and the unions have acquired greater independence of each other. In the United States, where the tradition and practice of independent political action is most pronounced, organized labour, while for the last thirty years tending to be more "comfortable" with the Democrats, is wooed by both parties and is regarded as a potential source of strength for either.

Important developments have also occurred within industry. When we are dealing with technology it is difficult to be certain when we confront a change of kind and not merely one of degree. Large-scale enterprise, mass production relying heavily on power machinery, repetitive processes using scientific methods of time and motion study, increasingly automated assembly lines, and the like have become commonplaces of 20th-century industry. Is the more advanced automation, using computer programming and other methods of electronic control, to be regarded as wholly new? The answer is a matter of taste. On the whole I regard these recent developments not as revolutionary, but as a continuation, possibly at an accelerated rate, of tendencies that have been at work for a long time.

I do not regard these technological developments so startling in their impact as the organizational and attitudinal changes that have accompanied them. Here again, it is quite true that some features of modern capitalism could have been seen in embryo 150 years ago; the joint-stock company, the principle of limited liability, the means for promoting capital formation and movement, both domestically and internationally, are now quite old. But the extent to which the modern corporation has developed a new professionalism, with specialized training and distinct careers for different classes of management, has basically altered the character of "business," and of the popular attitude toward it, that prevailed only fifty years ago.

The dispersal of industrial ownership was well advanced before World War II and has continued since. With this change the relationship between industry and finance has been substantially affected. This is particularly marked in the United States, although other countries, notably Britain, are developing the same patterns. Whereas only fifty years ago Marxists could write about the growth of "finance-capital," by which they meant the penetration of large-scale productive industry by banking interests, the situation today is almost exactly the reverse. The tremendous power to generate its own financing for capital investment inherent in the modern corporation, plus the growth of huge investable capital sums through the spread of pension and other broadly held funds, have put industry in a leading position vis-à-vis finance. Until the Thirties, and particularly before and during the Great Depression, it was common for industrial boards to be dominated by nominees of financial institutions; now the position is reversed.

The climate of business and finance also has been affected by the greater availability and the rapid spread of information of an economic character, both that relating directly to the individual business and that dealing with national and world economics. The frequency, the spread, and the range of statistical data, and the scope of their dissemination, continue to grow at a prodigious rate. The main problem now is to improve the presentation of economic data in the most "usable" form; it is only the absorptive capacity that presents any serious limitation on this process.

All this finally leads up to and back again to the question of the management of the economy which I have already touched upon in describing the Keynesian revolution and the macroeconomic approach to which it has led. In the Thirties a fierce controversy raged over the issue of economic planning. At that time the debate was largely provoked by the theories surrounding Russian attempts to manage the Soviet economy after the disasters of war and revolution, and the practices developed in the course of painful restoration of some semblance of economic order through the partial resumption of private enterprise during the period of the New Economic Policy.

The debate in the West was closely bound up with prevailing attitudes toward the Soviet Union, or toward socialism in the abstract, and was carried on largely in terms of good and evil: the virtue of individual freedom (and private enterprise) in contrast to the vice of slavery (and central planning). Today the voluminous literature of that period—only thirty odd years ago—is almost as incomprehensible to the modern student as that produced by the controversies between mercantilists and bullionists three hundred years ago. No doubt there are still some who might derive satisfaction from an attempt to rekindle these dying embers; but most people in Western capitalist countries now display a tolerant attitude toward central management of the economy that may in itself be the most impressive symptom of the change that has come over the economic order.

This new view of the relationship of government to the economy has been enshrined by a number of countries in legislation, for example the Employment Act of 1946 in the United States. In this measure the people's representatives accepted the government's responsibility for giving long-term direction to the economic forces within society, and for deciding which are to be stimulated and which are to be restrained. Moreover this view is no longer held to be related to any particular political ideology. In the sense here given the term "plan," there are planners in both political parties of the United States.

In Britain there are nuances. A trend toward the newly discovered virtues of the "natural order" has recently appeared within the Conservative Party, but it does not seem to be significant; and it is to be remembered that it was a Conservative Government which created the National Economic Development Council for the specific purpose of drawing up a long-term growth plan. The Labour Party is wholly committed to this process and, in taking over the government, itself assumed responsibility for the plan. Long-term planning has been an integral feature of French economic management since the end of the war; and in Italy the multiplicity of state and para-state organizations deeply involved in various industries makes planning inevitable.

The Human Condition

Over and beyond these areas of change, which lie primarily in the economic and political sphere, it is worth pausing for a moment to consider whether any of the more basic elements of human conduct have been subject to a similar process—and, if so, whether these changes may be of significance for the future of the economic order. Some of these are potentially of special relevance, since they stand in a mutually determining relationship to the economic factors we have under discussion. I would draw special attention to attitudes toward property and affluence, to the family, and to certain aspects of the accepted code of moral conduct.

The problem of equating such developments over the last two hundred years with the prospect for the immediate future, as with so many other aspects of human life, is that the frame of reference is already utterly different from that within which the conduct, ideas, and social arrangements of the past were molded. We can, for example, see reasonably clearly in highly advanced Western communities what is happening to the moral code that evolved in these same communities in the last part of the 19th century. Attitudes toward work (and work of different kinds), toward business, toward government and the professions, toward accumulation of wealth for the benefit of one's descendants —all of these are obviously very different from what they were fifty years ago.

It is somewhat more difficult to discern how less developed communities are going to react to the impact of modern industry and trade as they are suddenly drawn into the now virtually worldwide circle of social, political, and economic intercourse. What, if any, stages of social development will they skip, as they may well skip the railway age or the age of steam that marked the economic growth of older countries? Will they repeat the evolution of the West, or will the speed of their development involve the emergence of entirely new forms of social organization in which current Western forms are absorbed and modified by older types that in the advanced countries belong to ancient history?

These questions cannot be answered here. What can be said, however, is that the basic pattern of economic development for the world as a whole will be determined by the directions taken in countries already industrially advanced. These are the cultural and ideological trends that are most relevant in an economic context. And here, too, one can say that what is most striking in this sphere is the extent to which general economic changes appear on the whole to be unrelated to political organization or ideology. For example, there seems to be some coalescence between communist and para-communist countries and the mixed free-enterprise economies in such matters as the strength of the individual acquisitive instinct, in relation to excellence of managerial and administrative performance, or the urge for satisfaction of private as against social wants. Nor do changes in the significance of family ties, or the attitudes of adolescents toward cultural and material values, seem significantly different as between one type of society and another.

We now have a number—perhaps an embarrassingly large number—of guidelines for surveying past and present economic developments and for peering into the future. There are the many tendencies at work in all societies and which move in the direction of making the world one. We have the three groups of actual or potential tensions which are deeply embedded in man's nature and in the conditions under which men live together in society and nation-states coexist in the world order. We have specific developments of modern history which have determined the actual manner in which present-day economic activity is carried on, and the climate of opinion, including its own theoretical apparatus, which surrounds it. Broader cultural tendencies also have been noted which either affect the economic order or are determined by it. These lines might serve as the grid on a map to provide a framework within which we may choose particular points of reference as landmarks to guide us in our exploration of the future. The choice of these points of reference is necessarily a matter of taste. I do not claim that those I have chosen add up to a comprehensive treatment, or even a skeleton list of all the possible growth points of the economy and of economic theory. But they do provide a general framework in which I have placed those aspects which I regard as nodal points.

The rest of this essay falls into two parts. In one I deal with the chief domestic issues that are likely to preoccupy mankind in the coming generation. Here I draw a distinction between the desiderata of economic policy and the means for achieving them. In the other I deal with international problems, the issues that arise from the ever more pressing movement toward one world against the resistances interposed by national policies, whether these be rooted in real or imagined economic reasons. Here the distinction between desiderata (or objectives) and means of policy is less easy to draw: too often they are confused by the play of ideology and illusion. But some distinction can be made between the goals toward which events seem ineluctably to lead and the clash of current policies.

Finally, in a concluding chapter, I attempt to deal with the limits of economics, the shadow-land where politics and the other social sciences mix with economics under the guiding hand of philosophy.

Chapter 3 The Domestic Economy

THE DISTINCTION BETWEEN the internal, national economy and the theory required to explain and manage it, and the worldwide economic order has become an artificial one. In strictly objective economic terms it has disappeared so far as the larger part of the world's population is concerned (with the possible, and surely temporary, exception of China).

Again and again we shall see that national trends are limited or determined by international implications or consequences. Nevertheless, the distinction is valid from the point of view of the individual citizen. For what he, as a national of a state, is obliged to do and is capable of doing is to express his political will within the confines of his nation's own political power. This is not to say that in the process he may not be swayed by, or wish to influence, the course of events in the international sphere. In fact the more politically conscious, the more economically sophisticated he is, the more he will be aware of the interrelation between national and international actions and developments. But in the end it is the actions of his own government that he has to try to influence.

Sometimes the individual citizen can use his influence to a considerable extent. There are formal means for him to do so in parliamentary and other democracies of most Western, so-called capitalist, countries. But even under authoritarian regimes evidence is not lacking that on some issues and in some—often to the outsider very mysterious—manner, the wishes of the citizens can be registered and brought to bear on the actions of the rulers.

But whatever the process by which he affects the decision of the state, whatever its efficacy, and whatever the degree of sophistication he brings to bear in activating it, the average citizen is overwhelmingly concerned with what must be regarded as essentially domestic matters. It is a commonplace that in Western democracies elections are fought and won on such issues, except in the rare cases of war or crisis approaching war. In the elaborate processes by which the Soviet citizen exercises at least some influence on the actions of the state, it seems likely that everyday domestic problems preoccupy him just as they do his Western counterpart. It is on this basis that a valid distinction can be drawn between national and international problems, even though it is one the economics textbook will only countenance by introducing the fiction of the "closed" economy.

The Desiderata of Economic Policy

In enumerating the objectives which states may establish in ordering the economic lives of their citizens, there are inevitable differences of view as regards the total scope and the priorities within it. We have already noted the marked change that has come over public acceptance of what an "agenda" of public policy properly should be. No longer is the state expected to be merely the "night watchman." Responsibility for law and order and education has long since been joined by positive economic obligations. Which of these is to be listed first, however, is a matter of individual taste, and the choice reveals the political conviction of the chooser.

Some will give first priority to economic justice. For these the supreme task of the state is to remove at least the gross inequalities in the standard of living and in the opportunities for material and cultural advance enjoyed by all citizens. For others, security against the hazards of life and particularly the risks of economic change will come uppermost. This means in particular the provision of benefits in case of unemployment, sickness, and old age. For still others the average level of the standard of living itself will constitute the test of the efficacy of state action; they see the state's duty primarily confined to enlarging the size of the national cake; the precise manner in which it is shared becomes a secondary, and perhaps in the main a noneconomic, consideration. And there are those to whom the main duty of the state in the economic sphere is to reconcile the striving of the individual, his freedom to choose as consumer, worker, or entrepreneur, with the demands of a society which must accommodate the needs of large numbers and is being pressed by technological change toward still greater regimentation. These would put high on the state's agenda such matters as the regulation of monopoly and the protection of the consumer.

The distinction is still made between private consumption and public consumption. The argument here is that once the state has created the basic elements of an environment propitious for the exercise of individual drive and ingenuity, private acquisition will largely take care of satisfying the individual's own wants. (Of course people will differ in their view of what constitutes the basic environmental elements.) The obligation of the organs of public authority (above all, the state) is to see that social consumption is adequately catered to. This once could be seen as a strictly limited function, but the wave of urbanization has brought with it increasingly complex demands of education, transportation, health services, facilities for leisure pursuits—in general, the removal of public squalor.

Finally, for some people, the principal economic task of modern government is to shape its policies so as to contribute directly to the emergence and strengthening of a one-world economy. Admittedly only a small, sophisticated minority are presently so concerned, and even here the variety of views reflects the continuing clash between national desiderata and the pursuit of international economic policy.

Each of these groups of objectives may properly be included in our analysis, though the last named is probably best dealt with in relation to the consideration of worldwide issues. Nor does it matter particularly in what order we treat them. What is important is to attempt to distinguish the circumstances in which one or the other may be more intense, for this may give us some clue as to the manner in which they are likely to operate in the future.

For my part I believe that the grossly inadequate standard of living for the greater part of the world's population, and the continuation of stubborn pockets of poverty even in the most advanced countries, make the *size* of the national cake the predominant issue; in any event, the other requirements of economic policy will only be fulfilled in the measure in which the total national product grows. In terms of actual future problems of the economy no less than future developments in economic theory and economic policy, growth is undoubtedly at the centre: round this issue all others are grouped. I therefore put it first among the desiderata of economic policy.

Growth

Growth is not an end of economic activity. I have called it a desideratum because, although it is the means for achieving a number of ends, economic and noneconomic, it is itself the end result of a series of economic processes. It can therefore properly be regarded as an objective of economic policy.

Only relatively recently has growth become a fashionable word in economic discussion. It is true that the classicists knew about it and so did more modern economists such as Marshall. After all, Adam Smith had called his great work *The Wealth of Nations;* and he and his contemporaries and successors recognized that the size of the resources of labour, capital, and materials (land), which a nation could command, and the skill with which it employed them, would determine the sum total of its riches. And he also knew that these factors were capable of expansion under the impact of dynamic factors. Marshall added much to the classical body of doctrine by his distinction between partial and general equilibrium analysis, which allowed for the introduction of precisely these dynamic factors.

Some more recent economists dealt more explicitly with economic development, for example, J. A. Schumpeter. But his main interest was to isolate the elements in business enterprise which gave rise to economic development, rather than to deal comprehensively and systematically with all the factors, particularly government policy, that led to the achievement of economic growth. It is a measure of the change in economic interest that a little over fifty years ago, in

1911, a book could appear entitled *The Theory of Economic Development* in which, with the one exception mentioned, no serious study is given to any of the topics dealt with in the large and rapidly expanding "growth" literature that reflects contemporary economic thought. (This is not in the least to denigrate Schumpeter's pioneering effort; it was a great achievement even to have selected this subject at a time when the rest of the "Austrian" school from which he sprang hardly recognized its existence.)

It is worth pausing to consider what has been responsible for the great awakening of interest in this subject in the last few years. So far as countries just becoming independent were concerned, the postwar period naturally saw an immediate interest in economic development. But for the most advanced countries recovery and reconstruction took priority, and it was not until the first phase was achieved, by the end of 1952, that the possibilities of more rapid development began to command attention. Growth was then seen on an individual national basis rather than within the collective confines of the Marshall Plan, which had dominated the reconstruction period. In the decade that followed, marked differences in the rates at which individual countries advanced (not only in Europe and North America, but elsewhere, particularly in Japan) began to appear.

Discrepancies between countries and the apparently capricious economic fluctuations in particular countries seemed hard to explain. After spectacular advance in the immediate postwar period, the United States' rate of growth slackened. Britain never seemed to get anywhere near the rates achieved by some of her neighbours in Europe, particularly Germany and France. Nor did any of these economies maintain a uniform rate throughout the period. It is not surprising, therefore, that explanations were sought and theories developed.

At the same time, the initial concern for the development of the newer countries had given way to more systematic consideration. A number of changes contributed to this, apart from the inevitable development of the inherent aspects of the subject itself. Larger and larger sums were being channeled to the underdeveloped areas as loans or grants, and the lenders or donors, whether individual countries or international institutions like the World Bank, became more interested in evolving a systematic view of the best use to which these funds could be put—that is, in a theory of economic growth.

Toward the end of the decade, too, the newly created European Economic Community, having engaged in negotiations for the association of some of their members' ex-overseas territories (mainly French), became a factor in this process. The recipient countries, having more or less consolidated their political regimes after independence, also wished to tackle their own development plans and policies in a more coherent fashion. Soon, to cater to this demand, a literature developed, partly using the new macroeconomic technique, partly the achievements of economic history—particularly those which related to the development of early capitalism.

Finally, the study of growth in advanced and in less developed countries co-alesced and began to take the shape of a general theory. However, this is even now in its infancy and its further refinement and development will be one of the main economic tasks of the next few years. Perhaps the clearest demonstration that the subject had at last been accepted was provided by the decision of the Organization for Economic Cooperation and Development (OECD), largely on American initiative (it is said President Kennedy took a personal interest). to pledge all its members to a growth target of 50 percent during the decade of the 1960s. Since then, growth rates have been kept under as close scrutiny in all countries—but particularly in the West—as the fever chart of a hospital patient; and international comparisons are as eagerly followed as league standings by baseball or football enthusiasts.

One should not underrate the great potential political significance of this still growing and increasingly widespread concern. Perhaps the time has not yet arrived when in a democratic country parties change office on the basis of performance or promise in respect to economic growth. But certainly in the majority of the member countries of the OECD, and in Japan and Australia to mention only two of the others, this factor is becoming very important in the eyes of the general public and we can confidently expect it to be even more so in the future.

What then are the factors which determine growth and will do so in future? This is not the place to attempt to sketch in a full-scale general theory of economic growth. I would, however, distinguish four broad groups of factors that operate whether we are dealing with an advanced or with a less developed country (though of course their relative significance can be substantially different in individual cases). These are labour supply, productivity, capital formation, and government policy.

Labour supply is of course basic, as Adam Smith long ago pointed out. Today the theoretical analysis of present and prospective labour supply is greatly advanced and integrated with the modern theory of population and population movement. There are highly developed means for measuring and forecasting its total size, its structure by age and type, and for relating it to the demand likely to arise in particular sectors of the economy. Modern statistical concepts and techniques adapted to the use of electronic computers have made it possible to get a much higher degree of accuracy and speed in such forecasts, so that they can be utilized in the planning of government policy.

So far as the less developed countries are concerned the problem is not, generally speaking, one of limitation of growth potential by lack of numbers in the labour force. Indeed, in most, once the other factors that determine growth are taken into account, the prospective size of the population is deemed to be excessive.

In the numerical sense used here, the most striking feature about labour supply considered as a dynamic force for future development is the great discrepancies in the prospects of different advanced countries in the noncommunist world.

The United States, already the most populous of the advanced nations and still possessing the fastest growing population, has not yet reached the end of the well-known and often repeated process in which industrial development causes, and in turn is aided by, a relative (and sometimes even an absolute) decline in the agricultural labour force. The United States has the prospect over the next few years of a steady increase in population, as well as a continued move of labour away from the land at a rate similar to that of recent years. In the United States, therefore, labour supply is not a factor which should impose any limitation on economic growth. On the contrary, given the high level of economic development already achieved, the problem of absorbing new labour by appropriate changes in the structure of the economy will be paramount.

At the other extreme are other advanced countries, Britain being the most important. The prospects here are for a very much smaller increase; and for the two decades beyond, while estimates must be much more tentative, it is hard to see any substantial improvement. Nor has Britain a sizable reservoir of labour to draw from the land as a result of further improvements in agricultural technique or a greater reliance on imports. The proportion engaged in agriculture has already fallen to as little as 3.9 percent of the working population, much the lowest of any economically developed country; there is no prospect that any foreseeable change would release enough manpower from the land to make a fundamental difference. The problem of economic growth for Britain, therefore, will turn to a considerable extent on the possibility of enlarging the labour supply, or of compensating for its deficiencies by a more intensive exploitation of other growth factors, or by a combination of both.

Between these two extremes the picture is quite varied. Japan approaches most closely to the probable pattern of the United States, with the difference that a conflict may develop between further industrial development and an increase in food supply unless intensive cultivation can be extended more rapidly. France, too, has the prospect both of fairly rapid growth of numbers and a sizable reservoir of agricultural labour; in recent years, however, her very rapid growth rate has required fairly substantial reliance on immigrant labour, which the growing demands of other European countries will make more difficult to obtain in future. In Italy the early postwar years were characterized by what appeared to be a quite intractable problem of labour surplus, notably in the south. Emigration has alleviated this problem and continues to do so, but it is, above all, her own rapid industrial growth in recent years, including major development in the south, which has made the biggest contribution to absorbing Italy's growing work force. For the future, Italy seems reasonably well placed with a proper regional policy, well adjusted to handling the problem of labour supply as a factor in economic growth.

In Germany the absolute increase in numbers has not been able to sustain past rates of growth, nor is it likely to do so in the next two decades or so. In the past the major source of additional labour has come from the flow of refugees from East Germany; this is now virtually exhausted, and more recently West Germany has encouraged immigration from a wide variety of sources. Germany still has, however, a considerable reservoir of agricultural labour; she possesses the highest proportion in Europe of people engaged in farming, a good deal of it of a relatively inefficient kind. How far she will be able to draw on this is, therefore, bound up with the whole question of the future of European agriculture, about which more will be said later on. In Germany's case the problem is further complicated by the division of the country—a condition one may assume to have been removed before the end of the period we are considering. The present agricultural policy of West Germany (and the resulting agriculture/industry balance), having been evolved in the abnormal situation of a divided country, will have to be rethought not only in European terms but in terms of a united Germany.

For the smaller countries of Europe the prospect seems on the whole to be one of shortage of labour. For countries like Belgium and Switzerland this will continue an already difficult situation that has been ameliorated only by heavy immigration. It is not clear whether easement can be gained in these countries and others in a similar situation by drawing labour away from the land. Given their special geographical and social features, the politically tolerable limit of such displacement may not be far off.

In all the above I have not taken account of immigration or emigration except to the extent that primarily intra-European migration has already affected labour supplies. Immigration into Europe from the less developed countries, and particularly into Britain from the less developed parts of the Commonwealth, presents special problems.

Outside the "capitalist" and underdeveloped world facts on the existing labour balance are not so easy to ascertain or assess. The Eastern European countries appear to be in a favourable position. This seems to be due less to population growth—in which some slowing down may be expected to follow the rapid progress of industrialization and the raising of living standards—than to improvement of agricultural techniques and organization which is releasing labour for industry. In the Soviet Union, on the other hand, the prospects are remarkably similar to those of the United States, with the difference that the balance between technical improvement in agriculture and the opening up of new areas of cultivation, coupled with the increasing demand for food for an expanding population whose standards are improving, is not so likely to result in a substantial further addition to the labour supply from the land.

On the whole, then, labour supply should be a favourable factor for Russian economic growth; and given the ground that must be made up to approach Western living standards, the absorption of large numbers into the working population will depend largely on the proper management of some of the other factors of growth discussed below.

The picture that emerges from this survey is one of considerable diversity. In Europe, or in what is broadly called the Atlantic area, any view taken in narrowly national terms shows sharp discrepancies in growth possibilities insofar as these are related to labour supply. This is one of the more striking prospects for the next generation, but before we can assess its significance we must look at the other growth factors.

Productivity

Numbers are not, of course, everything. There is no close correlation between size of population and level of its economic advance, nor even between the rate of population growth and the rate of economic growth. Numbers are a predisposing factor, but it is their use which is significant. When I apply it here, I am using the term productivity in a very wide and not in a narrowly technical sense: included are all the factors (other than availability of capital and raw materials, or the efficacy of government policies, which are, of course, interrelated but will be dealt with separately) that determine the level of output of a given unit of labour. These factors are varied, covering the broad range related to the utilization of labour as such. They include education, vocational as well as broader technical training; the continued application of new methods for retraining and adapting labour to new production processes; and the speed and facility with which labour is moved from declining to growing sectors of the economy. The general management of labour and labour-market policy must be taken into account as well as the effectiveness of the organization of the work force in the individual factory and the factory's adaptation to technological advance.

Management itself must be included, since productivity ultimately depends in large part on the efficacy and imagination of those responsible for the initiation and supervision of industrial processes, their alertness to the possibilities of Schumpeter's innovation, and their responsiveness to changes in technology and to the condition of the market.

It must be clear that the same absolute labour supply can produce entirely different results in terms of growth, depending on the extent to which factors that determine its productivity are favourable or unfavourable. This condition is the result of an intricate process in which many complex factors mutually influence each other, and some causes and effects may be rooted in history. It is beyond the scope of this work (or any other restricted to the field of economics) to analyze these factors in any detail. Here it is enough to say that increasing attention will need to be devoted to these matters, particularly in those countries like Britain which will have to overcome some numerical inadequacy in the normal labour supply if healthy economic growth is to be sustained. In many cases labour and management must share responsibility for increasing productivity by jettisoning restrictive practices that grew up in an era in which the significance of growth to society as a whole was not appreciated, and awareness of the means by which it could be achieved was virtually nonexistent.

This general realization of what productivity means to growth, and a readiness by both management and labour to accept the consequences, is vital in every country. In the United States, even with its large labour supply, very high standard of living, and very high level of labour productivity, the trend cannot be slowed if all the benefits (including affluence of public goods and increase of leisure) that can flow from continued economic growth are to be obtained.

While an assessment of the force of the different factors that determine productivity in different countries is more difficult to make than are estimates of labour supply, enough has been done in recent years to show that here too there are substantial variations. Even in the advanced countries of Western Europe which have a similar industrial history and similar cultural traditions, there are marked differences from country to country; and there are even more significant contrasts between Europe and the United States. These differences do not necessarily work in a direction that compensates for differences in prospective labour supply; sometimes they clearly threaten to aggravate them. In general one sees here further evidence of potential disintegration in the future economic experience of the Western world.

Capital

Economic growth depends also on an adequate provision for investment; that is, setting aside out of current production the material means for increasing production in the future. As I have already noted, the decision on the right balance between the two, for nations no less than for individuals, is one of the most difficult dilemmas imposed by the human condition. To begin with, maintenance of the current level and rhythm of production (and of the level of consumption which it makes possible) demands continuing investment for the maintenance and replacement of equipment. To allow for the needs of an increasing population—even at an unchanged average level—some increase in the rate of investment is a necessary accompaniment of increasing output.

Then, if the *rate* of increase in the national product is to be raised, there has to be an actual increase in the investment set aside to sustain an expanding production in future.

Some of the investment needed for productive purposes, as distinct from that which provides the social infrastructure (such as hospitals) or that which is only indirectly related to production (such as schools), is provided by government in the form of public services. In the case of public utilities such as electricity, gas, or transport, which in many countries are owned by public corporations, government may participate directly in capital formation. But the bulk of the capital needed for manufacturing industry, including the industries supplying capital goods, is raised through a complex process involving a vast number of individual decisions. In the treatment of this subject in textbooks of economic theory much attention is devoted to the decision of the individual to "postpone present satisfaction" and thereby to provide savings out of his income which, taken together, constitute the stream of investable funds out of which capital is formed. This process of individual saving is, of course, still very important and, in the sense in which it imposes a limit on private consumption, it still provides a large part of the true basis of capital formation.

However, modern economic theory and analysis, starting with Keynes, has shown that a number of other factors in modern industrial society are especially relevant to this process and are of fundamental significance in any appraisal of future trends. These factors are distinct from the major additions and reforms Keynes was able to make in the basic theory of saving, notably the concept of "propensity to save," which he showed has a relation to income and thus to the volume of production. What I have in mind are improvements in our understanding of the process by which decisions as to the volume of investment are really arrived at. This is due partly to a better appreciation of the manner in which balance is achieved between the determinants of long-term and short-term factors in the economy, and partly to a more realistic appraisal of the working of the large private companies, the publicly owned or controlled corporations, and the financial mechanisms for raising capital, together with their relationship to government policy.

It is no longer possible to follow the elementary textbook theories and regard individual saving as in some sense the "prior" factor which determines what will be available for investment. This may have been an adequate view for the analysis of early industrial capitalism, though even this is being challenged by modern theory and historical research. Today it is clear that the major investment decisions in the economy, public and private, are more often than not the "prior" factor to which the individual balance between current consumption and saving has to be accommodated in one way or another—mainly through the mechanisms by which government manages to maintain the short-term balance of the economy. This is not to say that voluntary saving has ceased to be important; on the contrary in most countries, the more and the less developed *alike,* there are flourishing "savings movements" encouraged and supported by the government; and one of the constant preoccupations of public and private financial institutions is to devise new savings schemes with which to persuade the private individual to "postpone" some of his current consumption. But it is now recognized that there is nothing simple and clear-cut about the relation between investment decisions and individual saved funds.

The large industrial units are now in a position to generate large investable funds through the decisions by which they determine policies covering prices of their products, wages and other current benefits to their employees, the creation of pension and other reserve funds—and, finally, by the allocations they make when they distribute profits as dividends. To some extent these decisions not only determine the size of the funds they can hold back themselves for investment, but, through their effect on the income of employees and stockholders, and on the disposition of the income of the consumers of their products, they also have bearing on the "saving" that must underlie investment in general.

In taking its decision in these matters any large enterprise will be guided primarily by financial considerations in the narrow sense, rather than by any large view as to the congruence between the investment being planned and the available volume of saving. However, the managers will be concerned with estimating the demand for their products in future, *i.e.,* the prospective state of the market; and in making this determination they will, if they are part of a well-run enterprise, be taking account of certain general trends, which will (or should) include, *inter alia,* the probable balance between consumption, saving, and investment in the economy as a whole. The extent to which these broad assessments are made by private firms is growing, and it provides one of the most interesting subjects of speculation about the future of economic planning.

This, however, does not and cannot mean that the sum total of individual and corporate investment decisions will result in a true balance for the economy. Government still has to step in to ensure that, at least in the short-term, a balance is achieved. We shall discuss presently the possibilities open to governments in this respect and the tendencies that can be forecast in regard to planning for longer-term balance. It is important at this point only to note that in the initiation of the process by which investment necessary for growth is secured, the more significant decisions are not those of the individual consumer, but those taken by the large units, public or private, that operate directly on business enterprise.

It is now pertinent to ask what conditions are favourable to decisions as to productive investment and, therefore, to growth. Some were cited in the discussion of productivity: a spirit of enterprise and innovation, a readiness to change, perhaps a self-confidence that derives enjoyment from competition. These should produce an atmosphere which encourages scientific research and technological experiment as well as the application of new methods of cost-conscious industrial and financial management.

Other, perhaps more important, factors are less dependent on individual attitudes. I have already noted that private firms, particularly the larger ones, base their investment decisions on estimates that place their prospective fate within the framework of the probable future course of the economy as a whole. Thus, in their own terms, the general economic climate becomes of paramount importance. At this point the trend of individual business decisions becomes bound up with the forward economic outlook which in any modern community is largely determined by government views and government action. When one adds the weight of the massive investment decisions, which in whole or in part are the government's own, one can appreciate how important government policy becomes.

Another group of factors of some significance relates to the special nature of the financial mechanisms existing in any country at any time and their relationship to business, *i.e.,* mainly industrial enterprise. This subject has received a great deal of attention from historians of capitalist development as well as from fiscal theorists and from descriptive writers on monetary institutions. Their work demonstrates how the evolution of modern industry has gone hand in hand with the development of ever more elaborate and effective machinery for mobilizing savings, creating credit, and making funds available for investment. Countries, like Britain first and the United States thereafter, which were able to develop advanced financial institutions and a smoothly functioning capital market have had a great advantage in promoting economic growth.

Still, as I have already noted, the most significant single recent development probably is the relative decline in large-scale industry's reliance on outside finance. The large funds they have at their disposal have even produced a marked trend toward financial operations, often of a short-term nature, which are not directly related to their own industrial activities.

This trend, which seems likely to continue, may well have been responsible in part for the varying investment experience of different countries in recent years. For example, the absence of a highly developed capital market in countries like Germany or Japan (even after allowing for the effect of foreign investment) did not stand in the way of their achieving very high rates of manufacturing investment. Nor has the possession of such a market been enough to offset the other factors that have made for a relatively low rate of manufacturing investment in Britain. In France the position is somewhat different. Although her domestic capital market is a little more highly developed than Germany's, she has evolved somewhat different arrangements for providing industry with finance in which the government and governmental institutions play a large part. In the French model the provision of funds for manufacturing investment is designed to be more easily employed as an instrument of central planning.

It may well be, therefore, that in the future the existence of a highly developed capital market will be of less decisive significance than it has sometimes been in the past. This changed relation between finance and industry may be relevant in another regard. It could be argued that the financial interest is historically conservative in the strict sense of the term; that is, concerned primarily with the preservation of capital values. Its attitude toward innovation—and the risks attendant upon it—is therefore usually more cautious than that of industry, where technical factors may predominate.

There is evidence that in the United States in particular this distinction has been operative in recent years. While the American experience in regard to growth has not been exceptional, major advances in productivity have continued and have been promoted and sustained by heavy rates of capital investment. It is, of course, very difficult to isolate one factor from among many that operate together, but it is certainly permissible to speculate that some part of Britain's less satisfactory performance may have been due to a relatively greater influence of financial as against industrial and technological considerations. If there is any validity in this distinction, as I believe there is, it may be of some consequence in any assessment of future trends and issues.

Government Policies

It is unlikely that even twenty-five years ago anyone writing about the factors that determine growth would have regarded government policy as an important feature of his analysis. It is a measure of the great change that has come over the economy and our way of viewing it that this consideration should now occupy a central position. All the growth factors we have so far discussed appear in the end to be dependent in greater or less degree on government decisions. Governments can influence labour supply directly by demographic policies—though here their power is clearly limited and schemes to relocate people by fiat have been slow to fructify. But they make a sharp and rapid difference in the labour pool by means of migration policies.

In the case of productivity, the government's power, at least in the capitalist democracies, bears directly on the foundations only; that is, the direction in which education, research, and training are developed and encouraged. Beyond that, a Western government depends mainly on exhortation, or perhaps more on example. Whatever their political complexion, governments now operate considerable business enterprises, or at least enterprises having much of the character of business. The attention paid in these activities to the requirements of enhanced productivity can often set the tone for the economy as a whole. Even more important is the extent to which governments encourage or discourage (by positive or negative action) the retention of restrictive practices of both labour and management.

In our consideration of capital formation and the role of productive investment in growth, we have seen that the climate of the economy as a whole is of considerable importance in determining the shape of business decisions. This is quite apart from the direct bearing of the government's own decisions, which has been increasing as the portion of the national product that passes through the public purse has grown. The general shape of the government's economic policy, particularly in the fiscal and monetary field, will have much to do with the way in which other growth factors work out.

Here, however, we encroach upon the field of means rather than of desiderata of policy. In particular the question of the influence of the government's general economic policies, *i.e.*, those which determine the balance of the economy, brings us to the very difficult issue of the relation between short-term balance, or economic stability, and long-term economic growth. This will occupy us later, since it is undoubtedly one of the most important of the problems that will confront the next generation. The above summary is intended only to pass quickly in review the most important factors that determine the first of our economic desiderata: growth. Although these factors are at work regardless of the stage of development or the political structure of the country under consideration, a more detailed analysis would require study of the specific forms in which these factors appear in individual countries and at particular times. This will generally show that it is a combination of factors—sometimes mutually determining each other—which must be looked at as a whole before sensible conclusions can be drawn.

But, supposing all these factors are favourable and that the policies which are specifically concerned with growth are successful, what then is the gain that may be expected? I confine myself to the simple answer that more goods would then be available for more people and for more purposes. This means, in the first instance, that all the other economic desiderata, at least in theory, can be more easily attained. I am not now concerned with the less tangible objectives of human striving that have led many (who, it must be noted, are most often found among the better-off citizens of the better-off countries) to scathing denunciation of theories of growth and the accompanying concern for numbers and quantities. I do not deny that there are less-desirable features of growth associated with deplorable cultural developments (though it may not always be possible to show that it causes them.) To this problem I shall revert at other points in this essay.

Chapter 4 Economic Justice

I PROPOSE to consider the problem of inequality and the search for its attenuation and abolition first from the point of view of economically highly developed countries. This too is a large subject with a vast literature. It has preoccupied thinkers and statesmen and ordinary people for as long as there is recorded history. I do not intend to go back over this ground at all. Inequality has many noneconomic attributes and may have many noneconomic causes; it also has noneconomic consequences. All we are considering here is the significance of inequality in the economic order of the advanced countries; its ascertainable present and prospective future tendencies (is it declining or increasing?); the importance its abolition will have as a desideratum of policy; and the manner in which its existence or disappearance may influence the other desiderata of economic policy.

For this purpose some convention is required as to what we mean by inequality in the economic sense (including economic opportunity). This is by no means easy. Inequality could be measured in a variety of ways: dispersion round the average level of income; the sharpness of the discrepancy, regardless of any average dispersion between the lowest and the highest; and the application of similar measures to wealth rather than income. For those advanced countries that have a communist or near-communist regime, the basic statistics are hard to come by, and such quantitative information as there is must be interpreted in terms of income of all sorts—not only in money but in kind, to include what elsewhere are called fringe benefits.

For those advanced countries for which a great many data are available the distribution of income is remarkably similar. There can be little doubt that in these, as in other capitalist countries (and for all we know in the communist countries, too), the desire to see inequality reduced is widespread, and these days the objective stands unchallenged as a broad goal of government policy.

A number of questions naturally arise. First of all, is this desire well founded, or is it based on a sentimental misunderstanding of the process of economic development and of the role of equality in it? If there were to be any substantial doubt about the answer this would clearly be a factor of major importance in the future development of the economic order.

Putting the same point in another way, the question turns on how inequality is related to growth: can historical experience throw any light on the matter of whether, in the interests of growth, some measure of inequality must be tolerated (either at the top of the scale or at both ends, if I may so put it)? Alternatively, we could ask whether a higher degree of equality, particularly a less-heavy concentration of incomes near the bottom, would be more conducive to economic growth in the long run.

In the second place, there is the question whether the desire for greater equality is directed to (or, indeed, should be directed to) a twofold movement from the top and bottom toward the average level (I leave aside here the somewhat old-fashioned argument about distributism.); or whether its main aim is or should be the raising of the level of those below the average, regardless of what happens to those at the top of the scale.

These are very difficult questions and it may be that complete answers will not be available by the end of the period we are considering. First we will need findings—more definitive than those we have now—as to the causes of inequality in present-day society.

All I can do here is to sketch out a few elements of the answers that will be sought. For the first group of questions, those that relate broadly to the issue of how different degrees of inequality affect economic growth, history is not a very good guide. Early capitalism certainly appears to have been associated in the Western countries with the accumulation of private fortunes so that both in terms of income and wealth it must be said that growth was accompanied by, and presumably furthered by, inequality—this being accomplished by giving full rein to the acquisitive instinct. Nor can it be denied that this instinct is still very powerful in Western countries and is apparently no less so in many of the less developed countries, where early industrialization is often promoted by the prospect of glittering material prizes. Even the Soviet Union has found it necessary to allow the prospect of reward—at least in the sense of consumption, including some provision for old age—to operate as a spur to those factors which have a beneficial effect on growth.

It would be risky indeed to try to assess the probable future force of the instinct for individual betterment and acquisition, and, a fortiori, its relation to individual economic performance as this affects economic growth, entirely in terms of these experiences. For one thing, while there is no doubt still scope for greater appetites (in the broadest sense) and therefore for greater consumption in even the highest income brackets of the richer countries, one can already discern some limits to this sort of expansion. Moreover, attitudes are changing and the more exclusive forms of material enjoyment are clearly going to become the preserve of a relatively less and less significant class. What is even more important, the relation of income (and even wealth) to consumption as such, and to other rewards which are usually lumped together under the heading of status, seems to be undergoing a marked change. The factors which are at work in this area are highly complex and their analysis would certainly be the primary concern of disciplines other than economics.

The Income Scale

More important than the question of the motives, attitudes, and future position of those at the top of the income scale is the probable trend of the middle and lower income groups. Here the evidence, both historical and recent, seems to be clear-cut. There is every evidence that over the last hundred years a relative as well as an absolute improvement in the position of these groups has been conducive to greater productivity and to a more substantial contribution to economic growth. Perhaps the most striking evidence in recent decades can be seen in the effects of unemployment, which inevitably increases economic inequality, particularly through a rapid decline in the living standards of the poorer classes of the community. Almost invariably productivity during periods of unemployment has declined, while high employment (leaving aside for the moment what exactly that is and how it might in general be related to growth) has nearly always been accompanied by faster growth of productivity.

It would appear therefore that while the continued existence of very high incomes may need to be tolerated in a free society as one of the factors of growth, there is no reason to think that the widespread, deeply rooted, and irrepressible desire in all countries to reduce inequality by raising the level of lower income groups need in any way be inimical to growth. This is particularly so when we consider the facts of modern industry in which buoyant mass markets provide the essential stimulus to management to expand and develop production. Thus, the next few decades should see further efforts to bring the lower income levels of the community closer to the average—which itself will be rising.

Now questions arise as to the causes of this inequality and how it might best be removed entirely. This again is a question to which other disciplines must contribute. To some extent the answer, insofar as it can be provided by economics, is closely bound up with the question of incomes policy and labour market policy, with which we shall be much concerned in the next section. Apart from this, attention has recently been focused in the advanced countries on the question of poverty as distinct from the general question of economic inequality.

We have gone past the early welfare considerations of provision for old age, sickness, and unemployment, to consider poverty as primarily the product of a more fundamental lack of educational and, subsequently, of economic and social opportunity. Recognition of the first group of causes has been a powerful stimulus to improvements in social security over the years in all countries. But it is only relatively recently that stress has been put on the cumulative effect of inadequate access to educational and other opportunities in relation to economic inequality in the extreme form of poverty. In this connection the position of particular regions in which for special reasons there may be an abnormal concentration of poor or low-income people has begun to attract special attention in some countries. The social causes of poverty referred to above I must leave for others to elucidate; so far as the regional aspect is concerned, I shall have something to say when considering regional problems generally.

I have so far been dealing primarily with the richer countries. What of the less developed? On the face of it the problem here would seem to be completely different. In most of these countries in Asia and Africa the general standard of life is so low that it may be thought that words such as inequality or poverty have very little meaning in the Western sense. If we are trying to look ahead twenty-five years, however, it must be supposed that the process of economic development will have made considerable strides, and the question of maintaining and accelerating the rate of economic growth will continue to be an extremely important one.

The beginning pattern in most of these countries is a mass of poverty relieved here and there by the emergence of a slightly better-off class and made even more poignant by the existence of a minute class of the very rich. In dynamic terms, however, the problem posed by the lowest levels of income of the less developed countries is no different in kind from that which faces the richer countries. In some measure these countries probably will live through an experience similar to the one that the more advanced countries knew at an earlier stage in their history—a sequence of accumulation, growth, and possibly the building up of private fortunes.

In one sense the prospect differs between the countries which accept a framework of private property and a measure of private enterprise and those which, after the model of the Soviet Union or China, do not. In the latter, the building up and transmission by inheritance of large fortunes is presumably severely limited. However, insofar as inequality connotes a marked difference in the level of current enjoyment of shelter, clothing, food, leisure, and entertainment, the distinction becomes insignificant.

The debates in the Soviet Union at the time of the introduction of the New Economic Policy on the question of "enrichment" provide interesting arguments on behalf of the theory that growth can be stimulated by private material gains, and these are being repeated in the less developed countries. Here, however, a further problem arises for the developed countries that are aiding this development. All of these have a more or less acute sense of the need to diminish inequality in their own countries. But most of them also attach stringent provisions as to the purposes and manner for and by which public funds are to be spent, particularly when individuals may be the beneficiaries. A dilemma, therefore, arises between the well-intentioned desire to see abuses prevented in these aid programs and the ineluctable fact that development geared to large capital projects not infrequently results in the creation of considerable private fortunes in the less developed countries. At a later stage, we shall need to return to this question and to examine the arguments (which, of course, involve many other considerations as well) for and against tying development aid to particular projects rather than making it available for the general support of the balance of payments or even for social improvement.

Individual Security

Modern society is rapidly developing new forms of economic security to complement older concepts of social security. By economic security I mean the relatively new principle (only about twenty years old) which relates to the individual's expectation of a continuing availability of work opportunity, as distinct from the earlier concern with the terms on which he is able to take advantage of such opportunity; in regard to both, some combination of private and collective responsibility usually operates. Except in communist or near-communist countries (where the position is somewhat different because of the considerable degree of compulsory direction of labour) the state has not yet accepted complete responsibility for ensuring employment for all who are willing to work. Virtually everywhere the state has accepted responsibility for guaranteeing at least a minimum of social security, providing public funds to make up for the effects of unemployment, sickness, old age, and other special aspects of poverty. But, under the most generous and comprehensive of these welfare programs, there is still a substantial degree of individual responsibility for securing employment to insure a standard of living above some minimum subsistence level.

Collective responsibility in respect to economic security is well established so far as the terms of employment are concerned. The state supports the organization of workers to bargain for wages, hours, and working conditions, and it intervenes directly with legislation embodying minimum wage provisions, regulating hours of work, setting legal holidays, establishing safety standards, and the like.

There is not much that need be said at this stage about the history and present position of trade unions, of bargaining machinery, of legislation relating to industrial disputes, and all the other statutory or traditional limitations upon the free play of market forces in the relationships between employer and employed. We can see here evidence of acute flux, and in most countries a reexamination—sometimes a fundamental reexamination—is very much the order of the day. But I believe that this is due less to developments within the ambit of industrial relations (though some aspects, *e.g.,* the drive toward larger industrial unions in Britain, is one such feature) than to the impact of problems of general economic management upon the traditional relationship between the state, management, and workers. These developments link up with the acceptance, barely twenty years ago in the "capitalist" countries, of the state's role in ensuring conditions of full employment, and with the effect that this has had on the general position of public authority in the economic process.

It is now accepted by politicians of all persuasions that never again will a country in which the people can express their will accept large-scale and prolonged unemployment. Therefore, short of natural catastrophe or the aftereffect of major war, we are not likely to witness again mass unemployment on the scale of the Thirties. No freely elected government is likely to stay in power if it is thought to be tolerating the emergence of conditions of that kind. The full-employment White Paper (1944) of the British coalition government, and the Employment Act (1946) of the 79th American Congress, bear eloquent witness to the fact that deep-seated desires of the people (made urgent and vocal by the Great Depression) and the intellectual analysis of an underemployment economy associated with Keynes had jointly produced their final political expression.

Ever since, the rate of unemployment has been watched as one of the most relevant indices of a government's performance. Argument does, of course, continue about the permissible level of the unemployment rate. Aside from the inescapable social connotations, economists divide on the questions of when underemployment of resources requires some stimulation of the total level of activity or, on the other side of the scale, when a very high rate of employment calls for some degree of deflation—questions that often must be considered in relation to a country's balance of international payments. These are hotly debated issues to which we shall need to devote attention later on in the sections dealing with economic policy. The important point here is that general acceptance of a stable high level of employment as a major objective of economic policy has shifted the balance between collective and individual responsibility for securing work (an extremely important element in society's set of economic desiderata). This development has also impinged heavily on an area of public policy, pushing it well beyond the terms of wage bargaining (including other conditions of work) to matters hitherto governed largely by social and humanitarian, rather than economic, considerations.

Incomes Policy

This marked shift, which I believe to be most significant for the future, is clearly seen in recent developments in the United States and Britain in regard to what is known as incomes policy—more correctly (and more usually in

Britain) referred to as productivity, prices, and incomes policy. We shall need to go into this in some detail later on. At this point, my concern is to stress the new line of development which leads, on the one hand, from the desire for economic security to recognition of the government's power to affect decisively the level of employment and, on the other, from the traditional concern of the state with the individual welfare of workers to preoccupation with the total complex of the level of employment, the level of earnings and its relation to wage rates, output, labour practices, cost of living, and so on.

Less obviously perhaps, but not less significantly, a similar shift is taking place in the approach to social security. Its origins lie in humanitarian preoccupations and partake of the concern for economic justice. From the beginning of the modern system of social security there was some recognition of the effect of impersonal economic forces (and so of the diminution of personal responsibility for poverty), and this played an important part in securing general acceptance of increasing government intervention in areas once reserved for private philanthropy.

There is ample evidence that not only economic analysts, but also public and private policy makers are becoming increasingly interested in the financial and economic aspects of social security arrangements; for example, the actuarial considerations in pension systems are broadening into full-fledged fiscal analysis. To put it in perhaps oversimplified form, the evolution has been from a humanitarian and eleemosynary approach, through the actuarial concept which emerges once the number of people and the amounts of money involved became large, to a view in which social security policy is regarded as part of taxation policy in general and is therefore embodied in an approach from the standpoint of modern macroeconomic analysis.

Seen in this wider context, the issues are somewhat different from those with which economists, businessmen, and politicians in most countries have been accustomed to dealing in the recent past. The size of taxable capacity at any one time, the effect on incentives of transfer payments through taxation and social security benefits, the relation between payroll taxes and short- or medium-term management of the economy (particularly in regard to the relation between investment and consumption)—these become the major questions on the new agenda. The several methods by which funds can be raised to provide social security benefits can, it is now accepted, have a profound influence on the entrepreneur's investment plans; on his attitude to labour supply (hoarding of labour, incentive to more capital-intensive processes, etc.); and directly or indirectly on incomes policy. In short, like all taxation questions, those related to welfare also need to be answered with reference to general objectives of economic policy and to the role of fiscal management.

We can confidently expect this way of looking at social security to become dominant in the developed countries over the next few decades. The tendency will be enhanced by the concern which public policy increasingly will have with methods of capital formation, the techniques of the capital market, the role of private pension funds and personal insurance, and the responses of the "institutional" investor.

The technical problems that arise from each of these questions and sub-questions are many and varied, and it is fair to say that despite a sharp increase in intellectual interest there is, as yet, no fully worked out body of doctrine available. Thus, in academic economics, partly through the development of elements already present in current macroeconomic thinking and partly in response to the needs of policy makers, the next few years will probably see a considerable preoccupation with these new problems of public finance.

The final matter that should be touched upon here bears upon the relation between the level of employment (and economic activity generally) and growth. I shall return to this later in discussing questions of long- and short-term economic management. Brief mention here is appropriate because the political reasons (and their intellectual reflections) that led to the change in approach to social security are the same as those that led to present-day interest in the growth/employment problem: namely the concern with avoiding repetition of the large-scale unemployment of the Thirties.

The paradox of poverty in the midst of plenty was a familiar way of expressing the waste of productive potential through the unemployment of human and material resources in the Great Depression. The dramatic gains in technology and productivity during the war, when the use of all resources was pushed to the limit, created a new understanding of the stimulating effect the pressure of general economic demand could have, even in a time when specific shortages and bottlenecks were frequently disruptive and, therefore, retarding. Then, under the guidance of the New Economics, reconversion was accomplished with unprecedented ease after the war. Here was apparent practical proof that postwar depressions and the resultant unemployment could be avoided and a steady rate of growth achieved on the basis of a fuller use of labour and plant capacity. Perhaps the clearest indication of the possibilities of achieving not only a higher rate of growth but of doing so while continuously improving productivity and reducing cost has been afforded by the experience of the United States during the last few years, particularly after the 1963 tax cut.

Now that this remarkable process has achieved the status of a normal phenomenon in the United States, attention has swung round to the opposite question, namely, the extent to which low levels of unemployment are consistent with noninflationary growth—a problem of general economic policy I will deal with later.

Chapter 5 The Individual and the State

IN DEALING WITH economic and social security, I have already touched upon an extremely important part of the individual's relation with the state. Public authority can, by means of general economic policy, profoundly affect the parameters of the market within which the individual operates, even to the point of creating conditions in which, for large numbers, the gaining of a livelihood becomes impossible. Fiscal and monetary policy determines the rate of growth of the economy and thus the limits within which—given certain political rigidities formed by historical and ideological factors—the various sectors dependent upon the gross national product can hope to enlarge their share. Employment opportunities obviously are affected, but so is the potential for public investment in utilities or amenities, or the amount available for personal private consumption.

But over and above the general limitations imposed by economic policy as a whole, the state has a very considerable influence on the individual as a result of decisions arrived at in the process of executing political authority. These decisions sometimes may be related to specific issues submitted to the process of political decision-making by the electorate, but more often they result from the application of a mandate of a more general character to some particular problem.

The multiplicity of such issues is very great indeed. I propose to refer to three areas for brief treatment here, chosen because each covers a wide range of individual aims and activities that are influenced by the exercise of the collective power of the state; and also because each seems to me to be in a state of evolution which is likely to produce new and possibly very striking features over the next few years and decades. These areas are: the state's relationship to private, personal spending; the state's provision of public goods; and the state's position in regard to the direction and form of individual enterprise. Each of these has a large and still rapidly growing literature. I cannot hope to give a detailed account of the problems that arise for any one of them. I shall, therefore, limit myself to emphasizing what seem to me to be the most important and dy-

Private Consumption

namic features.

The individual's consumption of "private" goods and services has long been discussed, notably as the result of the work of the marginalist school that occupied the centre of the stage during the heyday of microeconomics. I am not here concerned with the refinements of this theoretical analysis either in its early pseudo-psychological form or in its later mathematical versions. What I believe to be much more significant is the extent to which, partly on the basis of the existing body of theory—substitution and indifference analysis, for example—and partly through new methods of empirical, statistical inquiry, new insights are likely to be gained in the broad patterns of consumer behaviour at various levels of social and industrial development of different societies. This seems to me to be a field in which not enough new work has been done and in which we may expect a considerable burst of activity in the future. Out of many specialized studies, both empirical and deductive/ mathematical, I would expect that before the end of the century there would come new and, one would hope, more searching replacements for the broad generalizations of Vilfredo Pareto, or of Ernst Engel (particularly Engel's law of the distribution of consumer's income).

There are two areas where fresh insight seems to be most needed. On the one hand, analysis is required of the behaviour patterns of individuals as consumers in the most advanced communities. Since the United States appears in this regard—for good or ill—to hold up a mirror in which those somewhat below her level can see their own future, it would be there that I would look for most new inquiry. On the other hand, the advance of less developed countries under new conditions of much more self-conscious concern with economic development, both on their own part and on the part of the richer countries, would seem to offer challenging possibilities for further study of how private consumption patterns evolve.

Many of these problems are, of course, also of a sociological nature. The oft-debated role of advertising in the advanced industrial countries (and how much reality it leaves to the concept of "free" consumers' choice) provides an example. So do the changing patterns of demand for food, housing, and clothes in developed, densely populated, and predominantly urban societies. Obvious questions arise as to their economic effects in stimulating new industries and new technologies of urban planning, building methods, food preparation and distribution, and their counter-effects in creating congestion and new relationships between the provision of public and private transport. There are questions about the means by which the directions of consumer demand may be influenced, positively and negatively, by education and by protection. Consumers' movements, sometimes state-guided and supported, may provide an important new feature in the total machinery of collective regulation of the economy that has grown up in most of the highly industrialized countries.

One may confidently predict that the state will not be able to divest itself of its new interest in, and responsibility for, these new problems. When an industry, such as advertising, has reached the dimension where in the United States its share in the gross domestic product is as great as the total GDP of a sizable European country, and where its effects are evidently great and widespread throughout the economy, it cannot hope to escape the attention of the state, even if there were not powerful social reasons pushing in the same direction.

The significance of the mere fact that very large numbers now must be catered to in such matters as food and entertainment has not, I think, been studied sufficiently deeply as yet. The canons of taste, the hierarchy of enjoyments, still presumed to exist in the industrialized countries are very largely the product not only of more rigidly stratified and (perhaps) economically more inegalitarian societies but also of small-sized communities. Clearly, a new Veblen will be needed to describe the tastes and mores of the leisure class of the year 2000!

As I have suggested, the emerging pattern of consumption in developing countries, from the point of view of the future, may be even more deserving of intensive study in the years to come. Here a perspective opens up which could be especially fruitful, particularly to those concerned with policy-making, to insure a proper balance between development of the industrial and social infrastructure, heavy and light industry, agriculture, and distribution (and their political and social concomitants).

The Public Sector

Economic growth brings with it a considerable increase in the amount of the national product devoted to social goods; that is, to that part of an individual's consumption provided by collective decision and not by personal choice—or at least by production that is in some way the result of a collective decision. Education, health, public transport facilities (roads and highways at least), and public amenities require greatly increased resources each year.

In the case of education, the basic requirements for subjects taught and pupils to be enrolled rise with the population; at the same time, there are increasing demands for an improvement in the quality of teaching, at least insofar as it can be translated into strictly measurable material terms, *e.g.*, pupils per teacher or classroom; and, finally, technological progress applies here as in other forms of consumption: visual and auditory aids to teaching, laboratory equipment, and new school and college design constantly add to the resources required.

The same is true of amenities generally: parks, museums, public libraries, the performing arts, and so on. There are, of course, fashions in these matters; and we may, at the time of writing, at least in the United States and Britain, be passing through a cultural up-phase. Nevertheless, insofar as an underlying long-term trend can be discerned in economic terms it appears to be upward too.

In regard to health, the demand for resources is stimulated by the great burst of medical research and by the emerging patterns of expanded social security. In countries such as Britain it is now accepted politically that the state must carry virtually full responsibility for health service; the surviving argument at the centre of political debate is confined to questions of marginal adjustment; and now the United States appears launched on the same course. All the factors mentioned in respect of education are also at work here—greater cost due to advancing technology, increased total demand, and pressure for improvement of the quality of the service.

In the face of these indisputable facts, however, it is still difficult to establish—and much more contentious—whether "public" goods are taking an increasing share of the national product; that is, whether expenditure on them is rising relatively to that on private goods, let alone whether it should do so! The evidence is conflicting and fluctuating. Measurement is difficult and data do not go back over a very extensive time span. Even for individual countries, where one can barely begin to trust what figures there are, the line tends to zig-zag. As between one country and another, no clearly consistent comparison, valid over a number of years, is now possible.

One is, therefore, thrown back on speculation and, above all, on discussion of what a desirable policy should be. Here the debate has been very active in recent years, and it is safe to say that it will grow still more intense in the decades to come. At one level the argument is couched in economic terms; at another the issues are drawn according to value judgments, and sociological and aesthetic elements are predominant. Both levels tend to coincide on such pressing issues as those raised by the growth of urban traffic or the provision of open space in relation to the need for public (or private) housing. The body of economic doctrine relating to these matters has been pretty well established in what is known as welfare economics, beginning with Marshall and Pigou. However, this branch of applied economics is beset by urgent problems which cry out for more and better theoretical work as they are thrust upon public authority for resolution.

First, there is the question of pricing for public utilities—universal, or near-universal, goods and services supplied directly to the consumer by a collective process whether or not the production is in the public domain (as it generally tends to be in many countries). This area is traditionally—for reasons known to all students of monopoly theory—subject to public regulation and heavily involved in fiscal policy. The call of these industries for investment of resources is heavy and, given technological changes of a highly discrete character (atomic energy; the discovery of deposits of natural gas; and sudden, politically oriented changes in oil policy are examples), it can fluctuate widely. In their impact on capital markets, utilities can greatly influence other investment, public and private, and their pricing policies can affect the scope left for private consumer spending and its direction. For these reasons, decisions about the scope and nature of investment in these public goods, and their pricing, are reflected importantly in budgetary patterns (and, therefore, in official policy). The regulation of demand translates into policy designed to preserve the equilibrium of the economy in the short-run and into wages and incomes policy.

Somewhat different in the specific issues they pose, though not much different in kind, are problems related to the provision of public facilities which serve consumers' wants indirectly (roads and airports) while greatly affecting directly competing services (railroads). This may involve to some extent social amenities as well as economically measurable values (urban congestion). In all the highly industrialized countries strenuous efforts are now being made to develop new forms of analysis of these issues and new methods for the regulation and control of public goods of this kind. Much interesting material has been developed already, but it is clear that there is a very long way to go in the development of practical instruments (parking fees and prohibitions, redirection of traffic, new electronic use-measuring and taxing devices) and the theoretical substructure on which they rest. Again, the rating "urgent" must be applied to economic research dealing with public regulation of the limits of free choice since this inevitably will become more comprehensive and will require more sophisticated methods.

The range of problems which concern public amenities in the wider sense has been put effectively before a wider public by Professor Galbraith's *The Affluent Society,* one of the most influential books in the general field of social studies of recent decades. It has drawn popular attention to the existence of public squalor amidst private affluence; and the fact that its title has given—as did Veblen's *Theory of the Leisure Class* (1899)—a new phrase to the language is indicative of its seminal influence. Unlike Veblen's work, however, Galbraith's is peculiarly the product of a critical approach to the problems of a relatively limited sector of mankind: the United States and the relatively few highly industrialized societies that approach the United States in their level of private affluence. Furthermore, as the author would be the first to agree, its appeals for a greater share of the national product to be devoted to "public goods," particularly amenities, cannot absolve the so-called affluent society from the task of removing the blemishes of private poverty at least as fast as it improves the general quality of its public life. Nor can the analysis of America in the Sixties have much relevance to the world at large, in which between three- and four-fifths of the population have not yet begun to emerge from a high degree of "private squalor"!

Individual Enterprise

The tendencies toward an increasing role for the state in determining the direction and form of individual enterprise have already produced the term "mixed economy" commonly applied to the United States, Britain, and the countries of Western Europe. The reference is to the coexistence of publicly owned and privately owned enterprise, and to the fact that private enterprise generally must operate within certain constraints imposed by public authority.

How novel the latter development really is can be argued at length but, I believe, fruitlessly. At best, the idea that there really was a golden age of free enterprise, when the last remnants of feudal restriction had finally disappeared and the interventions of the modern, democratic state had not yet made themselves felt, is an over-simplification; it could have had only limited validity for some countries during very short periods of their modern history. On the other hand, the Marxist, and neo-Marxist, concept of the inexorable march of industrial capitalism towards monopoly and increasing interdependence with "finance-capital" and the state "apparatus," with violent revolution to subjugate its overweening power the inevitable result, hardly provides any more useful an intellectual instrument. I am not persuaded that grand generalizations of this kind—relating to the proper way in which the institutional framework of the economic order should be constructed or to the question whether there is a clearly discernible historical process in which it evolves and changes—are necessary to a full understanding of the issues.

The significant fact is that in nearly all the major industrial countries the ideological contest over the ownership of business enterprise is now at a very low ebb. I find it hard to believe that it will break out again in full force in the foreseeable future, though this cannot be entirely ruled out. It seems more likely that questions of the most effective administration of the public and the private sectors (mainly in regard to particular areas, such as public utilities) will provide the primary source of intellectual debate and political controversy.

These issues will be sharpened by new scientific/technological advances. Forerunners may be seen in the application of atomic energy to the production of power; the aerospace industry providing new means of communication; new discoveries of already known sources of energy—oil, natural gas, etc.—all these raise anew old questions of the proper relationship between private enterprise and public authority. In all these instances characteristics of "natural monopoly" are present, and this has long been recognized as a factor calling for public regulation and "justifying" it against the canons of purely private enterprise economics. Moreover, in many, if not all, of these new developments the scale of the financial resources required is such that some recourse to public funds is virtually inevitable.

So it seems to me that in the next two or three decades the abstract issue of private versus public enterprise will give way to study and debate over precise methods of financial interrelation, pricing of products and services, proper rates of return on capital invested, and amortization. Although the problems will not be different in kind from those already encountered in relation to the existing range of "public" goods, the general area of the state's positive determination of the forms of enterprise is likely to be a very active one indeed—perhaps precisely because the simple black and white juxtaposition of public versus private ownership has ceased to be very meaningful.

In trade, in industry, and in finance, questions as to the regulatory functions the state should exercise have undoubtedly been increasing in complexity and will continue to do so, if only as a result of the much larger numbers involved and the consequently greater impact of any development in one sphere on the more closely interconnected network of economic relations. In all industrial countries, for example, the attitude to monopoly and restrictive practices is being looked at afresh. The historical experience and the current problems of different countries again show that no uniform set of theories or policies has yet been derived, nor can countries very easily be classified according to the degree to which they practice this or that form of regulation and intervention. Britain. for example, has only relatively recently followed the lead given long ago by the United States in pursuing an active policy of investigation and suppression of monopoly and restrictive practices. Yet, in a relatively short time, she has in some respects established an even more stringent antitrust regime—so much so that it is now often regarded as being an obstacle to the progress of industrial efficiency.

France, to take a different example, is not generally regarded as a country in which public regulation of enterprise is especially oppressive, despite the fact that she has under ownership all the usual range of public utilities. Yet her commercial banks are also, to all intents and purposes, fully nationalized, as is an important sector of the automobile industry. What is more important, a private capital market is practically nonexistent; and finance for the larger investment projects can be obtained only through the medium of state-controlled institutions. This, incidentally, as we shall see presently, puts a powerful planning instrument at the disposal of the state.

In the United States, too, a country sometimes looked upon as the citadel of unfettered private enterprise, the relation between the federal—and sometimes state—government and business is far more intricate than appears at first sight. It is true that completely public-owned enterprise is much rarer than in Western European countries which have a roughly similar political framework and level of industrial development. But, as I have already noted, regulation of public utilities and control of monopolistic practices has a long history in the United States. Regulation of banking, the stock exchange, and the insurance industry in many respects goes much further than it does in Europe. Legislation relating to corporations—including provision for disclosure of information, prohibitions due to conflicts of interest, and the like—is also often more advanced than that in effect in many an otherwise more "planned" European economy.

Most important of all, perhaps, from the point of view of potential future developments, is the impact of great federal spending programs on certain areas of business enterprise. Outstanding in this respect is the defense effort, not only because of its size but because it relates to the technologically most advanced industries with the greatest potential for growth and for producing a revolutionary transformation of the industrial structure as a whole. This influence is spearheaded by the overwhelming impact of the expenditure of public funds on scientific, technological, and even economic, research and development. One has only to think of the electronic and aeronautical industries to realize how important these new defense-oriented enterprises are; and, although they are very different from tobacco monopolies or state-owned coal mines and railways, they are no less acutely significant in the consideration of public versus private ownership.

In the European countries, too, government expenditures have mounted for defense, for scientific research, and, in partnership with private enterprise, for technologically experimental new industrial ventures. Over the next two or three decades the politico-economic problems raised by this trend will require much study. Even if more peaceful international conditions lead to some relative decline of direct defense expenditures, the pattern already created will, because of its technological aspects, continue to be the active frontier of state/business relations.

It would, however, be rash to conclude from this that the scope for private enterprise, including ease of entry and mobility, would necessarily shrink. The growth of populations and the increasing mass market (due both to the emergence of new wants and to the enlargement of demand for known products as the level of prosperity increases) should leave much opportunity for enterprise and ingenuity. Here, the size of the market will be of great consequence. The larger the market, the less likely is it to become dominated by a few producers and distributors for any length of time. In the United States, the largest of the advanced industrialized countries, the scope for new products, new techniques for old products, or new methods of distribution, has remained consistently large in recent years; and it has not by any means invariably been exploited exclusively by the large corporations.

We shall need to look at all these matters again in relation to economic policy; but before I close this chapter, a word might be said on how these issues present themselves in the perspective of the less developed countries of the world.

Here, too, it is difficult to find a consistent pattern either by comparing groups of countries with one another or by seeking for analogies in the history of older economies. The evolution of business enterprise in England from the 16th to the 19th centuries is unlikely to be reproduced in, say, India, even in telescoped form. As regards scientific advance or technological know-how, it has long been accepted that the revolution in methods of communication has made it unlikely that the full sequence of earlier stages of economic development will be repeated. Phases are apt to be "skipped," as the railway age is likely to be, in part at least, in many developing countries. Also, in regard to the matters here discussed—namely, the most appropriate form of organization of business enterprise—learning from the experience of older countries may lead to the nonappearance of earlier controversies.

In the face of these hazards, one generalization may, however, be in order. In most developing countries economic advance is taking place under the close and continuous guidance of the state, even where development is not undertaken directly on public initiative. This is clearly inevitable. The pace of the reform of old social, political, and economic patterns has been greatly accelerated by rapidly changing relations between developed and developing countries; the virtually total disappearance of the colonial system; the enhanced political weight in international councils of the less developed world; the consequent change in trading relations even as regards the old "colonial" products; the stirrings of political pressure for material improvement within the countries concerned; and the development of a consciously directed flow of technical and financial aid from the richer to the poorer countries—all this leads to continued internal central direction (and a form of planning which we shall discuss later) and calls for highly centralized dealings between governments.

This pattern is bound to prevail for many years to come. But the resolution of the problems to which it will give rise (and which one may predict will form a major preoccupation for the rest of the century) will require, on the one hand, the deliberate creation of some scope within the developing countries for private business enterprise of the modern kind, and, on the other, control of private exploitation and enrichment in the major sectors of the economy, which must continue to be largely centrally directed. To suppress or avoid undesirable forms of relationship between government and large business will be a major problem not only for the developing world but also for the advanced countries that are aiding them to accelerate their growth. To this subject I shall return later.

PART TWO

ECONOMIC POLICY

Chapter 6   The Rise of Planning

IN THIS SECTION I propose to examine the means by which the various problems I have broadly sketched can be solved or at least subjected to an attempt at solution. So far as possible, I shall deal primarily with domestic economic problems, leaving international policy issues to be discussed in subsequent chapters. This is, of course, a somewhat arbitrary distinction which inevitably introduces an element of artificiality into a number of the problems dealt with. It will, however, help the exposition.

The most comprehensive form of managing a country's economic order has come to be called economic planning. The term became current less than half a century ago, and it came into use in relation to the form of economic management developed in the Soviet Union, inevitably carrying with it highly ideological overtones. For a long time any discussion of the forms, methods, merits, and risks of planning tended to be political and emotional. This reached a climax in the Thirties when the prolonged depression in the capitalist countries, with its heavy unemployment and underutilization of agricultural and industrial productive capacity, led many to question the efficacy of the free market economy. This in turn led to a revival of interest in the Soviet economy, at that time again entering a period of strict central direction after the brief return to the market during the period of the "New Economic Policy."

In these circumstances the debate tended to embrace a logically mixed array of issues, including those of public versus private ownership to which I have already referred, along with the political forms of the communist state as opposed to those of political democracy. Little in fact was said at the time about the specifically economic issues of comprehensive economic planning.

Looking again at the literature of the Thirties, one is struck by the mixture of naïveté and mysticism with which both apologists and opponents approached planning. The essential irrelevance of the theoretical work of the period is illustrated by the attempts of the Marxists to deal with the role of money in the Soviet system and, on the other side, the effort, in the face of the most obtrusive evidence to the contrary, to prove the virtues of "consumers' sovereignty" and market equilibrium. This is not to say that some useful lessons were not learned. Economists acquired a deeper understanding of the role of the market

55

and made a more determined attempt to develop a meaningful macroeconomics, moving away from the crypto-normative aspects of marginalism. And,
perhaps, the inspiration for the budding science of national accounting grew out
of the interest in Soviet economic budgeting.

Here again Keynes and his followers had a major liberating effect. The development of macroeconomic analysis, and of the statistical techniques that go
with it, almost automatically created a new meaning for the term economic
planning and a new approach to its objectives and methods. Once a picture of
the whole of a national economy could be presented in words and figures—and
these of a more dynamic kind than the ones to which the physiocrats or the
classical economists had been limited—it was natural to seek to forecast economic evolution over a period of time.

Some of the elements in a Keynesian national-accounts table can be forecast
with a considerable degree of accuracy, and, since the interdependence of all
the elements is high, it became feasible to take the further step of forecasting
the movement of the whole pattern—at least under the saving assumption of "on
existing policies." At this point the temptation naturally arises to move on from
forecasting under the restrictive assumption and to speculate on the effects of
this or that change of policy on the total economic pattern. The process of
model-building is thus set in train.

In terms of economic science this has been a particularly active and fertile
field of endeavour in the last twenty years, and a great deal of progress has
been made in theoretical analysis. One has only to mention the advances in
input-output studies, in linear programming, in algebraic, geometrical, and even
physical and electronic methods of presenting possible movements of economic
aggregates, and to recall how recent these developments are, to recognize what
a considerable achievement this has been. At the same time, statistical techniques and their application to actual data have kept pace with theoretical advances so that today, at least in the industrialized countries, a great mass of
continuous material is available.

It is difficult to project what the future may hold on this theoretical front,
but there is no reason to believe that progress has come to a halt. The manner
in which a major change in one element of the national accounts (whether in-
duced by a deliberate policy change or in some other way) percolates through
the rest is not yet perfectly understood—nor is the quantitative relation between
one change and a consequential one. These are all matters that require further
theoretical work of a high order. New conceptual tools may also be developed;
and the use of computer techniques to provide quicker answers, and answers to
more complex clusters of questions, still has a long way to go. Similarly, statistical techniques can be further improved and undoubtedly will be; and all this
is bound to improve planning as it is now understood.

It is, however, by no means clear that the next twenty years will produce so radical a change in basic approach as did the last twenty in comparison with the preceding prewar period. The most important need, as now seen, would appear to lie in a different direction. For when forecasting "on the basis of present policies" stops, and when theoretical model-building on abstract hypotheses has come to an end, we face the really difficult problem from the point of view of economic management. This is, first, to determine the size of total resources and the pattern of use one wishes to achieve at some future date, and, second, to decide on the departures from existing policies that will be required in order to bring this about.

Largely through trial and error much has been achieved here also in a partial sense, as we shall see in our detailed consideration of economic policy objectives and methods. But much more remains to be done before there can be real confidence in the ability of economic planning to provide a reasonably accurate and comprehensive system for managing the economy. It is, therefore, in the analytical discovery of new relationships between individual policies and economic aggregates, the reexamination and refinement of already known connections, and in the development of a comprehensive total system that I would see the major task in this area of economics over the next decade or two.

State of the Art

In most advanced industrial countries economic planning with the means now available has come to be finally accepted by most political parties as the proper framework within which specific economic policies can be developed and employed for both long- and short-term economic management. For the purpose of this brief survey, I limit myself to a short account of the manner in which planning has developed in France, Britain, and the United States, since in these three countries most of the characteristic ways of tackling the problem of overall planning can be seen. With only secondary variations, their experience is repeated in other industrial countries, particularly those of Western Europe. Nothing could better illustrate the change in attitude toward economic planning in the last thirty years than a comparison of the practice in these three countries, all of which have preserved what are commonly regarded as the essential institutions of capitalism.

THE FRENCH PLAN

Historically, the French Plan is the oldest of the three. It developed as a central part of immediate postwar policy when the emphasis had to be on reequipment and modernization, and for some years these were the leading themes. The plan's first aim was to mobilize resources for investment and to direct them in such a way as to construct a secure base for general economic advance. This meant essentially creating the necessary infrastructure: railways, coal, gas and electricity, and later highways. The plan encouraged private enterprise or newly-created mixed private/public institutions to revive French heavy industry (steel, chemicals); and later it was instrumental in initiating the long delayed technological revolution in French agriculture.

As impressive results began to appear, the whole scope of the planning process was widened. The conceptual and statistical apparatus was strengthened and refined. Modern methods of national accounting (up to then not widely accepted nor appreciated in French economic thinking) were applied. The links between the planning organization and other departments of government were strengthened, and more regular and effective processes of consultation with the "interests—" particularly management and unions—were developed, as was the manner in which the legislature and the executive were to collaborate in the plan's evolution and adoption.

This is not the place to describe in detail the nature and procedures of French planning; the British National Plan, being the most recent and in many respects that most closely resembling the French, will give a better opportunity for a brief sketch of what is currently being done. What may be said here, however, is that the French Plan has not only persisted through many political changes in France but has clearly established its claim to having played a predominant part in postwar French economic reconstruction and growth; and that it is certain to continue as a major feature of the French economic order as far ahead as one can see. It has shown that it possesses a growth potential of its own, and it has greatly influenced French economic thinking in the last twenty years.

Indeed, the plan's contribution to the development of economics in France is as great as, and historically perhaps even more significant than, its contribution to actual economic growth. Before the war French economic thought was strikingly backward compared with that of the Anglo-Saxon countries, and also with that of many central European centres of economic teaching and research. Economic teaching was largely attached and subordinated to the teaching of law and was dominated by an exclusively historical approach. Only slight beginnings of interest in modern theoretical developments were to be discerned in France in the Thirties, when the great ferment was well underway elsewhere in the West.

Today the situation is strikingly different. While original contributions to economics from France are still relatively small, teaching and research are now largely imbued with the spirit of modern economics, and the general corpus of Keynesian and post-Keynesian economic work is widely understood in France. While other factors have contributed to this development (particularly the reform of the machinery of training and recruitment for the public service), I would give pride of place to the French Plan for having effected this revolution. Looking ahead, therefore, I would see further developments in the same direction in the years to come: a mutual strengthening of the theory and machinery of planning, and the advance of economic and statistical theory.

THE BRITISH PLAN

As I have said, planning is a recent development in Britain. While some academic work in the subject of economic growth can be found in the prewar period (outstandingly, as can now be seen, in the writings of Colin Clark), it was not until after the war that the government became interested in the subject. The first official attempt to look some years ahead and to set down a comprehensive statement of the probable development of the economy as a whole was closely linked to the requirements of the Marshall Plan (of which more later) and the so-called long-term, *i.e.,* four-year Recovery Program covering the period 1948-52. This was a brave attempt, undertaken not only by Britain but by all the European countries participating in the Marshall Plan.

This first effort was primitive in regard to the means (conceptual and statistical) at its disposal; it was also severely limited, first, by the purposes for which it was undertaken, and, second, by the low level of economic activity and the great uncertainties surrounding economic policy in the immediate postwar period. Since the program was designed to show how, given a certain amount of American aid, the economy could in four years become viable, *i.e.,* capable of continuing to work at a satisfactory rate without the continued injection of aid, it inevitably became part speculative forecast, part wishful thinking. It was (somewhat more than any government plan must inevitably be) essentially a political and diplomatic document.

Nevertheless, the program had an enormous educative value over and above the immediate and highly urgent purpose of making it analytically respectable and politically possible to mobilize large resources from the United States for the revival of the shattered European economies—which, as we now know, turned out to the inestimable benefit of the economy of the whole world. In Britain (and in all the countries concerned) Marshall Plan requirements familiarized politicians, bureaucrats, business men, publicists, and the general public with the notions of forward planning. It made everyone face up to the conditions of "viability," though in this respect its main lessons were to be, as we shall see, in the international field.

It is not entirely clear why this sound beginning of planning was not immediately followed up. One factor was undoubtedly the success of the Marshall Plan itself, the fact that by 1952 the aim originally set had been substantially achieved. Another was the fact that the British Plan was drawn up in an environment still dominated by severe wartime restrictions. This meant that attention was concentrated, in Britain at least, on the use of policy instruments which were to have only a limited life ahead of them, while at the same time there was only an uneasy realization of the inevitability of the freer and more competitive world economy just around the corner.

Whatever the reasons, more than ten years elapsed before these early starts towards planning were followed up. It was not until 1962 that the next step was taken. This was after a period during which the British economy had suffered from the difficulties of short-term economic management afflicted by recurrent cycles of expansion and contraction associated with balance-of-payments crises, and even in the upward phases had shown an inferior performance compared with other European countries. The establishment of a National Economic Development Council to draw up a program of economic growth, and to study the factors influencing it, was the first step in the creation of a new planning machinery. The next was the assumption by the new government in 1964 of direct responsibility for drawing up a plan, to be executed by a newly created Department of Economic Affairs. The first "National Plan" was published in September 1965.

The British Plan, though not fundamentally different from the French, brings out very clearly both the possibilities and the limitations of what has been termed "indicative planning." It is arrived at as a result of a combination of two different processes plus an admixture of a number of other elements. The major contributing elements are a theoretical model and what has been called "the industrial inquiry." The former is the application to the conditions of the British economy of a mixture of forecasting with the injection (and subsequent tracing out of the consequences) of some overriding policy objective—in this instance a healthy balance of payments and the achievement of a given rate of overall growth. The second strand consists of bringing together replies to certain questions concerning industry's own plans over the period of the government plan, made self-consistent as far as possible by uniformity of assumptions, and by a subsequent "dialogue" between the planners and industry representatives which leads to adjustments in the data first supplied.

To these two major sources are added other data. For example, the development programs of the industries in the public sector can be forecast with considerable accuracy, partly because of their long gestation period, partly because the processes of decision-making import a certain minimum time lag before changes can become effective. Government expenditure for education, roads, housing, or health also can be regarded as a relatively more stable element in the total picture, partly because they are directly under the control of the government, partly again because public programs once begun cannot be quickly changed. Sometimes, too, special policy decisions supply fixed points for forward planning; *e.g.*, in the British case the decision to keep total government expenditure within an annual rate of increase of 4¼ percent, or the decision to contain defense spending by 1969/70 within a total of two billion pounds.

All these elements, admittedly of a highly disparate nature, go to make up the total picture. Together they provide something which is a peculiar combination of projections, forecasts, and targets, as well as broad policy objectives to which the government is committed.

The ultimate objective of this form of planning in Britain, as elsewhere, is to employ a gradual process of refinement of each of the constituent elements to build up a rational framework for particular economic decisions made not only by the public authority, but also by private enterprise and, indeed, by the individual citizen.

THE AMERICAN ADAPTATION

In this respect, the United States presents at first sight a different picture. There is nothing called a National Plan. Nor is there a single authority, equivalent to the Commissariat of the Plan in France or the Department of Economic Affairs in Britain, with whom central responsibility in this field rests. The President's Council of Economic Advisers is probably the nearest equivalent to the DEA in Britain; yet the Bureau of the Budget also has crucial overall responsibilities and, for longer-term purposes, is responsible for a great many studies which, elsewhere, might well be regarded as coming within the purview of planning.

Since the passing of the Employment Act of 1946, a summary economic report is submitted annually by the Council to the President and transmitted by him to Congress. This is the nearest thing to a plan produced in the United States. But, unlike those of France, Britain, and many other countries, the report does not project more than one year ahead (though there are, of course, comments and statements on individual matters here and there which relate to a longer time span). This is not the only difference. Large elements of the President's State of the Union message, as well as the annual Economic and Budget messages, must be taken together with the Economic Report to obtain a comprehensive picture of the annual "forward look" for the American economy.

It would be very wrong, however, to conclude from this that the American economy is unplanned. The similarity will come out more clearly when we consider later the instruments of economic policy now in use in all the industrial countries, but some general points may now be made. First of all, the projections, forecasts, targets, and government commitments, which are the characteristic mixture of European planning, also are essential characteristics of the Economic Report and the presidential messages even though they cover a shorter period.

A series of governmental "programs" in the public sector, very often covering a number of years ahead, go to supplement this basic blueprint. In addition, the government sponsors, alongside private foundations and institutions of all kinds (and sometimes in combination with them), research and study projects which cover topics that in other countries are often deliberately made into integral parts of the "Plan"—*e.g.,* population growth, regional development, the industrial implications of technological developments.

Finally, and in some respects most important of all, American business (including both management and labour) has a long history of elaborate and effective forward planning for its own purposes against the background of the general data provided by government. This is a characteristic feature of the American scene which is rarely well appreciated abroad; it certainly is by no means fully established in Europe, where such planning is limited to the largest units of industry. No one who has studied the American economy can fail to be struck by the extent to which broad business decisions for a relatively long time now have been influenced by expectations concerning overall economic aggregates based on careful and highly sophisticated studies akin to those undertaken within the government itself.

Taking it all together, therefore, the differences between Europe and the United States are now more apparent than real. Much might, of course, be made of the different role played by the state in this planning process. In my view this would be mistaking the ideological shadow for the economic substance. Indeed, it may not be too hazardous a prediction to say that a future development in the United States is likely to be in the direction of more comprehensive forward "indicative" planning over a longer period of time in the European manner. Constitutional differences will, however, continue to impose somewhat different patterns.

OUTSIDE THE WEST

A rather more complicated picture is presented by the communist countries in Europe. Here, perhaps, the appearance presents more similarities than the reality. A study of all the changes that have taken place in planning in the Soviet Union and the Eastern European countries is not germane to the general theme of this essay. What seems to have happened, so far as one can judge, is that the practical planning methods employed have tended to become increasingly similar to those used in the West. While much may still be written in Eastern Europe to emphasize basic theoretical concepts derived from Marx, the preoccupations of the planners or their conceptual and statistical apparatus do not seem to be so very different from those in the capitalist countries.

Here, too, it is the balance of the economy as a whole over a period of time that is the centre of attention. How rapid a rate of growth of the total national product can be sustained; how much should be devoted to the development of manufacturing industry; how much to investment in the utilities or in economic and social infrastructure; how far can the rising desires of the population for consumer goods—durables such as motor cars, or soft goods like packaged food or nylon stockings—be satisfied against the competing claims of heavy industry or defense; how fast and by what means can agriculture best be developed (a problem they share both with the capitalist developed countries and with the underdeveloped world); what part shall foreign trade play in the total—these are some of the urgent questions the communists face, and they are no different in kind from those that planners elsewhere pose and try to answer.

The real difference, then, must be sought elsewhere. It lies in the means at the disposal of public authority to realize the planned objective or, put another way, in the sanctions available to it. The organization of society in the communist states is such that responsibility for the execution of the plan is as fixed and centralized as is that for drawing it up. Capital—both in financial and in real terms—and labour can be directed to the uses prescribed by the plan. This is not, of course, a method open to public authority in even the most thoroughly "planned" of Western economies which, while they can affect the operation of the market, must, in the last resort, work through it.

In the early days of the planning controversy this was often regarded as a fatal lack in Western economies and was used by ideologists to assert the ultimate incompatibility of capitalism and economic planning. It is doubtful whether, in the West, many people would argue this now. While planning in the Soviet Union has many remarkable successes to its credit, the failures are also numerous. Nor is it at all apparent that the former are due in any significant measure to the political and social framework within which the economic decisions were taken, rather than to factors for which a perfectly adequate economic explanation can be supplied.

Without wishing to enter into an ideological controversy, I should also say that the market as a mechanism has by no means ceased to exist or to play an important role in the processes of Soviet planning and economic management generally. And as the total and variety of economic goods grows, as well as the proportion this represents of the national product—in short, as society becomes more affluent—the need for the market becomes increasingly clear.

But it would be rash to push the argument about this apparent coalescence of planning very far. Some further increase in the similarity of techniques employed in East and West may well take place in the next few years. What is much less certain is how far the processes by which collective decisions in the economic sphere are taken and then carried out are likely to become similar. One may quite confidently predict that in the capitalist countries the essential characteristics of individual freedom will be preserved, even though this means that better methods will have to be found for disseminating knowledge and thus ensuring individual attitudes that support collective decisions. Nor should one exclude the effect of more refined decision-making methods themselves. How far the authoritarian compulsions now operating in the communist countries are likely to be lessened is less easy to predict since this question in the end is intimately bound up with the larger one of the maintenance of peaceful relations between states.

Much has been written in recent years on the subject of overall economic planning in underdeveloped countries, mainly in relation to the problem of economic growth. For my purpose here, only a few points need be made; others arise more appropriately in relation to the problem of aid for economic development. For reasons to which I have already alluded, economic development in the poorer countries is invariably under close central direction. This predisposes them toward overall economic planning—even if there were not compelling special reasons for each of these countries to endeavour to encase its economic policies within a comprehensive framework called a Plan. In fact, there is no developing country which does not have some form of plan, usually stretching over a five-year period, and the governmental machinery responsible for drawing it up and supervising its execution. In form, they vary from relatively loosely strung together programs for three or four more major sectors of the economy, to more elaborate designs containing the full panoply of model-building and national accounting.

In some respects these plans have some affinity with those of the communist countries. For example, the ingredient of "targeting" is much more prominent, as against that of forecasting. In regard to implementation, too, the power of public authority to impose policies is often considerable and, for obvious reasons, is virtually complete as far as capital investment is concerned. In many of these countries, too, the market mechanism is weak at best. Indeed, the creation of internal markets is for many of them rightly regarded as an important condition for the achievement of the desired rate of economic growth. The direction of enterprise, and of labour, is often a powerful weapon in the hands of the state, particularly where political democratic forms have not yet progressed very far.

Nevertheless, the main approach of these countries to planning is generally that of the capitalist countries; that is, it is based on the acceptance of strong elements of private property, free enterprise, and a considerable degree of freedom of consumers' choice. As I have already remarked when discussing the relation of the state to private enterprise, one of the main problems of these countries is to prevent the general impetus to growth from being used to establish positions of private privilege—economically, socially, and politically.

Overall economic planning can, perhaps, be a helpful instrument in this regard: as a check—both in the drawing up of the Plan and in its execution—against the excessive fostering of some one sector of the economy with old or newly created vested interests as the beneficiaries.

Moreover, comprehensive planning must lead to a strengthening of the general machinery of economic management, to a more rapid spreading of economic knowledge and understanding (itself a powerful safeguard against abuse), and it may perhaps even encourage the greater cohesion of economic and political democracy. It also supplies a useful point of contact with foreign economic expertise which can, in addition to its other uses, also serve as a check of the good sense and the integrity of domestic economic management.

For all these reasons, I would expect planning in the sense here described to grow rather than diminish in the underdeveloped world in the years to come. It is likely also to increase in complexity and to resemble more in technique the forms now prevalent in the advanced capitalist countries.

Chapter 7   The Instruments of Economic Policy

SHORT-TERM MANAGEMENT of the economy traditionally is accomplished by the use of two instruments: fiscal policy and monetary policy. Fiscal policy, through the annual budget, sets the stage. It determines the total volume of government expenditure, its distribution over different areas, and the manner in which the revenue to meet it is to be raised. These determinations have much to do with how the economy as a whole and its individual members will fare in the ensuing period—although recognition of the profound economic impact of the government's handling of its own annual household affairs is, as we have seen, a relatively new development. Monetary policy traditionally is designed to supplement fiscal policy and to make it more effective in the even shorter-term, often with particular reference to the balance-of-payments relationship between the domestic economy and the rest of the world.

Monetary Policy

Monetary policy as a conscious instrument of general economic manage-ment is not new; its bearing on the general level of economic activity was rec-ognized (and indeed was consciously developed for the purpose) long before the annual budget ceased to be regarded purely as a means of setting the pat-tern of the state's income and expenditure. In a sense, therefore, the theoretical revolution brought about by the development of macroeconomics has had less impact in this field. Nevertheless, here too there had to be big changes.

Until recently, monetary policy, at least as practised, continued to bear a close family resemblance to the quantity theory of money long after this con-cept had been replaced by more sophisticated doctrines. Traditional monetary policy had been closely tied in with the old gold standard and preserved many of the features of the classical "mechanism" long after the classical standard it-self had disappeared. The influence of the new theories of full-employment equilibrium was first felt in the field of fiscal policy, leaving monetary policy for some time isolated from the main stream and treated as relevant primarily to a country's international position.

Now fiscal and monetary policies have come to be considered—practically and theoretically—as indissolubly linked in their bearing on the domestic

66

economy as well as on balance of payments. It is something of a paradox that, while the macroeconomic role of monetary policy was never in doubt, it took some time to evolve the precise way in which it could and did operate according to the new economic doctrine.

The objectives of monetary policy are also undergoing a change. In the pre-war years it was primarily regarded, for domestic purposes, as an anti-cyclical weapon, and even there its efficiency was a matter of considerable debate. Doubts then expressed sprang primarily from different theories—monetary or otherwise—of the causation of the "business cycle," and they have even greater force now that cyclical fluctuations in economic activity, at least as they were understood thirty years ago, no longer hold the centre of the stage. Much present-day economic thinking seems tacitly to proceed from the assumption that the "business cycle" is dead, although few economists would express complete confidence that significant economic fluctuations have been finally banished. In any event the simple explanations which led to the most acrimonious controversies between different schools have no place in modern macroeconomics.

Once the problem of short-term economic management is posed in terms of preserving the highest level of economic activity (including employment) consistent with the avoidance of inflationary pressures, the relatively subordinate role of monetary policy becomes clear. This is not, however, to say that it does not play an important, and sometimes vital, part in sustaining the purposes of fiscal policy and preventing them from being frustrated, and for short periods monetary considerations may still take the leading role.

If the approach to monetary policy has changed, so also have the instruments and techniques for implementing it. Public authority now has an increasingly important part to play. This is partly due to the increasing influence government exercises over central interest-rate fixing, as well as over the central banking operations that determine the total volume of credit in the system. In the United States, the Federal Reserve System continues to be independent of the executive, an independence that is still demonstrated in practice from time to time. Nevertheless, it would be foolish to deny that there is a strict limit to the extent to which government policy and Central Bank-directed monetary policy can diverge for any length of time. In Britain ultimate decision on bank-rate policy is formally in the hands of the government, as it is in France and most other European countries.

The government's role has also been enhanced by the vast increase in its own needs for finance, both short- and long-term. This has meant that government, quite apart from legal or conventional processes cited above, has almost always and everywhere a decisive influence on the volume of credit available in the market, and on its price. One may confidently expect both these factors to grow in importance. For this reason alone the integration of monetary policy into the general framework of economic management can be expected to become even more significant in the future.

Another factor of recent years which is likely to be even more prominent in the years ahead is the growth of international cooperation in monetary policy, a subject which will be treated later in a wider context. This is not a novel aspect of economic policy; even the classical mechanism required the observance of certain "rules of the game" for relating domestic policies to international monetary movements. In the disturbed days of crises and depressions of the Thirties the practice of close cooperation between central banks became very firmly established, and this practice was continued in the postwar world, first to handle inconvertible currencies and exchange-rate disturbances, later in a process of gradual progress towards widespread convertibility and fixed parities. Today such cooperation is continuous and taken for granted.

There is, however, still debate over how far this cooperation is limited to technical aspects and therefore leaves something to be desired in terms of necessary objectives of monetary policy in a modern setting. This question not only raises the issue of the relationship of central banks and treasuries but also involves larger considerations of international economic cooperation now that economic policies have new and wider desiderata as their objectives. I shall, therefore, deal with this later when discussing the international economy and its problems.

Fiscal Policy

The revolution which the other traditional arm of economic policy has undergone is well known, and I have already referred to it on a number of occasions. Although the forms in which economic analysis is brought to bear on the construction of the national budget, its subsequent presentation, and the execution of policies to subserve it may differ from country to country, essentially the process is always the same. An estimate is made of the economic prospects ahead on the basis of a national-income analysis, including the assumption of existing policies, especially prospective revenue from existing taxes. Where the balance of payments is of special importance, as in Britain for example, particular attention is paid to the forecasts relating to international trade and to their interconnection with domestic aggregates, particularly with the level of demand and of employment. Given certain desiderata, a judgment is then made as to the extent to which the level of demand is likely to be above or below the level consistent with the general balance of the system: a certain rate of growth of GDP, the state of the balance of payments, etc. The result provides some measure of the total which, by fiscal means, would need to be injected into, or taken out of, the economy—the fiscal means being either changes in government expenditure (not always easy to accomplish in the short term) or changes in taxation.

That these new methods can be efficacious is now established beyond any reasonable doubt. In Britain, where they have been practised with remarkable consistency and continuity for the greater part of the postwar period, they have proved to be capable of achieving a particular result with a high degree of certainty, provided they are applied quickly and with sufficient force. Perhaps the greatest triumph of the new theory to date is to be seen in the unanimity with which modern economists in the United States advocated a cut in taxation before and in the early days of President Kennedy's term, the relative speed with which it was adopted, the results which flowed from it, and the extent to which these corresponded to predictions.

Nevertheless, many doubts remain about the extent to which reliance can be placed on the new fiscal approach. The British experience, though intellectually somewhat satisfying, is for practical purposes far from reassuring. It could be argued that the situation was made special by the balance-of-payments problem that overhung the total economic picture throughout the period, and that fiscal policy (supported by monetary measures) was used to redress short-term balance-of-payments crises. Even so, while it proved relatively easy at times to create a sharp downturn in economic activity and at other times (as in 1963-64) a considerable upturn, the newly orthodox weapon of fiscal policy did not create conditions of steady growth and provide a consistent improvement in the balance of payments.

More generally—and here the experience of the United States is particularly apposite—it cannot be said that the new policies have been tested in a sufficiently wide range of conditions to justify final judgment on their adequacy. Opportunities to do so are already presenting themselves and will doubtless continue to arise. But there is also an understandable hesitation, in facing real issues of economic management, to accept exclusive reliance on these measures. Dangers are inherent in the deep-seated human desire for the philosopher's stone that solves all problems, and there can be a fatal fascination in self-contained systems of analysis, however useful and elegant they may seem. We know the lurking pitfalls of ultimate irrationality that lay concealed behind all the great systems of the past. In this instance there is tangible reason for doubting the infallibility of analysis which yields almost automatic answers as to what "to take out of" or "put into" the economy—a process which might lead to what I have termed the disease of "macroeconomicosis."

Because of this sense of inadequacy, attempts are being made in a number of countries, notably Britain and the United States, to find means for supplementing macroeconomic fiscal and monetary policy with more specific measures and instruments for influencing the economic process. In this context fiscal measures designed for more long-term economic objectives will naturally also find their place.

The trend I expect to become more pronounced in the next few years stems not merely from general malaise over fiscal policy as such, or even more philosophic doubt about the adequacy of the use of only "broad spectrum" instruments of economic policy. Apostles of *laissez faire,* who in the Thirties charged, "scratch a planner and you will find a dictator," will doubtless sound the alarm at this search for instruments capable of a sharper focus in influencing the economy. It is already argued that this is a symptom of the inevitable disease of planners, at best the result of an unjustifiably "technological" approach to economic and social problems. We shall return to this point in the concluding section of this work; here it must suffice to say that one can find fairly obvious practical reasons for the search for such policy instruments without invoking elaborate sociological or psychological explanations. The tendency is another manifestation of increasing recognition that existing economic policies, and the instruments by which they are implemented, already are capable of changing otherwise expectable effects of general fiscal or monetary measures.

The composition of the government's own expenditure, in financial and in real terms, is a striking example. It must be clear that when expenditure in the public sector reaches, as it does in some countries, one-third or more of the national product, general fiscal policy decisions, even though they do not alter the expenditure-revenue balance, produce marked results through the detailed changes they effect in the public expenditure-revenue pattern; and it is these which can have the most important bearing on the overall condition of the economy. Cutting back the defense program in order to increase school construction, highway improvement, or subsidy for home owners can have as important a bearing on the economy (certainly in the somewhat longer term) as decisions to increase total expenditure, raise more revenue, raise the debt ceiling, or go for higher direct taxes rather than expanding indirect levies.

In every major government program important decisions constantly must be made about the proportion of income to be devoted to current expenditure and to investment. Aside from their direct fiscal impact, the workings of these budgets may determine the shape of the infrastructure—and of the enterprises dependent upon it—for years ahead. Education, for example, depends almost entirely on the public purse, and the private economic sector depends almost entirely upon the educational establishment to supply personnel with the special skills required by a dynamic, rapidly changing economy.

If the objectives of fiscal and monetary policy could be limited to the maintenance of some sort of balance in the economy in the short term, these troublesome factors could perhaps be left out of account; and we could content ourselves with refining the means which have been employed in the postwar period "to keep the economy on an even keel." The difficulty with this analogy, as with most others, is that it deceptively simplifies the problem. Keeping the economy on an even keel is a problem not only of influencing its conduct in the light of expected developments, but also of reacting appropriately to the unforeseen—and the unforeseen is often the fruition of individual policies embarked upon at an earlier stage. Timing is of the essence here. The government is constantly and inexorably involved in taking decisions whose influence over the economy will only become apparent some years hence, while fiscal and monetary policy decisions inevitably take effect within a short space of time.

The trouble is that the objectives of economic management simply cannot be constricted within the scope of "short-term balance." There are certain desiderata which have, for good or ill, acquired general acceptance and aroused expectations which have become political "facts of life"; and now we must recognize that many of these desiderata—balance in international payments, high level of employment, rapidly rising living standards, and a high rate of growth—are not spontaneously consistent with each other.

It follows from this that general fiscal and monetary decisions more often than not involve a conscious decision to give one desideratum priority over another, thus varying the place where the equity risk of economic management falls. Moreover, the points at which desiderata of this kind can, at least temporarily, be reconciled may not vary greatly in accordance with short-term policy decisions, but can be located only in terms of specific decisions that set a course from which there can be little deviation for an extended period.

Consideration of long-term or "structural" problems in the economy, and of policies appropriate to them, along with those of short-term balance is becoming a characteristic feature of the modern approach to economic management. This, of course, means finding ways to bring together in a meaningful manner both general and specific instruments of economic policy. The problem has appeared most clearly in recent years in Britain, where the long persistence of a balance-of-payments problem has directed attention to the need to improve the competitiveness of industry through structural changes thought necessary to achieve it. But it is not unknown elsewhere. As the context is widened to include more general economic or social objectives, it will obviously become significant in every country.

The need for more specific policies may be seen by reviewing the history of three that have played a part, or still do, in most of the advanced industrial countries: regional policy, industrial policy, and incomes policy.

Regional Policy

Before World War II a number of countries had identified certain protracted economic problems on a regional basis. In Britain, Italy, France, and Germany, depressed areas were defined and singled out for special treatment, and the fashion spread to the United States, particularly during the days of the New Deal. But these forerunners of present-day regional policy were relatively narrow in conception; specific local problems gave rise to them, and they predated the macroeconomic approach to economic policy. In nearly all cases relief and reconstruction were paramount. Sometimes it was a case of bringing into the mainstream of national development areas that for historic reasons had been left behind in the course of modern development and had preserved an antiquated economic (and often social) structure. Remedy was often sought in initiating works to mobilize some unutilized resource: the draining of marshlands, the opening of disused mines, or in the American Tennessee Valley a comprehensive program of flood control, navigation, and hydroelectric development. Britain developed regional schemes to cope with exceptionally heavy unemployment caused by the impact of the depression on areas in which economic activity was highly concentrated in only one or two sectors—coal mining and shipbuilding, for example.

It was not until the postwar period, when governments had become generally committed to full-employment policies and adequate growth had become both the objective and the badge of good economic management, that a different approach to regional problems began to emerge. The relief and reconstruction aspect has not entirely disappeared; it provides a motivating force for such programs as Appalachia in the United States, and the Italian *Mezzogiorno*. But increasingly a wider view is taken of the relation between regional development and general economic growth. This can be seen clearly in the regional policies developed under the aegis of the Commission of the European Economic Community for a number of areas in the Community's member countries.

The regional policy Britain embarked upon in the Sixties shows not only the changed approach but indicates the direction in which we may expect regional policy to evolve in the next phase. The essential basis is recognition that regional imbalance is embedded in the current level of economic activity and in its prospective future development; without correction, the usual determinants of industrial location will perpetuate it. Thus attention is now being paid to the underlying reasons for the cumulative growth of certain industries in particular regions. Governments in Britain have been preoccupied for some time by the compelling fact that, whether measured by differential unemployment rates, by population shift, by trends of urbanization, housing densities, or traffic congestion, striking economic differences can be observed between different parts of the country: the Southeast of England being in the lead and the Northeast and parts of Scotland well in the rear.

Attempts to redress the balance can, of course, be attacked on the ground that they interfere with the free play of market forces. However, what is now known about the economic theory of social cost, external economies, and diseconomies, and all the other developments in the framework within which market decisions work, has made that sort of argument largely irrelevant. The novelty of the new approach to the correction of regional imbalance lies in the fact that it is equally concerned with high-activity and low-activity regions, and that in the case of the latter it puts the emphasis on the potential for overall regional growth and development rather than on the provision of temporary, and not necessarily economic, outlets for unused resources.

Regional development thus becomes an integral part of general economic planning rather than a welfare exercise. Interesting problems naturally arise, first as regards the setting-up of new planning machinery to give effect to this new approach, and secondly as to the policies to be applied so that its operation will achieve a better balance throughout the country. The former need not detain us much. Essentially the solution adopted in Britain consists in the establishment of a number of planning regions and the creation in each of a Regional Economic Planning Board (composed of the official representatives in the region of the government departments concerned) and a Regional Economic Planning Council, representative of (though not directly responsible to) the primary regional interests: local government, industry (both management and unions), education, and so on. Each Council, served by its Board, is to draw up a regional plan within the framework of the National Plan; and the total network is meant to provide a means for collecting regional data and opinions for the guidance of the National Plan, as well as to inject the major features of the plan into regional thinking.

Perhaps the most interesting aspects of this machinery from the point of view of possible future developments are, first, the extent to which more general issues of planning, apart from strictly economic problems, are likely to occupy an important place in the work of these bodies, and, secondly, the functions the new network of regional-national relations is likely to have in relation to the more general evolution of the machinery of local government.

For Britain, at least, it seems probable that if the present machinery continues (and there is no reason to think that it will not) it will be used increasingly for what is known as general environmental planning. This will include such matters as transport, as well as amenities. Of course, the wider the scope, the greater the issues that will arise in relating the new responsibilities of the planning bodies to the long-established ones of existing elements in the structure of local government. It is, therefore, perhaps not just coincidence that Britain has created a Royal Commission to consider the future of local government.

Regional planning and development within the framework of national policy inevitably poses problems in the financial sphere. In countries with a federal structure, such as the United States and the German Federal Republic, the allocation of resources and taxing powers is, of course, a constant problem. But in Britain, too, the issue has become one that will require continual reexamination in the light of changing economic requirements and conditions, both national and regional. The matter of financial relations abuts on issues of a political order, but it is germane here in terms of its impact on key fiscal measures—as, for example, in the plan urged in the United States for some kind of comprehensive federal/state tax revenue equalization program.

The most important specific methods of implementing regional policy are those in which the economic (or, more specifically, financial) incentives and disincentives for enterprise are altered. This, however, is best considered in relation to industrial policy, to which I now turn.

Industrial Policy

I have already had something to say about the relation between the state and business and about the varying frontier between public and private enterprise. The subject of industrial policy covers policies relating to all forms of business, *i.e.,* trade and commerce as well as industry in the strict sense of the word. It perhaps can best be defined as the complex of government policies (other than the most general means of monetary and fiscal management of the balance of the economy) that directly affect the different sectors of business enterprise. It covers, therefore, the considerable ground between direct management by public or para-public bodies and the application of more general and indirect instruments of economic policy.

It follows that the characteristic features of industrial policy are that it is selective and discriminatory, and that it bears directly on one or more specific sectors of business. Its area is large, and, contrary to some popular belief, it is by no means wholly novel. Regulation of entry into trades, location of factories, and legislation concerning the safety of those employed go back to the earliest days of modern industry. The scope and complexity of measures of this kind have grown in recent years, it is true, but direct government intervention, restraint, and control are still exceptions rather than the rule. That the trend should be extended in times of war or in near-war conditions is, of course, inevitable; otherwise, acceleration tends to be the result of special circumstances, such as prolonged depression, though here, too, the growth usually has deep historical roots.

While agriculture does not, strictly speaking, fall within the scope of industrial policy, it provides the outstanding example of wide, intensive, and long-standing state regulation and intervention. Since the future of agricultural policy is very much bound up with the evolution of the world economic system as a whole, I propose to deal with it later on.

One of the earliest attempts to set up major constraints within which business must operate was directed toward the prevention of monopoly. Here, the United States led the field for a long time, but other countries have followed suit. In Britain, there are a Monopolies Commission and a Restrictive Practices Court, and in the European Economic Community regulations designed for similar ends have been employed in this effort to create a unified internal market. These interventions go at least as far as any that have been known in the United States.

It would, however, be very rash to suppose that we can yet see a stable pattern in this field. The need to preserve competition in the interest of the consumer and of industrial progress, and the pressure toward the larger industrial unit required to take advantage of the cost-reducing possibilities of modern technology, produces a conflict not yet satisfactorily resolved either in economic theory or in the practice of governments. This can be seen at work most strikingly in Britain. The structural regeneration of British industry is widely held to require, *inter alia,* the creation of larger industrial units, some reduction in variety, some concentration on "long-runs" of production, and similar developments that may well conflict with existing legislation and regulation of restrictive practices or of mergers.

This will continue to be an important area of discussion and innovation in the next few decades. The crucial factor that will condition the possible solutions is, I believe, the future evolution of the size of the market. This will depend on institutional (*i.e.,* semipolitical) developments as well as on the general rate of growth of economic activity. In the United States the conflict seems to be largely contained at present, mainly as a result of a large domestic market and of extremely successful economic growth policies which have provided an ever enlarging scope for improved productivity without precluding continued opportunity for new enterprise. It will be a major problem to ensure that both these two possibilities are preserved in the industrial countries of the world.

The last three decades have seen increasing preoccupation with the means by which the state might use its influence so as to achieve certain specific purposes in the private sector which extends beyond primary industry. The collapse of large segments of the banking system in the United States in the Great Depression led to almost revolutionary changes in the structure of banking and finance, the regulation of financial markets, and to a variety of legislation governing corporations in general. The upheaval of those New Deal years effected a lasting political change, one which at a stroke brought the United States—its strong noninterventionist tradition notwithstanding—well to the fore among the advanced industrial countries in the scope and depth of its regulation of finance.

In the United States and elsewhere the depression led to a search for

employment-creating policies which have left a legacy of permanent enlargement of the area of public or semipublic enterprise. In more indirect ways, too,
through efforts to preserve large corporations or whole industries from collapse, the state became involved in reconstruction and subsidy schemes which
provided precedent for later, more permanent developments.

The increasing emphasis placed on the achievement and maintenance of an
adequate rate of economic growth naturally has led to study of the factors which
promote or impede such growth. Intercountry comparisons have become fashionable to the extent that they constitute a further source of pressure for new
growth policies. Unsatisfactory performance by one country in comparison with
others, particularly when it has been a more or less consistent phenomenon over
a period of years, also tends to direct attention to structural problems, *i.e.,* those
that almost by definition are not easily tackled by general instruments of economic management geared primarily to short-term phenomena.

The usual result of this intensive study of the growth problem is the elaboration of new suggestions in the general field I have called "Industrial Policy." In
simple terms, the problem usually resolves itself into one of changing the pattern of resource use. "Growth points" have to be identified. That means picking
out activities in industry and trade (and ancillary or conditioning activities of
the state) that—on the basis of forecasts for population changes, trends in demand and world trade, and so forth—hold out the greatest prospect of rapid
expansion. Their reverse counterparts are the industries and trades, and the related activities undertaken by the state, that are likely to shrink in any future
period under review. The ultimate determinants of these changes are, of
course, those which have always produced the ebb and flow of economic activity: technological change based on new scientific discoveries, population movements, changing economic and other relations between countries (often themselves influenced by their own varying rate of economic evolution), and the
broad cultural changes (including those of demand) which go with them.

The novelty is that policy makers no longer accept adverse consequences of
these changes without making an attempt to influence them in some manner.
The political, sociological, and other reasons why popular notions as to what
constitutes an adequate rate of growth have become such powerful political
factors are beyond the scope of this essay. That they have done so, however, is
self-evident, and we can assume the search will go on for new policies to meet
the aspirations they engender. It can only lead to further theoretical and practical endeavour in the area of industrial policies as here defined.

CONDITIONS OF GROWTH

A clear idea of what is involved can perhaps once again be derived from examination of recent developments in Great Britain. Prevailing dissatisfaction

with the postwar performance of the British economy, and with the policies by which it was managed, centred not only in the frustrations of the "stop-go" cycle but on the consistent failure to achieve a high growth-rate compared with other countries. This was not merely a matter of national pride. Here was a country with a very high standard of living, the result of a long history of industrial and commercial achievement matched by progress in politics and education, which spread the egalitarian idea that economic comfort and security should be the objective of all rather than the privilege of a few. As a result, private and public consumption, and the investment required to sustain it, were constantly pressing upon the limits of available resources.

At the same time, Britain was saddled with large commitments all over the world for defense and foreign-policy purposes (including aid to developing countries); and a radical change in her underlying world-trading and financial position produced a precarious balance of payments. Against this dismal background there was no choice but to launch a search for new industrial policies to provide for the constantly rising social objectives now accepted, in practice, by governments of both the major political parties.

The essential condition for faster growth was seen to lie in changing the general structure, attitude, and operating practices of British industry. These included slow and incomplete introduction of new technology, antiquated operating methods, and ineffective management-labour relations often conditioned by mental attitudes shaped before full employment became the generally accepted objective of policy. The consequences were low productivity, ineffective industrial organization, and a lagging adaptation of publicly provided infrastructure—*e.g.,* transport and education—to the needs of a modern economy.

It was recognized that to change all this would be a formidable task. It involved, above all, changing human attitudes. Exhortation and education were two obvious methods, but their effectiveness must always remain very limited. Labour market policies were renovated and intensified. These included measures designed to make the transfer of labour from declining to flourishing employment markets easier to accomplish. Training schemes were multiplied and more carefully focused; redundancy and severance-payment schemes were introduced; the drawing up of manpower budgets was stimulated and special attention was paid to redeployment possibilities for particular industries. The regional policy described earlier was enlisted as a further potential stimulus to faster general growth. A great drive was launched to change the attitude of management and trade unions to restrictive practices that prevented the best utilization of labour and held back increase in productivity.

This produced a new network of relationships with industry designed to bring new ideas in technology, labour relations, and structural and production policies to the fore, and to relate them to the conditions of individual industries. The National Economic Development Council has already been mentioned as a milestone in the evolution of planning in Britain. Within it there have been created some twenty National Economic Development Committees covering most of the important industries and the vast bulk of the employed population. The total network provides an interesting example of the new pattern in government/industry relationships. Tripartite structure prevails throughout: the committees, like the Council itself, are made up of members representing management, unions, and government, with an admixture of independent persons. They act as a unique combination of research and discussion groups, sources for the dissemination of knowledge, and agencies for elaborating and proposing new measures for industrial improvement to be undertaken either by government or by industry itself.

Finally, this concern for greater growth through changes in the operation of industry and trade also has affected the direction of thought in matters of fiscal policy. The stimulation of capital investment by the tax system, or the possibilities of influencing the utilization of labour in different industries by such devices as employment or payroll taxes and subsidies, are instruments now being actively studied and experimented with after being little used in previous decades. Here, too, regional differentiation is employed in order to create financial incentives and disincentives to achieve particular objectives of industrial policy.

What of the future of all these attempts and the devices to which they have given rise? It is perhaps significant that direct measures designed to influence industry have been most to the fore in countries like Great Britain, which is faced with rather special structural problems resulting from the failure of the market, upon which the whole industrial process is focused, to expand as rapidly as the needs of the community required. In the United States, and in the European Economic Community, the search for new industrial policies has been much less evident. If it follows from this that a continuously growing market is of significance in determining the eagerness with which governments turn to industrial policies, then future developments will turn very largely on patterns of world trade, regional groupings, and the like.

There are, however, intrinsic forces for expansion in the industrial policies already in being. New methods of contact between government and business (like those elaborated in Britain) will themselves make cooperation closer, and this, in turn, will increase the opportunity for still further governmental experiments at least in consultation. One cannot be so sanguine about the effect on business of discriminatory fiscal devices; this question is bound up with the more general question of the future of taxation policy.

I have at an earlier point committed myself to the view that the essential features of what we call capitalism are still maintained in the advanced Western countries (however much they may be circumscribed by planning and other policies) and will continue to be characteristic of these nations in the future. The question may, therefore, be asked whether the expansion of industrial policies, including discriminatory fiscal devices, which I expect to take place, is consistent with this view. Does it not connote a gradual shrinkage of free enterprise and the rights normally associated with private property and private capital formation? I do not think so. The very essence of these industrial policies is precisely that they are designed to work through the private enterprise mechanism rather than to replace it.

These policies provide a means of buttressing indicative planning by the use of incentives and disincentives, though it must be recognized that there is a paradox here. For the less indicative planning is successful by itself—*i.e.,* through a mainly educative process—the more it may demonstrate the need for more specific policies, including industrial policies. Yet these, by their very nature, make more difficult the achievement of the plan by a spontaneous process of voluntary adaptation of individual business policies resulting from deeper and more widespread understanding of national or collective requirements. This, however, is a much broader question of social and political structure. It is further illustrated by another major new development in economic management: incomes policy.

Productivity, Prices, and Incomes Policy

In Britain, and increasingly in other countries, the older term, Incomes Policy, is being replaced by the more precise Productivity, Prices, and Incomes Policy. This represents a relatively new feature of governmental policy thinking, but it has quickly become highly fashionable in many industrial countries. Once again the theoretical roots can be traced to the revolution brought about in modern economics by the work of Keynes. At least three strands can be identified: two are directly connected with Keynes's own analysis, the third stems from the elaboration of his whole system in recent years.

In the analysis of the financial phenomena of World War I, to be found in a number of Keynes's writings, and especially in passages in the *Treatise on Money* (1930)[1], there are quite explicit theorems linking money, wages, real income (*i.e.,* that involving price movements), and the calls of the government on resources for its own purposes, with personal consumption as the residue. The purpose of the analysis was different in detail from that which recent problems have made necessary: it was to demonstrate what virtuous war finance meant in terms of the profit inflation-income inflation pattern of the Keynesian theory of the day. A further development of this same line of thought—this

[1] Macmillan, London, 1960.

time inspired by the theoretical pattern of the *General Theory*—can be seen in Keynes's ideas on financing World War II. In both cases, the theoretically seminal element was to be found in the interrelation established between the various broad uses of the national product and its reflection in the movement of incomes and prices.

Today, with a more complete theoretical framework at our disposal, we can see more clearly the various problems involved in the pattern of resource allocation through time where specific policy objectives have to be achieved, such as an improvement in the balance of payments; or where dynamic factors, such as increases in productivity, have to be taken into account. Keynesian theories have made us familiar with the notions of the inflationary gap and the deflationary gap. Incomes policy has been evolved as one possible further instrument for preventing the emergence of either of these symptoms of economic imbalance. What it amounts to, very briefly, is an attempt to ensure that average money wages do not increase at a faster rate than the average increase in physical productivity. The price aspect must necessarily be associated with this. If the rise in money incomes is in some way to be restrained, this will not accord with principles of justice and, therefore, will be politically impracticable, unless prices are at the same time put under some form of control to prevent real incomes from being eroded.

The crucial new feature of our economic situation which led to the adoption of "incomes policy" is the general acceptance of the maintenance of full employment as a major objective. Once this is done one of the variables in the process of adjustment in a dynamic economic situation, namely the volume of employment, has been rendered wholly or partially inoperative. The danger of incomes getting out of line with changes in output is, therefore, ever present.

Naturally, in a democratic society (taking the term in its largest sense as one in which the pressure of individuals to improve living standards as output grows is a major political force) the likelihood is that incomes will outrun increases in productivity. As I have already indicated, this problem can arise both in the general course of a dynamic change of the economy or for quite specific short-term reasons, such as a deterioration in the balance of payments. These two sets of factors, of course, are nearly always connected.

Once again recent events in Britain provide a useful case study, closely paralleled by developments in the United States. At the beginning of the Sixties British governments attempted to break out of the frustrating "stop-go" cycle by turning their attention to the behaviour of incomes in the "go" phase, and seeking to restrain them as an additional means of closing an emerging inflationary gap. A new policy was evolved, which was first called a "pay pause." The later development of a "guiding light" principle was probably influenced by the most complete statement of the theoretical basis for the policy, *The Problem of Rising Prices,* a report by a number of distinguished economists produced for the Organization for European Economic Cooperation.

The policy did not in fact succeed to any significant extent. It ran into severe political trouble through being first, and most vigorously, applied in the case of public employees. The government could, of course, most readily influence this area, but only by laying itself open to charges of unfairness. Nor did the creation of a National Incomes Commission, to provide "an impartial and authoritative view on the more important or difficult pay questions," have more than a mild effect in slowing down the rise in incomes.

A fresh attempt to make the policy more effective was made by the new government that came to power in October 1964. Its first fruit was a "Declaration of Intent" signed by representatives of government, management, and trade unions, which, whatever the subsequent evolution, or success, of the policy, deserves mention as a landmark in the economic education of those primarily responsible for the conduct of the economy. Though linked to the immediate economic state of the country, it enunciated as a basic objective "urgent and vigorous action to raise productivity throughout industry and commerce, to keep increases in total money incomes in line with increases in real national output, and to maintain a stable general price level." It stated the penalty for failure to achieve these objectives as "a slower rate of growth and a lower level of employment."

From the time of this Declaration of Intent—December 16, 1964—the policy continued to develop through a number of stages. In February 1965 a statement was issued describing the machinery to be created to give effect to the policy set forth in the Declaration. This consisted of a Royal Commission, known as the National Board for Prices and Incomes, which would examine prices or groups of prices for goods and services and would review claims and settlements relating to wages and salaries and other conditions of work. The initiative for referring cases to the Board was kept in the hands of the government. The Board was not to have any powers of compulsion; the voluntary basis of the policy was to be preserved, and "persuasion and the pressure of public opinion" were to be "relied upon to ensure that the findings and recommendations of the Board" were accepted.

The next step followed fairly rapidly with the announcement of the members and the terms of reference of the Board, and a statement of the criteria to be applied in considering price and incomes cases. These were set forth in a White Paper published in April 1965, which is of considerable importance in showing the manner in which factors of economic analysis interact with political and administrative considerations in the formulation of government policy in one of the most difficult fields of modern economic management. The most important aspect of this elaborate statement was the emphasis, on the one hand, on the need to absorb cost increases by increased efficiency in order to maintain price stability, and, on the other, on the need to maintain "the average rate of annual increase of money incomes per head" in line with a norm which would be consistent with stability in the general level of prices. (The norm was stated, at the time, as being of the order of 3 to 3½ percent.)

By September 1965 it was clearly felt that the pressure of public opinion— as epitomized in the report of the National Board—had not been sufficient to slow down the increase in incomes to a level appropriate to the continued need to cure the balance-of-payments deficit and to restore the lack of financial confidence thus engendered. The government announced its intention of introducing—on a statutory basis—a compulsory "early-warning" system for prices and incomes; and by November 1965 the details of how this was to operate—on a voluntary basis until legislative powers could be secured—had been worked out in consultation with management and unions. The bill to provide for the necessary powers was introduced in the spring of 1966 and, while still retaining the voluntary basis for the policy, made it possible, after consultation with both management and labour and subject to certain parliamentary procedures, to invoke powers which would enable the government to enforce a total delay of four months before a projected wage or price increase could take effect.

The final phase in this long story was reached in July 1966, before the bill was passed, when the government, as part of a series of emergency measures to disinflate the economy in the interests of the balance of payments, added a new provision (limited to a life of twelve months only) under which it could direct that specified prices, charges, or rates of remuneration should not be increased, or to reverse increases that had already taken place. In the end, therefore, and under the pressure of a severe balance-of-payments crisis, the government, while preserving the earlier policy (which it was intended should become a permanent feature of the economic order) had felt obliged to buttress it, as a strictly temporary measure, with reserve powers of a wide-ranging kind, more severe in character in some respects than any used even in wartime.

The experience is described here at some length because it has taken this particular aspect of economic management further in Britain than it has gone in any of the other highly developed industrial countries facing similar problems. In the United States, for example, a comparable policy has developed to the stage of the British "criteria" (or "guidelines" in Washington's terminology) but without the creation of an independent body to apply them. The President's Council of Economic Advisers is, appropriately, regarded as the custodian of the guidelines, although, in practice, important cases tend increasingly to involve the President himself at a quite early stage. Other countries, too, particularly Germany, are beginning to experience the inflationary pressures from which, like the United States, they had been relatively free for a considerable period.

At this writing, the radical new development of policy in Britain, the great increase in the number and importance of cases being dealt with by the existing means in the United States, and the increasing search for effective new machinery in Germany and other countries, have not yet reached a point where a clear prognosis for the short-term success of incomes policy in general can be made. Some reflections are nevertheless in order on the longer-term significance, on the means used for trying to implement the policy, and on the probable future course of development over the next two or three decades.

A Policy of Self-Restraint

It must be recognized that in one way or another what is being attempted here is a major, and quite unprecedented, modification of the market economy without an impairment of its essentially free character—that is, modification by means which do not, in the last resort (and excepting the temporary crisis powers in Britain) involve actual direction of final settlements in matters that had hitherto been regarded as reserved for free individual bargaining. Another way of putting it is to say that a new factor is being invoked in the continual struggle of economic policy to maintain a dynamic balance in the economy. This factor is individual self-restraint in the strictly economic sphere. The justification for self-restraint is that in the absence of such restraint, frustration of national objectives of policy, and inevitably, therefore, of individual aspirations also, must be the result. It is, in my view, hard to overestimate the potential significance of this development for the future shape of the economic order, at least in the developed, so-called capitalist, countries.

The elements of this incomes policy are not wholly new. Not only were there theoretical bases in the work of Keynes to which I have already referred, but the conflict between full employment and stable prices as a practical danger had already been pointed out by other economists and politicians, many of whom had recognized that if this danger was to be avoided, excessive wage increases would have to be kept in check. This meant at the least that trade unions would have to act with a sense of social responsibility. Perhaps even more important, experiments to give effect to a "responsible" incomes policy, *i.e.,* one which linked wage movements to productivity, had started long before the recent developments in America and Britain which I have described in some detail. In particular, the Swedish incomes policy, and the concomitant changes in trade-union structure and practice as well as in the techniques of wage bargaining, has been developed very much in line with the progress of theoretical thinking.

We are, I believe, faced here with a tendency which may well become the major testing ground for the survival of some of the familiar and generally highly regarded features of our Western communities. Involved are: the structure of trade unions as well as of employers' organizations; the methods of collective bargaining, with their long and often turbulent histories in industrial societies; the role of the state in the processes of price-fixing and income determination in what remains an essentially free-market economy; and, in the ultimate, the methods by which in a democratic state the pattern of resource allocation through time is to be determined.

It is possible that recognition of the magnitude of the issues involved in the creation of a successful incomes policy (that is, one retaining a basically voluntary character) will lead to a revival of older controversies over "planning" versus the "free-market." But there are at present only few signs that this is impending, and while one cannot exclude the possibility that it may become again a major aspect of politico-economic debate, I would myself doubt this. The debate, in my view, is more likely to concern the practical problems of working out a reasonably consistent pattern that would have some hope of reconciling the different forces at work, rather than the theoretical validity of *laissez faire* or the potential horrors of interference by central authority with the individual acquisitive instinct.

This is not to say that I regard the coming debate as less important or less likely to be stormy. At the moment of writing, it looks, indeed, to be the most vigorous, not to say vehement, controversy that is in store for most countries. Nor is there any chance that circumstances will develop in a way that will make it less relevant. It is true that there is increasing discussion now about what is "full" and what is "over-full" employment. But I doubt whether even some loosening up in this respect can greatly diminish the possibility of a conflict arising between expectations of security of employment, the strengthened bargaining position of unions that results from governments' commitment to this objective, the inflationary dangers inherent in that situation, and the claims of satisfying ideals of social justice.

PART THREE

THE INTERNATIONAL ECONOMY

Chapter 8   The Bretton Woods World

IT IS NOT POSSIBLE to think for very long about the economic order without becoming aware that nearly all current problems of any magnitude are profoundly influenced by international considerations. Again and again in the preceding pages we have seen how quickly a seemingly domestic problem acquires an international character, at least to the extent that international factors are involved in any possible solution. This is not, however, a condition peculiar to the present century. Economics and its problems are actually creations of the modern age of international commerce and finance. What is novel is the pervasiveness of the international characteristics of the problems that shape national economies, and the increasing strength of the impulses, technological and ideological, tending to create worldwide economic interdependence.

It is a commonplace that the world is daily getting smaller. The transmission of ideas and the movement of people now take place with an ease and rapidity that can only be seen as revolutionary when compared with the communications system used to consolidate the nation-state a few hundred years ago. For this reason alone, one would expect strong uniting tendencies to be at work, often conflicting with accepted national institutions, techniques, and modes of thought. There is no longer any real barrier to the spread of ideas exploding out of the great advances in science and technology; what stands in the way of their universal application is continuing difficulty, rooted in historical reasons, in adapting the political, economic, social, and cultural infrastructure to absorb new developments imported from other environments. This is the source of mounting tension between the developed and the less-developed countries, and it is bound to give rise to many more complex international problems than those of the past, precisely because of the rapidity with which the new unifying tendencies make their impact felt.

As between the more highly developed countries, the situation is somewhat different. Here, by definition, the infrastructure is broadly similar; the problem of absorbing—one from another—new developments in science and technology is therefore not particularly acute. At the same time, the developed countries exhibit most clearly the complete interdependence of modern economics. From this standpoint there can be no argument against the evident need for

87

creating and maintaining a strong, cohesive network of institutional relationships that will maximize the benefits of a world economy and minimize the
damage that might result to one economy from unfavourable developments in
another.

We have seen that few, if any, of the major domestic objectives of economic
policy can be attained or made secure without involving action of some kind in
the international sphere. In one sense, then, the international economy does
not seem to be subject to any independent desiderata. So far as economic considerations are concerned, international policies can be said to be instrumental: ends and means are not easily distinguished, the policies are designed to
subserve the broad objectives of the national economic order we have already
discussed. Therefore, we must examine the problems in this field by somewhat
different methods than those we have used so far. I propose, first, to review the
broad features of the economic world which was constructed only twenty years
ago, after World War II, and then to examine one by one some of the major issues that have continued to create tensions and difficulties and are likely to be
the mainsprings of future developments.

A few words are necessary to remind ourselves of the background, of fact
and of economic doctrine, against which the architects of the postwar system
had to work. Classical political economy was international, partly because its
noninterventionist laissez-faire doctrines fitted well with an "open" international economy, and also because most of the early economists were keenly interested in the creation of an international political order that would guarantee
peace and reproduce on a world scale the legal and institutional framework
in which the law-abiding citizen of a national society could conduct his economic activity freely and securely. This, then, was an overriding desideratum
in itself, though not primarily economic. The classical predisposition was for
an international economic order modeled as closely as possible on the ideal domestic one. Free trade was clearly a basic characteristic, along with a single
monetary system and freedom of movement for the mobile factors of production, capital and labour.

The prescription for the free movement of goods and people was relatively
easy to write: one simply urged the abolition of the artificial barriers inherited
from an earlier period and the prevention of new ones, allowing only relative
prices and transport costs, together with national cultural factors (in the case
of labour), to determine distribution across national boundaries. A monetary
system that subserved these objectives (and made possible free movement of
capital up to the limits of efficacy of the institutions for capital formation and
distribution) required a more positive construction. The gold standard and its
classical "mechanism," as it was significantly called, supplied the answer.

It is a matter for debate how often, in how many countries, and for how long, the classical gold standard, and the process of international monetary and economic adjustment that went with it, actually existed in the form in which it was described in the textbooks. Like so many of the solid structures of economics, it represents an abstraction from reality; and the attempt to make that reality, in its historical manifestation, conform to the theoretical picture is a well-known temptation to which economists readily succumb. The essential prerequisite of a gold standard (be it a specie standard, a gold bullion standard, or even a gold exchange standard) is that the countries who base their money on it should maintain a fixed monetary value per unit weight of gold. In modern times the general tendency toward the maintenance of a gold standard, in the sense of this basic condition and regardless of any particular form it may take, is not more than a hundred years old, though in Britain it had prevailed somewhat longer.

It is worthwhile, for our later discussion of issues of future economic policy, to dwell briefly on the interrelation created between the economies of individual countries by the common adherence to gold as the ultimate standard of reference of their own money. In textbook terms, the process of adjustment, starting from a position in which countries are in payments equilibrium, worked something like this: Suppose there is a disturbance of this equilibrium through one country's exports falling while its imports rise. (There are, of course, other reasons for imbalance.) Money flows would then be engendered which would, provided all the monetary authorities concerned observed the rules of the game, result in raising interest rates to diminish the volume of credit in the debtor country, and in opposite changes in the creditor country. Price relationships would thus be changed: in the debtor country, deflationary forces would make exports more competitive; while in the creditor country, inflationary forces would create a greater propensity to import. Thus, the original cause of the imbalance would be nullified and the movement to which it gave rise reversed.

This is, of course, a highly simplified account of a theory with a vast literature, but it displays the essentials of the nexus that, according to classical political economy, bound countries together and made their domestic economies interdependent. Price movements alone were not the full story. A whole complex of factors determined the level of economic activity of the countries so linked. Domestic demand (whether for consumption goods or capital goods), relative employment levels in different industries, wages and earnings, and investment prospects and intentions would all be affected by the mechanism once a change was set in motion by an imbalance of international payments and by the consequent moves of the monetary authorities.

Having got this complicated piece of economic theory down to its essentials has two advantages. It enables one to judge more clearly the relative merits and demerits of the various current proposals for reform we shall consider later. It also enables one to realize how much the working of the classic system depended on whether the monetary authorities of individual countries did in fact observe all of the rules of the game. It is here that the idealization of the past so readily breaks down, for during the last fifty years (and, indeed, before that) the rules were constantly breached by one country after another. In both debtor and creditor countries (or, as we would now more appropriately call them, deficit and surplus countries) the consequences of faithfully maintaining the gold standard mechanism were increasingly seen to be unacceptable to the domestic economy and its political epiphenomena. Here, too, the progress of democracy meant that more and more numerous sections of the electorate were called upon to bear the burden of the adjustment process, while they were also acquiring the political power to refuse to do so.

The great testing time for the mechanism, even in the highly complicated form in which it subsisted in the Twenties, came with the Great Depression and continued into World War II. By this time classical monetary theory was substantially discredited because economic reality was so patently in conflict with its basic postulates. It is not much of an exaggeration to say that in 1939 a large section of received economic theory, at least that which dealt with international trading and monetary arrangements (in some respects the most important segment of economics), lay in ruins—as did the actual network of relationships which it set out to explain. It is not relevant here to discuss in detail how this came about, how economists came so completely to ignore—at least in their purely theoretical writings—the tremendous importance of individual countries' changing roles in capital-exporting or importing activities and in the structure of their capital markets, or the interplay of political, ideological, and economic forces in the management of their domestic economies. It is enough to note that the war of 1939–1945 was a watershed, and, afterward, there was a new beginning in international economics.

The Great Vision

Wars are traumatic experiences for institutions as well as for people. They make possible vast changes achieved at a pace which would seem utterly inconceivable in normal times. But wars do not take place in an ideological vacuum; the last world conflict certainly applied a major shock to the economic order, but we can see very clearly the intellectual antecedents of much of the new thinking to which it gave rise.

The Beveridge Report and the full employment White Paper in Britain have their origins not only in Keynesian economic theory but in the pamphlets of the followers of Lloyd George at the time of the Great Depression. The Employment Act in the United States has its roots in the measures and the thinking of the New Deal. In the international sphere, too, the lines go back to Keynes's *General Theory* and, perhaps even more pointedly, to his *Treatise on Money*.

Whatever the antecedents, the last few years of World War II saw a remarkable attempt, unprecedented intellectually or institutionally, to erect a new international economic order on the ruins of the old even while the issue of the war itself was still joined. All wars, of course, awaken new hopes of better human arrangements, the prospect of a charter of peace and security and economic justice and well-being to follow the ultimate triumph. But the splendid economic vision that found expression in what came to be called the Bretton Woods agreements was no emotional by-product of a time of world crisis; the doctrines these agreements embodied grew out of a vast amount of economic thinking and practical expertise that constitute a high-water mark in human attempts to order the world economically.

The United Nations Monetary and Financial Conference which took place at Bretton Woods in 1944 actually resulted in the setting up of the International Monetary Fund and the International Bank for Reconstruction and Development, but I apply the term Bretton Woods symbolically to a whole array of elements. The list includes the conference in Havana which gave birth—a stillbirth, as it turned out—to the International Trade Organization (ITO); it also includes the critical American and Canadian loans to Great Britain and the various lend-lease agreements concluded by the United States with many of her allies. Taken together these provide the outstanding example of the new economic world that is still coming into being—"the Bretton Woods world."

Seldom can there have been concentrated for the ordering of human affairs so comprehensive a combination of economic and political vision, of administrative and technical expertise, of idealism and interest, of the old and the new. In retrospect it can be seen that here an attempt was made to preserve the essential features of a free-trading world and of a semiautomatic monetary system, while combining with it a number of new control features; and to provide the whole system with new institutions to ensure its proper functioning. The new features derived in large part from recognition of the limitations imposed upon the automatic working of the international monetary system by member countries' tendency to deal with their domestic economies in accord with desiderata established by internal political processes. Also, the Bretton Woods architects took into account the practical trade and finance arrangements that had grown up in the depression and post-depression years to restrict greatly the automatic forces of the system. They consciously allowed for an elaborate series of special and exceptional departures from the main principles they enunciated, but in so doing laid down a carefully worked-out code of conduct. Finally, the Bretton Woods system, though constructed before the war was over, attempted to take realistic account of the situation in which the countries concerned were likely to find themselves when the fighting stopped. This required the planners to consider the possible state of their economies, their internal political pressures, and their financial and economic strength in relation to one another.

In a sense, the part of this remarkable agglomeration of agreements, arrangements, and institutions that demonstrated most clearly the power of the new economico-political ideology, is that which never saw the light of day. The new economics is symbolized by an agency that was elaborated and finally agreed upon quite a bit later than the institutions that emerged directly from Bretton Woods, namely, the International Trade Organization.

The concept of the ITO—the element in the postwar structure dearest to the American heart—was at once the most and least advanced in its theoretical appreciation. The concept embodied ideas put into the form of a Charter, first by a preparatory committee of the United Nations Conference on Trade and Employment in Geneva in the summer of 1947, and then by the Conference itself in Havana (1947-48). These developed out of a sharp clash between conflicting economic philosophies. At the conference table each of these seemed to be closely associated with one country or group of countries; but in truth, the real battle of ideas was taking place within each country and was reflected within each national delegation.

The Americans had emerged as the leading protagonists for this new piece of international machinery. It related to their effort in the various lend-lease agreements (particularly the one with Britain) and in the British loan agreement, to enshrine free-trade ideas (a mainstay for many years of the economic policy of American administrations) in international instruments, and thus make them common international action. But in pressing for ITO, the framework within which these ideas were discussed was widened to include a very large number of countries. Other views were propagated and tensions were set up that, in the end, produced something very different from the pure doctrines of reduction of trade barriers, rights of establishments, proper treatment of foreign investments, etc., which the Americans had sought.

Thus we find that the ITO Charter begins by extolling the goal of full employment. The Charter of the United Nations (in article 55) already contained a full employment pledge: the ITO was in part designed to ensure its implementation. In a sense, the ITO Charter was the international counterpart of the full-employment policies already present in many national policies. In this context, however, it was a paradoxical development, for the full-employment objective of national policy had its origin in what could almost be called a revolt against the constraints imposed by membership in an international trading and financial system; the domestic version had basically more affinity with commercial and financial measures based on national autonomy than with those designed to circumscribe the freedom of national action and to restore a large measure of free international trade.

Nevertheless, this is what ITO was in part designed to achieve, and the incorporation of the objective of full employment into the principles and rules of an institution concerned with international trade must be accounted a major change in the general climate of economic opinion in which international economic relations would be conducted henceforth.

The Havana negotiations also produced a series of provisions relating to economic development and reconstruction. It is worthy of note that the sections of the Charter dealing with these matters, and with full employment, precede those dealing with commercial policy. Restrictive business practices and international commodity agreements also were dealt with. In fact, the ITO Charter, despite many imperfections resulting from heavy international bargaining, represented a remarkably up-to-date assembly of prescriptions for the conduct of international economic relations. These, when combined with those of the Bretton Woods institutions, might well have given the world a solid basis for ordered economic advance.

The New Arrangements

At Bretton Woods the principles of international trade and employment and general development policy were translated into practical arrangements to assist reconstruction and long-term development and to reorder the world monetary system. The most urgent postwar needs were conceived as falling into three distinguishable categories. There was, first, the need for immediate relief and rehabilitation. The special agency concerned with it, the United Nations Relief and Rehabilitation Agency, was to cope with that first phase; thereafter, following what was then known as the "UNRRA period," the emphasis would shift to reconstruction and then to the development of productive resources.

It was recognized that the need for funds for these purposes would be far greater than could be supplied by international movement of private capital alone; and the risks, too, were judged to be very much in excess of any that private investors could be expected to carry. The creation of a new type of international investment institution was called for: the International Bank for Reconstruction and Development (the World Bank). It was authorized to make loans (or to guarantee them) for reconstruction or development projects either out of its own capital resources or by helping to mobilize private capital. The capital funds of the Bank were provided by the member governments, and investment risks were shared in proportion to their contributions.

A unique and important feature of the Bank's financial structure is that only a small part of its subscribed capital (only a tenth being paid in) is directly used for its loan operations. The existence of large uncalled funds provided backing that enables the Bank, either by guarantees, or through borrowing from private investors, to mobilize considerable nongovernmental resources.

This use of government resources to further private capital formation achieved one of the main objectives of the architects of the Bretton Woods agreements. By putting an obligation on the Bank to insure that its loans were for productive purposes (in general, geared to specific projects of reconstruction or development), and by providing that such projects should be judged from the point of view of their economic urgency, it was hoped to avoid the chief errors of international lending in the interwar years. Together with the international sharing of the risk, these principles of the Bank's operations were designed not only to encourage directly a flow of private capital, but to create a favourable climate in which private capital movements through ordinary institutions of capital markets would be resumed. Thus the Bank supported one of the objectives to be enshrined later in the ITO Charter.

Subsequently, the Bank was supplemented by two other international financial institutions. In 1956 the International Finance Corporation was set up, and in 1960 the International Development Association. The former was designed to encourage the growth of productive private enterprise in member countries, particularly the less-developed ones. This it does by providing financing (through subscriptions to stock and/or loans) in association with private investors without government guarantee, as well as in other ways. The IDA can be said to lie on the other side of the spectrum: it is designed to promote development on more liberal terms of repayment than does the Bank itself. Its members are divided into two groups: Part I countries are the more developed ones, which supply the whole of their subscription in convertible currency; and Part II countries, the less developed ones, which supply 90 percent of their subscription in their own currency. These funds may not be used without the member's permission. Part I countries (except for the purposes of their dependent and associated territories) are contributor countries; Part II countries are recipient countries. As supplemented by these two ancillary institutions, the Bank created at Bretton Woods was capable of becoming a powerful instrument for international cooperation through the promotion of economic development.

The third and, in some ways, the most important of the postwar creations was the International Monetary Fund. Its purposes are set out in the six clauses of its first article; like all such preambular declarations of international instruments, this reflects the heavy negotiation that went into it and the multifarious and not easily reconciled objectives its creators had in mind. The charge is to promote monetary cooperation through permanent machinery for consultation, to facilitate growth of trade and promote high levels of employment, to promote exchange stability and eliminate exchange restrictions, to help correct balance-of-payments maladjustments by making funds available to members, and thus to shorten periods of disequilibrium and to lessen their severity.

The IMF operates in three ways: it regulates the conduct of members in certain respects, it consults and advises, and it provides a source of finance in case of need. In its regulatory activities, that is to say those which govern members' practice in regard to exchange rates and restrictions on international payments, the Fund was intended to work in harness with the ITO: the former looking after the currency aspects, the latter the commodity and services aspects of international exchanges. The basic inspiration for this part of the Fund's work is liberal. The inevitability of restrictions on trade and payments in certain circumstances is recognized, and specific provision is made for changes in exchange rates in the case of "fundamental" disequilibria. However, the general assumption in the Fund's articles is that the most desirable pattern of international economic relations is one in which exchange fluctuations are kept to a minimum, in which there is the highest degree of free trade in goods and services, and in which payments are settled on the widest possible multilateral basis.

At the same time, the Fund does not shut its eyes to the existence of imbalances, to their causes, or to the domestic economic, social, and political difficulties to which their adjustments might give rise if these were to be achieved by means too rigorously inspired by multilateral standards. For this reason the Fund is able not only to consult with countries on the domestic policy implications of their international obligations but is endowed with substantial financial facilities which it can put at the disposal of members for the purpose of smoothing the path of adjustment towards a new equilibrium position.

It is not my purpose here to elaborate further the provisions contained in the Articles of the Bank and the Fund or in the stillborn Havana Charter for the ITO. Nor do I propose at this point to go into their shortcomings: these will be looked at later when we consider the unfinished agenda of international economic cooperation for the next few decades. The important thing here is to recognize the remarkable scope of these postwar institutions. They were designed to deal with a very great range of problems indeed; and one must emphasize the considerable, and in some respects revolutionary, intellectual innovation they embodied. Perhaps the most far-reaching and significant step in that direction (demonstrated more particularly by the Fund) was the attempt to reconcile autonomy in domestic economic policy with the obligations imposed by international rules of conduct.

Keynes, the intellectual begetter of the Bretton Woods principles and one of the principal architects of the institutions themselves, had little doubt that this reconciliation had been accomplished. In a speech in the House of Lords in which he commended the Fund agreement, he listed three desiderata of domestic monetary policy. These were freedom to ensure that the exchange value of a currency was determined by its internal value as set by domestic policies (and not the other way round); freedom to control the domestic rate of interest so that it is unaffected by international capital movements; and ability to resist deflationary forces engendered by outside influences. Keynes thought that in the Articles of the Fund all three of these desiderata had been fully safeguarded. However, even at the time, doubts were expressed; and today it is precisely in relation to this supposed reconciliation that there is the greatest controversy.

The second point that must be made is that even though imperfect, the three institutions did, in conception at least, provide adequate machinery to meet all the major problems in the period of immediate postwar reconstruction, and, more important, for the subsequent ordering of the world economy for a considerable time thereafter. Moreover, they were supposed to operate within a framework of gradually expanding trade and financial activity of a private character, for which they would have created a propitious climate. And yet, within a few years, most of the problems they were designed to resolve were still weighing upon the world as heavily as ever.

Why the Vision Faltered

In analyzing the reasons for the relative failure of this grand design we can distinguish a number of factors that operated outside the institutions themselves but in the environment in which they were placed and, at the very least, greatly complicated their task. Then there were the inadequacies in their own structure which became increasingly obvious as the postwar world developed. Of course, these two sets of factors cannot be strictly separated. The unfavourable environment not only aggravated the problems to be overcome but also set up tensions which made the internal deficiencies of the machinery more significant than they might otherwise have been.

Probably the first and most basic of the external factors that militated against the success of the Bretton Woods concept was the split between East and West. Harbingers of what was to happen were evident during the war not only in the politico-military aspects of the joint effort but in the economic field, too. The lend-lease relationship between the United States and the Soviet Union was marked by difficulties and frictions as the war neared its close. Above all, inside UNRRA and in the relief activities conducted under the aegis of the military authorities, fissures began to appear which clearly showed that the Soviet Union and the Eastern European countries associated with her had an entirely different conception of the pattern of the postwar world from that entertained in the West.

The political background of the years 1945–46 must be remembered. The widening split between those who had won the war as allies was paralleled in many European countries by violent dissent—in some instances seen as foreshadowing imminent radical change. Not surprisingly, then, the Soviet Union and most of the countries associated with her refused to join new institutions designed to restore and maintain stability, even though they had collaborated in their creation. The culmination came with the refusal of the Soviet bloc to participate in the Marshall Plan in 1947.

The consequences of this split have been described and analyzed often and at length. Here all that need be recalled is that the Bretton Woods institutions ceased to be universal; and the multilateral (albeit with safeguards) trading and financial arrangements which they were meant to provide for the world as a whole were, from the beginning, confined to one part of the world only.

The other great factor which was not sufficiently recognized at the time, and which made the success of the new arrangements immeasurably more difficult to achieve, was that the physical and economic devastation in Europe was very much more extensive than had been allowed for in all postwar plans. The first loans made by the World Bank in 1947, amounting to nearly $500 million, were in the nature of emergency assistance to four Western European countries. And they no doubt prevented a very severe drop in production and possible total economic collapse. But loans on this scale were almost irrelevant in terms of world needs, not only for relief and rehabilitation but, above all, for reconstruction. (This was long before there could be any thought of economic development in the strict sense of the word.)

The architects of the Bretton Woods Agreements had seriously underestimated the physical destruction, and the attendant dislocation of trade and industrial arrangements, and of governmental and administrative machinery. These were so great that there could be little question of general reconstruction and modernization without, first, substantial assistance simply to sustain essential imports of food, fuel, and raw materials for which the United States and the dollar area generally were the only possible source of supply. Thus one of the key parts of the new machinery from the beginning was unable to carry out its true function without some auxiliary mechanism first being brought into play.

This unforeseen and crucial economic weakness of Europe highlighted the overwhelming economic superiority of the United States. It had, of course, been clear to the drafters of the Bretton Woods Agreements that the economic strength of the United States would be vastly superior to that of any or all the other members of the Bank and the Fund; and the articles of these two bodies and various agreements and understanding that went with them reflected this realization. Both institutions were located in the United States; the President of the World Bank had to be (and continues so) an American since the bulk of the funds of the Bank had to come from the United States; the voting provisions of both institutions departed from the normal United Nations "one country, one vote" rule and were drawn up on the basis of contributions of capital or on quotas. The Fund articles contained scarce currency provisions, clearly drafted with the dollar in mind, and so on. Even so, the full measure of American economic advantage had by no means been gauged.

One forecast, regarded with reason as somewhat hazardous, but correct as it fortunately turned out, was that the United States would not, as she had done after World War I, retreat into political and economic isolation. If, by some mischance, this too had been proved wrong, there is no telling what kind of a world we would now be faced with. As it was, the United States, despite many false starts caused largely by her own domestic political difficulties, remained fully committed to the principles of the new world order and participated fully in most of the new institutions which she had helped to bring into being.

There was one major agency she did not join, and her failure meant in effect that this one, the ITO, did not see the light of day. It is not difficult to see why this should have been; and by no stretch of the imagination can the American failure to ratify the ITO, disappointing though it was, be compared with the lack of U.S. participation in the League of Nations. The trouble about the ITO was that it had taken too long to bring it to the point of delivery. By the time the Charter was signed, in March 1948, long after the Bank and the Fund had been created, the shortcomings of the prevailing conception of the postwar world, political and economic, had already become painfully obvious.

We have already seen that the Bank had had to devote substantial funds to provide immediate balance-of-payments relief before there could be any question of embarking on the longer-term reconstruction and development operations that were meant to be its real job. The Fund saw one of its basic purposes seriously impaired when in August 1947 the British Government suspended the convertibility of sterling. The verdict had to be that one of the critical commitments of the loan agreement had been entered into prematurely. And the loan agreement itself, although an absolutely indispensable part of the postwar structure, virtually proved that the new multilateral agreements and institutions were incapable, by themselves, of setting the world on the right economic road. Finally, by the time the Havana Charter was signed, the Marshall Plan had been launched and was being debated by the Congress. It is no wonder the blueprint for a new trade pattern failed to get much of a hearing.

Thus, as we reappraise the sum total of achievements of those first few postwar years, we see both the immense advance over the theory and the practical arrangements of the preceding generation, and the near-tragic deficiencies that ultimately robbed them of full success. But human ingenuity and political courage were not exhausted by the creation of the new multilateral institutions. The British loan, the Marshall Plan, and the General Agreement on Tariffs and Trade provided devices to plug some of the holes left by the inadequacies of

Bretton Woods and the absence of an ITO, and helped offset unforeseen, or insufficiently assessed, unfavourable political and economic developments. It is worthwhile touching briefly upon these three additional factors in the postwar pattern for the sake of the lessons in intellectual history their conception provides, and because they each set in motion forces that are still with us today.

Plugging the Gaps

The British loans from the United States and Canada (totaling five billion dollars) were designed to provide a breathing spell of five years, by which time the British trading position and balance of payments might be restored, and her economy made capable of subsisting without further outside assistance. It was hoped that these funds would be used up at a declining rate in the first three years, and that a further two years would enable Britain to develop an appropriate balance-of-payments surplus. In strictly financial terms, the conditions of interest and repayment attached to the loans were not ungenerous. But the main counterpart to the loans was to be British support for a rapid restoration of a multilateral trade and payments system (the loans having, it was thought, provided the essential interim financial easement). This involved an obligation to restore convertibility of sterling for current transactions and to remove quickly the discriminatory trade practices built up during the war. In both respects, therefore, the loans were of a piece with the rest of the postwar structure then built up: in practice they supplemented the new financial facilities, in purpose they were inspired by the same liberal economic philosophy.

Yet, once again, the real problem turned out to be much graver than anyone had foreseen. By August 1947, a little more than a year after the U.S. loan had been ratified by Congress, Britain had used $3.5 billion of the loan, $1 billion in June and July of that year only; and it had become clear that the convertibility and nondiscrimination obligations would have to be abandoned. Much of the drain on the loan funds had in fact been due to demands through London as a result of this premature institution of convertibility. It is interesting, though idle, to speculate what the position would have been if the British loan (together with the many other loans provided by the American and other governments to other allies) could have been used exclusively to prime the economic pumps of recovery and reconstruction, leaving the longer-term to be taken care of by the new postwar institutions. As it was, these imported financial resources bore the stultifying accompaniment of a rush to trading and financial conditions the enfeebled British economy could not tolerate.

Another auxiliary mechanism, and a surrogate for the ITO, was established by GATT, the General Agreement on Tariffs and Trade. This has had a modest but at the same time steadily useful history and it continues to this day to exercise a favourable effect in promoting the oneness of the international economy. It had come into being before the official end of the ITO, which took place in December 1950 when the President of the United States withdrew the Havana Charter from Congress, and it began its effective life roughly at the same time as the Bank and the Fund. GATT had to do duty (in a more restricted framework of functions and powers) for the more comprehensive organization which was intended in due course to replace it. Without a permanent organization and long-term binding commitments as to membership, GATT has been able, through a series of multilateral tariff negotiations during the last decades, and through the exercise of consultative and complaints machinery, to bring to life many of the commercial policy provisions of the original ITO Charter and significantly to reduce the restrictive effects of tariffs and discriminatory devices in world trade. Other provisions of the Charter, for example, those relating to agreements for avoiding excessive fluctuations in the prices of primary commodities, have led a more precarious existence. We shall look at the present position and future prospects of international cooperation in both these fields later.

The Marshall Plan was the most important of the arrangements that illustrated the inadequacies of the general postwar economic structure even as they helped make it work. For a number of reasons it is worthwhile looking at this great effort at international cooperation. I have already cited it as a far more potent factor in achieving a reasonably viable postwar world than the more far-reaching arrangements it had to supplement. It bequeathed a significant new Organization for European Economic Cooperation, which in enlarged form (as the Organization for Economic Cooperation and Development) now includes North America and Japan as well as European countries. It has had, and continues to have, an intellectual and a practical influence on both national and international economic planning that is of the highest importance. Its educative influence on governments as well as on influential private citizens probably has not been equaled, at least in intensity, by any other piece of international machinery for many decades. For these reasons, whatever the future practical importance of the OECD may be, the Marshall Plan and its sequelae stand among the more important forces operating in the economic order of the Western world.

The Marshall Plan was designed to provide Europe with American aid on a vast scale and at the same time to set the European countries jointly and severally on the road to self-help as well as closer cooperation. In both respects it succeeded beyond expectations. In three years, instead of four, and with a total amount of aid of about $12 billion, against the originally estimated need of $19 billion, productive capacity and output had been greatly increased, standards of living were improved, barriers to trade within Europe were considerably reduced, and conditions created for a major step forward in the liberalization of trade between Europe and the rest of the world. Balance-of-payments positions were made much healthier, internal financial stability was restored in large measure, and in general, an environment was created in which the higher hopes that had inspired the Bretton Woods Agreements no longer seemed utterly impossible of fulfillment.

Above all, the net effect of these developments was to reduce very considerably the great disparity in economic strength between Europe and the United States, and to create some prospect of a more evenly based partnership for the future. These developments had also instilled a strong habit of cooperation into the European member countries, had greatly contributed to creating a basis for nondiscriminatory treatment in every respect between former allies and enemies, and had made many of those involved begin to think of their problems as common.

Like other bonds forged between nations under the pressure of great need, these too tended to loosen once the immediate objectives had been gained. Other forces began to operate after the first three years or so of the Marshall Plan; its own cohesive tendencies, though they persisted, became less compelling. We must now turn to an examination of the situation as it presents itself in the late Sixties.

Chapter 9 The Problems of International Trade

THE PREVAILING PATTERNS of international trade, already strained by years of depression and crises in the Thirties and the defensive, illiberal measures they produced in most countries, were finally shattered by the war. Their restoration or replacement became the task, on the one hand, of organizations with long-term functions and, on the other, of arrangements intended for the interim but often with tendencies to exercise a continuing function. What is the sum of accomplishment of these devices in the nearly twenty years of their operation? And to what new developments and tensions have they given rise?

I do not propose to examine the first of these questions in any statistical detail; the effort here is to analyze briefly and in general terms the extent to which a new, more extensive and liberal trade pattern has emerged and the means by which it has been achieved. I then propose to describe the limitations to which the reconstructive tendencies became subject, the reasons for these limitations, and the problems which have thus arisen. This will enable us to go on to a discussion of each of the major new problems in world trading relations in turn, and thus to isolate and analyze the forces that are most likely to be responsible for shaping the future.

The task of freeing trade in the strictest and narrowest sense in the first phase after the war fell largely to two institutions and the particular methods of international cooperation they had evolved: OEEC (Organization for European Economic Cooperation) and GATT. Broadly, the difference between them was that the former operated primarily within a European framework and in respect to direct restrictions on trade, while the latter worked virtually worldwide (with the significant exception of nearly all the Soviet bloc countries) and was concerned mainly with the reduction of tariffs. This is, however, a generalization which needs to be qualified. The OEEC did attempt, particularly in the later stages, by agreement as to general rules of conduct in the matter of trade and payments, to go beyond the original task of reduction or abolition of quantitative import restrictions; and it also began cautiously to formulate an intergovernmental consensus on trade relations between Europe and North America. Similarly, GATT, although its major, tangible achievements are most clearly demonstrated by successive rounds of tariff-cutting negotiations, did lay down rules covering a multitude of conditions and situations in international trade—including state trading, exports, and so on. In the earlier years of its existence, before the problem of the developing countries had moved to the centre of the stage, GATT's tariff bargaining of necessity had its major impact on trade between highly industrialized countries and, therefore, particularly on its European members.

The distinction between the basic orientations of the two institutions is nevertheless worth making, because it gave rise from the beginning to certain differences of approach among countries to the general task of freeing and expanding trade. For example, early attempts by some countries to urge OEEC into the field of tariff reductions, albeit on a European basis, encountered opposition by other countries, particularly Britain, on the ground that this field, with its necessarily worldwide implications in bargaining terms, had to be reserved for GATT. This attitude undoubtedly provided an additional reason (though, of course, not the major one) for European countries anxious to move toward a more closely integrated European economy to seek new arrangements and institutions outside the framework of OEEC.

Neither OEEC nor GATT—at least to start with—was able to deal with the specific trade problems of the developing countries, let alone to satisfy their aspirations. To them, OEEC was essentially "a rich man's club"—though after its transformation into OECD it became an important means, through its quasi-autonomous Development Assistance Committee, for coordinating the aid policies of the developed countries. GATT, with its inevitable concentration in its earlier years on tariff bargaining, could offer little to the developing countries (not all of whom were, in any event, members) whose main interests lay in the trade and pricing of primary commodities, the protection of their own infant industries, and special measures to enlarge access of their developing secondary industries to the markets of more advanced countries.

Means of Regulation

These, then, are the problems I regard as particularly significant in the development of the new trade-regulating institutions in the first decade or so of their existence. First was the general problem of their partial, indeed fragmentary character—that is, of the absence of any means for effectively promoting the creation of a suitable trade and payments pattern in a comprehensive fashion; second was the inadequacy, as it seemed to many countries, of OEEC as a means of integrating the European economies. The third was the absence of any organization which could deal with the specific trade problems of the developing countries. Highlighting these inadequacies inevitably must give a somewhat unjust impression of the considerable achievement of the two institutions I have mentioned. As a preface to further discussion of the deficiencies, I propose to consider the sources from which subsequent developments have sprung. It is well to consider what, notwithstanding their limitations, both OEEC and GATT have been able to accomplish.

I have already said something about OEEC as the vehicle of the Marshall Plan and its tremendous role in rehabilitating the productive apparatus of the war-shattered European countries and restoring their domestic and international industrial, commercial, financial, and economic administrative structures. I have also stressed its great value in training a generation of European officials and other public men in cooperative attitudes and methods. In the field of trade especially the European countries have succeeded in a relatively short time in ridding themselves of virtually the whole apparatus of quota restrictions and other discriminatory trade practices. Through the instrument of successive payments agreements and the establishment, first, of the European Payments Union, later the European Monetary Agreement, they have been able to make rapid strides in multilateralizing European payments and in establishing a high degree of transferability of European currencies.

As for GATT, it can rightly be regarded as one of the most successful international institutions ever created. Certainly, when its relatively modest apparatus is set against the high degree of observance of its rules of nondiscrimination, of its requirements for consultation and for the actual outlawing (save on the basis of stringent conditions applying in exceptional situations) of certain trade practices, and the net effect it has had in reducing tariff barriers, it compares very favourably with many more grandiose international ventures.

It is, therefore, not to diminish what they have done that I return to what OECD and GATT, along with the rest of the postwar institutions, have not been able to accomplish. For what characterizes the situation in international trade since 1947–48, and has become particularly obvious in the Sixties, is the clear evidence that the world economy has had to make do with a second-best institutional framework. I shall return later to the broader question created by the absence of a comprehensive plan for dealing with international economic problems and an articulated means for carrying it out.

As regards Europe, I am for the moment concerned only with the OEEC. From a relatively early date in the trade liberalization program on which the OEEC had embarked, the issue of its place in the process of tariff negotiations became an important one. Two forces were at work to bring this problem to the fore. As quota restrictions were removed, and so created a general framework within which trade could expand, the significance of the tariff as a protective device became more obvious. The European countries had considerably differing tariff levels, and the so-called low-tariff countries not unnaturally pressed for some progress on this front too. The more OEEC's own liberalization program progressed, the more urgent did this problem become and the greater the resistance of the low-tariff countries to embarking upon a further stage for the dismantlement of quotas.

But GATT was the recognized medium for tariff negotiations and was, in fact, engaged in a number of rounds of bargaining at the time that this issue was debated in OEEC. There was the powerful argument against attempting to duplicate the work of GATT with all its elaborate machinery for multilateral negotiations. The British, in particular, were against blurring the lines of division between the two institutions, partly out of regard for organizational order, but mainly because tariff negotiations (particularly in GATT) carried a general obligation to extend most-favoured-nation treatment to all the parties, an obligation which clearly precluded purely intra-European concessions. In any event, those countries in Europe, like Britain, whose trading interests were worldwide were concerned to ensure as large a scope for mutual concessions as possible, including, particularly, concessions from the United States.

The United States itself was ambivalent on the subject. While anxious for general political reasons to promote closer European economic integration, most American officials did not wish to see the European countries engaged in trade matters which would move the enterprise in a direction that clearly involved discrimination against their own country. But here was precisely the other powerful tendency that made itself felt inside the European trade discussion. The creation of a preferential European tariff area was regarded by many Europeans as no more than a natural consequence of the great disparity in economic strength between the United States and Europe, and therefore as a perfectly proper pendant to the European Recovery Program. Others, even at that time, recognized a new European preference area as a powerful instrument for further economic (and later political) integration. The resulting conflict of views helped to slow down the activities of OEEC considerably while the integrationist forces in Europe developed other means for promoting their aims.

The Impact of Defense

For the sake of completeness, though it is not directly germane to this exposition, I should, however, mention here developments in the defense and foreign affairs field. Coinciding with the critical situation developing in European economic cooperation, and virtually paralyzing OEEC for some years, were the development of the North Atlantic Treaty Organization (1949), and the outbreak of the Korean War (1950), with its consequent pressure on raw material supplies. A result of the war was the organization, under British and American leadership, of the International Materials Conference, an *ad hoc* organization designed to prevent a general scramble for supplies that would produce excessive price increases. It demonstrated once again the fragility of European institutions when pressures mounted on a worldwide scale. In retrospect, it can be seen also to have had a profound impact on the developing countries, then having just attained, or reached the point of attaining, political independence. These developments contributed to a growing consciousness of their continuing dependence on raw-material prices for their basic income, and of the power this left in the hands of the industrialized countries.

The advent of NATO not only had a directly weakening effect on OEEC, but more generally on the intergovernmental pattern of economic cooperation that had been built up in Europe. The effect of the more institutionalized pattern for the Atlantic Alliance, combined with an enlargement and acceleration of the defense effort carrying an inevitable impact on the economies of the member countries, was to strengthen centrifugal tendencies already at work. The integrationists in Europe saw further proof of the weakness of existing methods of cooperation and took this as an incentive for their efforts to proceed on a narrower European basis but in a more intensive manner. On the other side, countries like Britain, either because of wider economic, political, and defense responsibilities or because of reluctance to go too far on what might become a "federalist" path, were ready to put less emphasis on existing European institutions and to rely more heavily on the new Atlantic arrangement which they hoped might become the main focus of cooperation, even in economic matters.

The experience of OEEC in the years of trade liberalization policies, European integration moves, a Far Eastern war, and the upsurge of the Atlantic Alliance illustrates vividly the intricate interaction of political and economic factors in the international sphere. I shall have more to say later about this, especially in relation to the growth of regional groupings, the role of the United States in European affairs, and the very important and difficult part played by Britain in these developments.

The other great problem which could not be handled effectively through GATT and OEEC in their early years was that of developing a trade policy peculiar to the developing countries. The Havana Charter had fully recognized this need, and, as a complement to the activities planned for the World Bank and individual national efforts at economic development, had contained important provisions of special interest to the developing countries. These were, apart from the section dealing with development itself, a series of rules concerning commodity agreements. Even though these did not amount to a self-consistent program of positive economic and trade development, they would have had an important influence on events if they could have been put into operation by a single major international organization. As it was, the implementing machinery never came into being, and, as I have already pointed out, GATT had perforce to concentrate on the more immediate commercial policy problems of the advanced countries.

Commodity policy was not altogether neglected; under the guidance of various United Nations agencies some measure of general supervision over individual negotiations for agreements was attempted. It is fair to say, however, that the commodity problem was seen in terms that had become familiar before the war rather than as an aspect of the general problem of development, and was not considered in close relation to trade policy as a whole. Only a few individual agreements were attempted, mainly those—wheat, sugar, tin, for example—for which some basis in prewar experiments at regulation already existed.

Thus the world emerged after the first ten years or so of postwar reconstruction with major issues of international trade unresolved, and with new ones arising or visibly threatening. I would cite six problems, or more properly groups of problems, confronting world economic practice, and the evolving theory of international economics.

There is the question of regional economic groupings, their mainsprings, their prospects, and their significance for world order, economic and political. There is a rather special problem, but one which deserves separate treatment because of its significance for international trade and its central importance in some of the regional problems: the question of production and trade in the foodstuffs grown in the temperate zones of the world. Much turns on the future prospects of the less developed countries, and there is an allied problem of the future of long-term international capital movements. There is the problem of the future organization of the world's monetary system, the question of international liquidity as it is often called nowadays. Finally there is a group of problems in which political and strategic factors play a very important role. Here are involved the questions of the impact of defense policies and alliances on the domestic economic situation in individual countries as well as on international groupings, and, of course, the future of the East/West economic relationship. I propose to analyze these groups of problems in turn. The degree of detail will vary, depending on the significance I attach to each as seminal in relation to the future of the economic order. This, of course, involves individual taste; and opinions may differ on the accuracy of my own estimate as to the time scale involved for the unfolding of the particular problems in each one of these groups.

Chapter 10　Regionalism

I DO NOT PROPOSE to examine here the details of the various attempts which have been made in recent years to form regional economic groupings as such, but rather to consider the general tendency toward what has come to be known as economic integration, using as an illustration the most significant example of it, that in Europe. The larger concept of a world economic order, and the limited practical manifestations so far, are not wholly at odds. Once the world economy had been fragmented by war and an inducement created to reestablish "oneness," it was not unnatural for this to express itself first in attempts to bring more closely together national economies which, because of geographical contiguity and other common features, appear to offer an easier prospect of early success.

I have already touched upon the essential internationalism of classical economic thought (buttressed in the case of many of its practitioners by a positive commitment to political federalism); and we have also seen how limited was the achievement of a truly worldwide economic community; and how quickly what had been achieved was blown apart by the war.

It is very much to the credit of those responsible that while World War II was still raging the minds of many leaders should have been turning to the post-war problem. With the experience of the worldwide depression still very fresh and with overwhelming evidence of its fatal consequences to amicable relations between nations, the creation of an integrated world economy drew its inspiration from political rather than narrowly economic motives. "Never again" was the watchword, and it applied not only to war but also to the collapse of the international economic order, which were seen to be inescapably related.

We have already considered the attempts made in this direction on a world scale. As a by-product of this effort, particularly under the Marshall Plan, special impetus was given to close economic cooperation on a European scale. The United States, as the begetter of the Marshall Plan and the supplier of its sinews, played an extremely important part in this process; and indeed, from a very early stage, European integration became a declared objective of American foreign policy. The motivation was complex, and economic only in part.

It was obvious that European recovery was impossible without the vital component of American aid. Although accepting this necessity, neither the Congress nor the Executive was anxious to see aid grow any larger, or go on any longer than was absolutely necessary. To an enlarged European market was ascribed important healing and reconstructive power; it, therefore, could in some measure be regarded as an alternative to American dollars. At least it could be argued that the more integrated the European market became the sooner would the European economy be able to stand on its own feet.

This was the economic background for critical political decisions. The Marshall Plan was conceived and put into operation at a time when the division between the Soviet bloc and the West was rapidly becoming extremely acute. Political conditions in many European countries were precarious, and the installation of openly Communist or left-wing governments susceptible to Soviet influence was widely feared by many of those in Europe working most closely with the United States. The economic strengthening of Europe by aid as well as by her own united efforts, growing ever more effective as a result of market integration, came to be considered to be an essential precondition to successful, long-run resistance to the spread of Communism.

A third factor, more difficult to identify with any particular interest and certainly less measurable, can be seen in a certain ideological attitude: the belief that the economic results the United States had achieved on the North American continent by the creation of a single market must be applicable and highly advantageous to Europe, too. Even though cultural and political differences were acknowledged as obstacles, it was argued that the creation of at least a customs union would speed the process of recovery and bring nearer the time when Europe could begin to close the technological and economic gap that now separated her from the United States.

Thus, from the very beginning of the European Recovery Program, United States pressure was continually exerted in the direction of more ambitious schemes of integration. In Europe, this pressure was welcomed by some countries, particularly the Netherlands, and later Germany and France. Nevertheless the United States was ambivalent as this movement began to present among the obvious consequences of closer European integration the prospect of intensive trade discrimination against the donor of Marshall Plan funds. Integration in Europe and American pressure polarized and brought into the open inherently conflicting concepts and tendencies of which, for a number of reasons, historical as well as contemporaneous, Britain became the main protagonist. I have already cited some of the reasons for this in discussing the respective roles of OEEC and GATT in trade liberalization. In addition, it may well be that having emerged greatly weakened but victorious from the war, Britain did not show a predisposition to radical change comparable to that of countries which had suffered defeat or occupation. From the beginning the

British saw the basic impetus for European integration as political, even though it manifested itself initially in the economic sphere.

If any one man is to be regarded as the true creator of the modern movement for European integration it is Jean Monnet. His influence over a wide range of economic and political developments during recent decades can best be likened to that of Keynes in the prewar era, even though the French statesman operated in somewhat different spheres and with different instruments. Monnet's objective was always the ultimate political unification of at least a large segment of Western Europe. He has argued for this in terms of the area's own essential interests as a means of pacification and prosperity; as an essential precondition for a more lasting partnership with the United States; and, more recently, as a step toward reestablishment of amity with Eastern Europe. But he and the European statesmen associated with him (and largely impelled by his persuasiveness) concluded that under the conditions obtaining in the immediate postwar period a frontal assault on nationalism in the political arena was unlikely to succeed.

Hence, the economic "sector" approach was chosen, with the first example provided by the so-called Schuman Plan for the integration of the coal and iron and steel industries of Western Europe (paradoxically, these by tradition are the most used to international agreement and yet the most often associated with ultranationalist political tendencies). The Treaty of Paris which set up the European Coal and Steel Community was followed by Euratom, the community for the peaceful exploitation of atomic energy. But the essentially political long-term purpose of the Schuman Plan could never be in doubt; and it became patent to all when a few years later the abortive attempt to create a European Defense Community was launched—an attempt clearly inspired by a political objective and which went to the very heart of national sovereignty.

The doubts of Britain and some other countries, notably the Scandinavian, about the pace of progress toward European economic integration were powerfully reinforced by its political overtones. They were reluctant to be involved in these wider objectives, and, in part at least, this was the reason Britain declined to join in the Coal and Steel Community. On the Labour Party side, there were fears for the fate of the nationalized British coal industry and the soon-to-be nationalized steel industry in an environment of privately-owned and managed continental industries. On all sides there were reservations about subjecting these key industries to the supervision of an entirely new type of politico-economic organ, the High Authority, endowed with unprecedented powers clearly superseding in important respects the sovereignty of national governments. Even more deep-seated reasons were discernible by the time of the debate over the European Defense Community.

Much of British thinking in the immediate postwar period was influenced by, as it seemed, an ever-present danger of flagging American interest in Europe, of a retreat into isolationism by the United States which would repeat the tragic history that followed World War I. Britain was acutely conscious of dangers from the East and the doubtful capacity of Europe, alone or in combination with its overseas territories, to withstand them. Thus enthusiastic moves toward European integration were thought likely to provoke similar moves on the other side of the Atlantic, notwithstanding the fact that many Americans who could by no stretch of the imagination be regarded as isolationist were leading proponents of European integration.

Whatever the precise mixture of these motives, the opportunity for Britain to be "in on the ground floor" of European integration was missed when she did not join the European Coal and Steel Community. The next fifteen years of European economic and political history were to be profoundly affected by that decision and to be marked by successive attempts by Britain (and others) belatedly to come to terms with the emerging European institutions.

The Basic Arguments

Before I sketch out some of these developments, a few words must be said about the most prominent economic arguments for and against integration on a regional basis heard throughout the period and certainly relevant for the future. By whatever route one approaches the problem, whether economic or political, there are certain characteristics of economic relations between nations which test whether, and to what degree, economic integration has been achieved. One can, in fact, distinguish several degrees of integration between economies that are otherwise distinguished by separate political sovereignties. This is a somewhat schematic expository device, but it is useful for describing and analyzing an existing situation or a historical process. Complete integration might be looked upon as a state of affairs in which the economic relations within a single unified state are reproduced as between two or more separate states.

If we begin with trade we may consider the first degree of integration to have been achieved when the countries which belong to the integrated group have abolished all restrictions on the movement of goods and services among them. The group thus constitutes a free-trade area. A higher measure of integration is reached by a customs union, which adds a uniform commercial regime (particularly tariffs) vis-à-vis those outside. When complete freedom of movement of capital and labour is also present within the customs union, a common market may be said to exist. This, however, will not be really effective without harmonization of economic policies to an extent which removes at least the gross factors that might distort competition among members, *e.g.,* freight rate policies, legislation in regard to monopolistic practices, and so on. At this point a wider economic union can be said to have come into being. Finally, full economic integration can be said to exist when unified policies in monetary and social matters as well as in fiscal policy have also been established.

With this sort of schema in mind, it is not difficult to see how powerful forces are mustered to keep pushing countries along the road to integration once a start has been made. A free-trade area may be the first step, one involving only a limited range of commodities, say industrial products. It is quite likely, however, that the balance of advantages among members may be thought uneven at this stage, and thus pressure may develop to include other goods, *e.g.*, agricultural products. Then, if each member is free to have his own commercial regime with other countries, difficulties may arise through diversion of goods and services which will distort group trade channels and patterns. Similarly, impediments to the migration of labour and capital may impair or wholly negate the advantages thought to have been obtained by the free-trade area or customs union. And so the process continues.

There is no theoretical reason for integration to stop except at the most subsidiary kinds of economic policy which can be left to local autonomy. In practice, too, pressure at each stage can be expected to be progressive; so that as the movement passes one stage the likelihood of its having to proceed to the next is enhanced, even though at the same time the difficulty of so doing also increases, since at each point more vested interests are involved and political questions relating to the surrender of national sovereignty are intensified.

The promoters of the economic integration of the six countries which joined the Coal and Steel Community were well aware of these considerations. When they started on the long negotiations which led to formation of a European Economic Community (EEC) based on the provisions of the Treaty of Rome, the so-called sector approach had assumed a new form: it related no longer to individual branches of industry, but rather to successive areas of economic policy. The Treaty of Rome (1957) was conceived as a dynamic instrument for the progressive achievement of each stage in the process of integration as I have outlined it above, beginning with a customs union in industrial goods, going on to embrace a common agricultural policy and increasing freedom of movement of labour and capital, and proceeding finally, it was hoped, to complete economic union. From the outset the ultimate objectives were common fiscal and monetary policy, industrial and regional policy, management of the short-term balance of the economy, and medium- and long-term economic planning. These would be first harmonized and eventually unified.

It would, I think, be unfair to the intellectual capacity and the political imagination and ingenuity of the "founding fathers" of the EEC to assume that they believed that this process could be smooth, or that the successive stages could be passed and a lasting measure of integration achieved without a much greater surrender of political sovereignty than was openly and avowedly conceded at the outset. But they placed their faith in two important considerations, both of a political rather than an economic character. They believed the attitudes of member countries to a particular problem would be fundamentally altered once it had been made common to all as a result of the creation of the economic community; it would then represent an issue to be jointly resolved, rather than the subject of bargaining between opposing interests. Moreover, they believed the institutions they had created under the Treaty of Rome represented an entirely novel, not to say revolutionary, mechanism for regulating the relations between nations. In the counterpoise between an independent "supranational" Commission (as distinct from the traditional intergovernmental secretariat), with the exclusive power to initiate and propose, and an "intergovernmental" Council of Ministers, which alone had the power to decide, they thought they had devised the instrument needed for turning all problems into "common" problems, and thus had set in motion an irreversible and progressive process of integration.

A number of specific questions are raised by this outline as to what economic integration involves at various levels, how it relates to political sovereignty, and what was the main principle on which it was based so far as the "six" of the EEC are concerned. In the first place we must consider, without belabouring the details of its history, how far the EEC's evolution to date has conformed to the basic ideas of its founders. In the second place we must inquire into the problems the existence of this grouping has created for the scope and practice of economic cooperation on a wider European basis. Finally, we must examine the likely future role and development of the EEC in regard to the desiderata for the evolution of the world economy.

So far as the internal history of the EEC is concerned, while it is much too early for a final answer, the record to date gives a fair measure of support to the claims originally made for the new construction. It is true that there have been a number of crises, including one which brought progress to a halt for a year and a half. It is true also that the transition from one stage to another has been marked, as could be expected, by a sharp intensification of the pressure to go forward, as well as by resistance to the further restriction of national freedom of action. These tensions have called into question the very essence of the new mechanism, as it concerns the power—and practice—of the Commission. The result has been virtually to put into abeyance consideration of an extremely important constitutional provision for the next phase of the Community; this has profound implications for the speed with which national sovereignty can hereafter be eroded, for the issue is one of weighted majority voting on policy matters.

Nevertheless, it seems to me that the Community has shown so high a degree of viability under great stress that it would be difficult to explain this by the pressure of supporting national interests alone—be they French farmers or German industrialists. There is evidently a source of power in the institutions themselves, including, of course, the attachment of important sections of public opinion to the ideas enshrined in the Treaty of Rome and the vested interests of those involved in its operations. But above all I think there is a powerful dynamism in the mechanisms by which the Community has its being. This is essentially an instrument for creating the conditions in which national sovereignty is automatically—and progressively—restricted in regard to economic decision-making without, formally at least, requiring overt political action to further abandon national sovereignty each time a community decision is made.

I would repeat, however, that the final outcome of this process cannot yet be placed beyond all doubt. A challenge has been made by the French Government to the basic conception of the Community. Even without the French challenge, as the progress of integration began to involve such vital areas as taxation and currency, there was bound to be a limit to the process of spontaneous or implied surrender of national political sovereignty. The powers of the Commission have continued to grow, for example, in such matters as management of the considerable funds accruing from agricultural import levies and, later, from customs duties, and this gives new point to glossed-over questions of democratic control of this appointed, yet independent, body. Sooner or later the process of economic integration will require that the issue of political integration—that is, actual federation—be squarely faced.

When and how this will come about cannot be accurately predicted, but the issue is inescapably on the agenda of the next few decades. In the meantime the issue complicates, but does not for the moment dominate, relations between the EEC and other countries in Europe and elsewhere. This subsidiary problem will continue to be acute, and may become more so, before it has to be resolved simultaneously with that of political integration. Britain, while by no means the only other country affected, was and is clearly the most important; and it is useful to consider this question in terms of the past, present, and future relationship of Britain to the European communities.

Britain and EEC

As regards the past, much has been written about the complicated and sometimes dramatic turns in this story, and we can pass over it quickly here. The main interest the subject has in the context of the present work is that it exhibits with unusual clarity the indissoluble connection between political and economic factors in the relations between countries.

The British attitude to the "continental" integrationist movement underwent several changes during the thirteen years from the launching of the Schuman

Plan in 1950 to the veto by President de Gaulle of British membership in the EEC in January 1963. Lack of belief in the survival value of "supranational" plans and institutions, indifference, fear, hostility, benevolence, and anxiety to join, alternated and commingled; and opinion within successive governments, as well as among the public at large, was rarely uniform and clear-cut. Nor were the reasons for this lack of clarity hard to find. I have already referred to the difference in continental and British historical experience in the immediate past. Britain, free from hyperinflation, unmarked by occupation or defeat, enjoyed considerable stability in general patterns of resource-allocation and economic expectations in comparison with many continental countries. This was to create special difficulties of adaptation for Britain in the postwar world.

The specifically economic arguments involved in determining the appropriate relationship for Britain and the EEC institutions were never easy to isolate from the political and psychological; they turned mainly on two subjects which were, in part, related: the system of agricultural support developed in England after the war, and her trading relations with the Commonwealth. The question of diminishing or abolishing, on a mutual basis, tariff protection on industrial goods was relatively less obdurate. It was only in the earlier years, when the general system of Commonwealth preferences was still regarded as powerful and long-lived, that this also constituted an important obstacle to progress. Jointly, however, these two factors persuaded British governments that participation by Britain in a customs union (requiring uniform tariff treatment vis-à-vis nonmembers) was out of the question. The British agricultural support system was closely geared to her special pattern of trade relations, particularly those with Commonwealth countries, and this reinforced opposition to membership under an arrangement in which a common agricultural policy would be linked to a general customs union.

The purely domestic aspects of the British agricultural system provided a primarily political rather than an economic obstacle, reflected in the fact that both the major political parties in Britain showed considerable reluctance to risk a major divergence of view with the farming community. The wider questions involved in economic union, such as social legislation, systems of taxation and fiscal policy, or monetary matters, did not enter significantly into the calculations for the greater part of the period we are here reviewing, since even within the relationship then being evolved among the European Six, these were regarded as belonging to a much more distant prospect.

Once the strength of the movement on the Continent was realized, and Britain's interest lay in finding some means of coming to terms with it, the efforts of successive British governments were directed to maintaining some kind of wider framework for economic cooperation within Western Europe as a whole, and more specifically to a pattern of trade liberalization which would not exclude her from the benefits of general tariff reductions while at the same time not calling in question her existing pattern of agricultural policy and Commonwealth trade.

Seen in retrospect, these efforts, which culminated in the negotiations for a Free Trade Area from 1956 to 1958, are understandable as actions dictated by the immense problems of adjustment to the radically new conditions Britain then faced. The fact that they now appear to have been destined to failure from the beginning is the sort of historical hindsight that is easily come by. At the time, however, the twists and turns of British policy obviously appeared to the Six as nothing more than an attempt to get the best of all possible worlds with the minimum of commitment.

Thus were added suspicion and animus to what were in any case extremely difficult problems of substance. And so attempts to create a general European Free Trade Area came to failure. As second best, seven of the members of the OEEC formed, in 1959, the European Free Trade Association, almost wholly confined to industrial goods, with only a minimum of agricultural arrangements included in response to pressure from some of the member countries. Provision for general economic consultation was also made, but this falls far short of the objectives of the Treaty of Rome.

The creation of EFTA simply formally registered the existence of two trade blocs in Europe, and it was hoped that in due course means would be found to bring about some association between them. But, for a variety of reasons, the British attitude was tempered much more rapidly after the creation of EFTA than might have been thought likely; and by 1961 membership in the European Community had become the objective—not fully avowed at first, but increasingly obvious—of the British government. After some months of soundings of the European Six and the Commonwealth governments, there followed some sixteen months of negotiations which progressed remarkably well until they were finally brought to a halt in January 1963 by the French President's imposition of a political veto on British membership—that is, an objection to British participation not directly or even significantly related to any of the substantive economic issues then under negotiation.

The French Veto

This is not the place to trace the course of these negotiations or to analyze the causes of their failure which lie in the political rather than in the economic sphere. From the point of view of the future course which Britain's relation with the Community might take, some aspects of the negotiations, however, are significant. In relation to many if not all of the so-called economic-union problems then identified, little serious difficulty was thought to arise. This applied, *inter alia,* to social legislation, industrial regulation, and even to migration of labour, although there would have been difficulties of adjustment and some transitional period might have been necessary. This is not to say that this was the end of the story. It is of the essence of these economic-union problems that their relative urgency changes, partly as a result of progress within the EEC itself, partly as a result of changes within Britain or in the world generally. For example, strictly monetary questions, *i.e.,* those that might arise out of a proposal for currency union, were not on the agenda in 1961–63, but clearly would be very likely to be on a future occasion.

It is also worth noting that the Common Agricultural Policy as evolved by the Community was found to be a perfectly adequate (indeed to some analysts, an excessively protectionist) method of looking after the British farmer. Conviction that this was so was no doubt an important factor leading the British government to embark on negotiations in the first place. Some political issues would undoubtedly still have had to be faced; for not only the level of protection he enjoys but the method by which it is determined (including the manner of his access to the Government and its decision-making process) is something to which the organized British farmer attaches importance. For this reason, at the very least an adequate transition period would have been required.

By the time the negotiations took place, a loosening in the general pattern of Commonwealth trade had already taken place and more could be seen coming; and the relative importance of particular aspects had changed. For example, the preferences enjoyed in Britain for their industrial exports by some of the advanced countries of the Commonwealth had clearly declined in importance as negotiating priorities. The reciprocal preferences enjoyed by Britain remained a somewhat troublesome point. On the other hand, the impact on Commonwealth trade of the Common Agricultural Policy and the regulations which were being evolved under it remained a matter of great importance to Britain and her trading partners, including some (the U.S., Argentina, etc.) outside the Commonwealth. For a country like New Zealand, with her overwhelming dependence on the British market for food exports, it could have been a matter of life and death. For Britain, too, the implications of the whole complex of the agricultural, and the related financial, regulations were very considerable in impact on the cost of living and on the balance of payments.

There is another issue among the many on which negotiations took place that should be mentioned here; namely, the relation of the less developed parts of the Commonwealth to Britain and to the members of the Community as affected by the Community's own arrangement for regulating trade with the associated territories of her members, nearly all also in process of development. At this point all that need be said is that a broad general solution on the basis of the possibility of association on the same terms being made available to Commonwealth countries was negotiated and that this question would not, therefore, have formed a major obstacle to British membership.

In some ways the most significant problems raised by the British negotiations and by the manner of their failure related not only to the relation of Britain (and of her EFTA partners) to the European Economic Community, but to the future character of the Community itself and to its relation to the world economy. I have already mentioned the challenge represented by the terms in which the French position was defined at the time of the last great crisis in the Community's affairs, and by the compromise solution which was arrived at. The character of the French veto as well as the subsequent French attitude inside the Community itself can, not unreasonably, be seen together as demonstrating not only the view of European integration taken by the present French government but also as the expression of certain antithetical elements within the concept and practice of economic integration.

Here there was an apparently inevitable clash between the built-in tendencies toward progressive integration, with their attendant pressure for greater political unity, and the French desire to limit these possibilities by retaining control over the pace of development within the intergovernmental parts of the machine, a desire pushed finally to the extreme of a veto over important new forward steps. This is not merely a major difference of approach between France and her partners; it inevitably raises the question of what kind of an economic community and what kind of political development in Europe a consistent application of the French approach is likely to produce.

It has been claimed by some in Britain, who have applauded the French attitude as being in line with Britain's own reluctance to follow the "supranational" path, that one result is likely to be a reversion to the straight intergovernmental negotiation and agreement with which we have long been familiar, in particular as it was practised in OEEC in the first few years of its existence. I myself regard this as highly doubtful, even if this were the intention of the French (which is by no means certain). The scope of integration marked out by the Treaty of Rome—and not so far questioned by the French—is far broader than anything so far attempted in intergovernmental relationships; on analytical grounds the concept is hardly likely to be consistent with the sort of "conference in permanent session" that intergovernmental arrangements represent. Finally, the progress already achieved has gone a great deal further than is usual with the latter method.

Admittedly not much has yet been done in such difficult areas as currency union; and the medium-term plan (though significantly produced as the joint work of the Commission and of intergovernmental Committees of the Council—and, incidentally, showing close similarity to planning efforts in France and in Britain) could perhaps be dismissed as being in the nature of a research effort rather than a genuine achievement of joint policy making. Against this, what has been done in the customs union—in the harmonization of taxation policy, in migration policy, and in other areas—has produced a substantial degree of interweaving of national economies.

Above all, the Common Agricultural Policy is deliberately designed to be executed and managed from the centre, that is, by the Commission; and even if the Commission's planned powers in regard to the income of the Community were to be severely restricted, its influence on agricultural policy would be bound to be very great. A further reason is that private enterprise, industrial, commercial, and financial, is developing constantly stronger cross-links of all kinds among the member countries based on, and thereby giving further encouragement to, unified direction of policy. Again, there is no evidence that the institutional mechanism of the Treaty of Rome—with its reliance on the counterpoise, as I have called it, between Commission and Council—is fundamentally affected, even if for a time in practical operation the powers of the Commission are restricted.

If one concludes, as I do, that there is no good reason to assume that the Community will, under the impact of French action, change its fundamental character, the question arises as to what the end result of the French challenge is likely to be, or even is meant to be. One immediate answer is simply that the pace of progress in the Community may well slacken or, at least, vary considerably between the several areas of activity involved. It is not easy to think of any general criterion by which this might be determined. Where, for example, the management of the short-term balance of the economy is concerned, much would depend on the conjunctural situation in particular countries at a particular time as to whether the interplay of national interests will produce a balance of forces in favour of collective, communal solutions, or not. Again, in the field of monetary matters, while close consultation among the Six is already normal practice, one cannot forecast with certainty how fast actual institutional arrangements might progress, particularly given the uncertainties in the world situation in this respect.

The more important aspect turns on the question of how the total balance of national interests will now develop within the Community, and at what point the issue of political integration in Europe can once again be actively taken up. This, in turn, is bound up with the question of the relationship of the EEC with other countries, particularly with the United States and Britain, not only in economic but in political matters. In other words, I think it much more correct to regard the clash of philosophies in the EEC as not being simply one between economic nationalism and integration as far as the Six themselves are concerned. Insofar as recent developments show a revival of nationalism, this seems to me to be directed more toward determining which national interest will predominate in the Community and the general direction in which the Community's policies shall be impelled, rather than tending to loosen the bonds that hold the Community together.

To put the brake on the Community's progress and, in particular, to restrain the powers of the Commission is not at all inconsistent with this view. For if the character of the Community as a political entity is to be deliberately molded in accordance with one nation's views, it is necessary that the Community's own development should be under some control other than that of its own immanent forces. So to that end the determination of the pace at which European integration takes place in the political sphere should be separated as far as possible from integration in the economic sphere in order to be susceptible to a higher degree of direct control on the basis of national policy. In short, I believe the question to be not whether there should continue to be a fairly well-integrated European Economic Community, but how and to what purpose it should be controlled.

The Outward Look

So far as these purposes are concerned there are, no doubt, purely political and strategic aspects involved which lie outside the scope of this study. On the economic side, it was fashionable at the time of the British negotiations and immediately after to speak of a choice between an outward-looking or inward-looking Community. As in the case of all such pat terms, it is not easy to define precisely what was meant. Inward-looking is perhaps most readily defined as protectionism, and outward-looking, therefore, as liberal. There is, of course, in principle no reason why an economic union of X members should be any more or any less liberal or protectionist than one consisting of X + Y members. Nevertheless, leaving aside all political, psychological, or propagandist overtones, there was a sense in which it could be argued in the early Sixties that an enlargement of the EEC, particularly by the inclusion of Britain, would have promoted more liberal tendencies toward the rest of the world. A successful negotiation at that time with Britain and, say, some of the Scandinavian countries would have added to the membership of the EEC more countries with a vital interest in foreign trade on a worldwide basis. This presumably would have strengthened the liberal elements in such critical areas as the so-called Kennedy round of GATT tariff negotiations.

In the matter of agriculture, too, the inclusion of Britain with her strong interest in imports of foodstuffs from the Commonwealth and other primary producing countries, or of Denmark with her highly efficient production and trade in livestock and dairy products, would have been bound to result in a pattern of commercial policy more liberal than that which the Six were likely to establish on their own. Where trade with the less developed countries was concerned, the inclusion of those from the Commonwealth would, both in respect of tropical products and in regard to simple manufactures, have widened the circle of countries benefiting from association and thus resulted in a more liberal and fruitful trade regime.

It is not yet possible to be completely positive on this question. As I said, in economic theory there is no reason to expect a grouping like the Six to be more outgoing in trade negotiations rather than less. There is, perhaps, good ground for expecting any new grouping, while struggling to establish its identity, to regard its external tariff or its system of agricultural protection as the most effective means available and, therefore, not to be very receptive to negotiations with others. Historically, the evidence is not very clear, though the *Zollverein* certainly was followed by a prolonged and intensive protectionist tendency in Germany. There is also the fact that an emerging customs union, having to achieve a compromise between a variety of national interests, is likely when it comes to negotiate with outsiders to do so on the basis of its own highest factor of protectionism rather than of that of the lowest common denominator of liberalism.

In practice, the evidence concerning the Community's attitude, apart from that produced during the British negotiations, is not yet decisive. There has certainly been delay in completing the "Kennedy round"; and in general the tendency has been that which might have been expected, namely, that the desire of some members to make progress in international negotiations for trade liberalization has been used by others in order to press for concessions in the internal arrangements of the Community. In the course of the British negotiations, the Six, as a group, did not show particular eagerness to adopt a liberal attitude, for example, in relation to the simple manufactures of the developing countries; in some respects they displayed a more protectionist bent, in this regard at least, than Britain. On the other hand, the British negotiations were complicated in a variety of ways, and they came at a time when the Community was hardly feeling entirely secure, so that it is not altogether fair to judge from that experience. More recently there has been some evidence that there is a real desire on the part of the EEC to see progress made in GATT.

There is, however, another, and more complex, aspect of the outward/inward-looking problem which goes back to the political factors upon which I touched before. In the broadest politico-economic terms the postwar period was for a long time dominated by a twin vision: the consolidation of Europe and the creation of an Atlantic Community. A full discussion of what this means and of the problems it involves would clearly trespass on other fields. What needs to be said here is that until the veto of January 1963, the general assumption on both sides of the Channel, and on both sides of the Atlantic, had been that integration in Europe in one form or another was consistent with the consolidation of the Atlantic Alliance into an ultimate Atlantic Community.

There were, of course, differences of emphasis and of method: broadly, the view of many of those in Britain who could be absolved from any charge of being hostile to European integration was to lay the greater emphasis on the Atlantic concept, wishing to proceed to it without an exclusive concentration on what was regarded as the intermediate, purely European, stage. Many of the "Continental integrationists," on the other hand, believed that the Atlantic Community required a partnership of near equals, thus stressing the need to achieve considerable progress in European integration first.

Since 1963, for the first time since the war, the compatibility of these objectives has been called in question, if not explicitly, certainly in practical terms. While at first confined to the political, and, especially the defense sphere, the view that there is an inherent contradiction between these aims has more recently emerged in economic and financial matters and I shall have something more to say about it in that connection. In a larger sense the question of regional integration in its relation to the desideratum of a consolidated world economy must in the practical terms of contemporary history still be regarded as open. But we may be able to form a clearer view on this question when we have further considered the other great unresolved issues of the international economic order.

As a postscript to this discussion of European integration, I should perhaps add that regionalism is not of course confined to Europe. Attempts at free-trade areas or even economic unions have been made elsewhere at various times. Some, such as that in Central America, have a longer history than the European, going back to abortive attempts, 140 years or so ago, to form a Central American Federation, and in a more recent, economic, manifestation, to 1951. I have thought it most useful, however, to concentrate this discussion on Europe. Here the general issues of economic regionalism can be most readily discerned as a force determining the great issues with which the world will have to grapple in the next twenty-five years.

Chapter 11   The Agricultural Problem

THE TREND TOWARD regional economic integration, as exemplified in EEC, has not created a new agricultural problem, but it certainly has brought an old one very much to the fore. Historically, agriculture has played a complicated and often difficult role in domestic economic policy and international trade. Prior to the period of classical political thought, land occupied a very special position in economic thinking; the immediate forerunners of the classicists, the physiocrats, regarded it as the ultimate source of all wealth and built the whole of their theoretical system on this concept. It was not until the time of Ricardo that economic science was emancipated from this intellectual bondage.

Among the general laws of classical economics, a central place was given to the doctrine of comparative costs and, with it, the belief in the wealth-creating effects of the international division of labour. Practical acceptance of the principle that free trade, including free trade in foodstuffs, was most likely to result in optimum use of resources was much slower in coming. Even in England, the home of classical economics, it was not until the abolition of the Corn Laws by Peel that a free-trade regime was finally established. Once in being it was remarkably durable, remaining virtually intact until the Great Depression of almost a hundred years later.

It was not until the second half of the 19th century that trade in foodstuffs, along with trade in general, became worldwide. This was the era when European settlers, with the aid of European and, later, North American capital, opened up great areas of hitherto unexploited cultivation: the United States Midwest, the Canadian West, Argentina, and Australia. Between 1876 and 1929, roughly half a century, the quantum of food exports more than quadrupled. Apart from these new sources of supply, technological development in food processing and transport, the spread of liberal economic policies, a falling death rate and a rising population, industrialization, and the steady increase of real incomes were all part of this revolutionary change in temperate zone agriculture, which was also accompanied by greatly expanded output of agricultural products in the tropical areas of the world.

The great upsurge of world trade in foodstuffs tended to mask the persistence of special and protectionist agricultural policies. Nor do the spectacular growth curves tell the whole story of the impact of the cycle of wars and depressions. Wars have always given a powerful stimulus to greater production, and to intensify efforts to achieve a maximum measure of self-sufficiency in agricultural supply. The dislocations of trade in the Napoleonic Wars, for example, saw the emergence of the sugar beet as a major continental commodity. Actually, the trend toward an increase in the international trade in food was slackening all the time. If we take the quantum of exports in 1913 as 100 we find that in forty preceding years it had trebled, while in the forty following years it had risen only by 54 percent; in the Twenties and Thirties food exports ran at about one-third above the 1913 level; in the Fifties they were only 15 percent higher.

The present position of temperate-zone agriculture shows marked similarities in all of the advanced countries. There has been a relative decline in the importance of agricultural production in the economy as a whole demonstrated in the sharply declining percentage of the population engaged in farming, and in the percentage of the gross national product contributed by agriculture. At the same time, rapid technical progress has produced absolute increases in output that have been enough—and, on occasion, more than enough—to meet the market demand of larger and more affluent populations.

There are, of course, variations in the rate of these movements among the advanced countries, and they are confined wholly to temperate-zone agriculture. There has been no general decline in the relative importance of tropical agriculture and of food production in the less developed countries. As a result, the problems of adjustment, which in the advanced countries have often led to action to mitigate or retard the consequences of economic change, have not been present in the less developed countries. However, other disrupting factors, which we shall discuss later, have been operating there.

Ever since the depression agriculture in all the developed countries has been characterized by attempts at protective devices which would prevent agricultural production patterns from being determined primarily by relative cost factors. It is an interesting question why these efforts to insulate agriculture from the effects of the cold winds of economic change should have been so persistent and so widespread. Some of the reasons are obvious: they lie in the technical as well as in the social conditions of agricultural production. Agriculture is tied to the soil; the mobility of capital is low, and that of labour sometimes completely absent. But there are also powerful institutional and ideological factors going back to primitive cultures which still endow agriculture and the rural way of life with a unique psychological influence profoundly affecting political attitudes. The remarkable fact is that the political weight of the agrarian interest is rarely closely correlated with the numerical importance or economic influence of those engaged in farming. In Britain, for example, the political weight (with all parties) of the "rural vote" cannot be measured by the small proportion (less than 4 percent) of the total working population in agriculture, or by the roughly similar percentage of the agricultural contribution to the gross national product.

The special position of agriculture in the economy gives rise to other paradoxes. There is no clear correlation between the degree of protection and/or subsidization of agriculture in one country as compared with another that reflects the relative importance of agriculture to either. Nor is the relationship between efficiency and degree of protection, or with general trade policy at all uniform. Switzerland, for example, has a very highly protected agriculture and a generally liberal trade regime. In Denmark and New Zealand, agriculture is of vital importance in the economy, but there is little, if any, subsidization. Some sectors of British agriculture are among the most technically efficient in the world, yet the degree of subsidization is high. It is clear, therefore, that a variety of factors are at work; some part of the explanation undoubtedly is to be found in political and military history.

Measurement of the degree of agricultural protection as between different countries is an extremely complicated matter and no accepted method has yet been devised, nor does one seem in sight. A special group under the auspices of GATT attempted the task some years ago but the subject still remains one more adaptable to exploitation in diplomatic negotiation than to objective scientific research. We have to rely on examination of the broad consequences of different methods of agricultural protection, domestic and international, while recognizing that no uniquely valid comparison is likely to emerge. But whatever may be the explanation for the persistent tendency to protect agriculture and whatever may be the methods used, the arguments that have been adduced in favour of it generally have been uniform and easy to state. Broadly speaking they have been of three classes: social, strategic, or economic (relating in recent years more particularly to the balance of payments). Each one has some force in some countries at some time, though none can be said to be exclusively relevant to agriculture as distinct from other important sectors of the economy. These arguments are important here only as they relate to the methods of protection to which they have given rise, and the dynamism thus engendered in terms of the international economic order.

Systems of Support

Domestically, the protection of agriculture does what would be done by the protection of any other sectional interest; it gives this particular sector of the economy a claim on national resources which must, by definition, be greater than would be the case in the absence of special measures. It also inevitably reduces international trade in the protected commodity or commodities. In other words, the object and result is to change the pattern that would result from the unimpeded working out of the international division of labour and thereby to achieve a higher level of domestic agricultural output than would otherwise be the case.

This happens, whatever the methods adopted, although from a political and administrative view the methods can be of considerable importance. The most telling and analytically useful comparison is perhaps that between Britain and the European Economic Community; what is done elsewhere in the advanced countries can quite readily be likened to or contrasted with these two systems. Broadly speaking, in the countries of the European Economic Community the state support of agriculture has taken the form of managing the market by means of direct intervention and/or by the control of imports through tariffs, levies, and quotas, or by a combination of these methods intended to raise the farmer's return to whatever is considered an adequate level. In Britain, the system that has been in operation since the immediate postwar period has allowed market return to find its own level, interventions at the frontier or otherwise generally being absent, while the desired level of income is achieved by giving the farmer direct subsidies—the so-called deficiency payments. Of course, these are broad generalizations; in the Community's Common Agricultural Policy, which is based on the methods long used in continental countries, subsidies are not wholly absent. Nor has the British system ever consisted exclusively of deficiency payments; in the case of milk and dairy products, for one example, a much more complicated system of market management has obtained. The weight of the contrasting patterns, however, is as indicated.

One major advantage claimed for direct subsidy is that it is most consistent with a democratic political system—the best compromise, that is, between a largely free-market economy and politically irresistible support for a sectional interest. The direct subsidy makes the cost of agricultural support plain to every citizen. An educated electorate in a democratic system, it is argued, prefers to have the cost of supporting agriculture (or anything else) borne by taxes, so as to be able to see exactly what it is spending, and to maintain direct, popular control over the level and direction of the expenditure.

A subsidiary form of the argument is this: a direct subsidy, though a burden on the taxpayer, is, like all direct taxation, progressive; the managed market approach of support for agriculture hides the cost in the price the consumer pays and, like all indirect taxation, is almost certain to be regressive. Further, since subsidy leaves the market substantially free, the benefits of competition are maintained with their presumed incentives to efficiency in production and marketing. Most important of all, the system allows a fair degree of (indeed, formally, often complete) freedom of imports. It is, thus, less objectionable to one's trading partners because it is less destructive of foreign trade. It means that foreign, as well as domestic, competition has to be reckoned with, and this helps to preserve the advantages of cheap food. Furthermore, it means that there is also always available a yardstick for measuring the true economic cost of agricultural support through the continued existence of an outside "free" world-market price.

These are formidable arguments. Most economists today share the view that if the benefits of full international division of labour have to be sacrificed it should be done in a way that still leaves the highest possible degree of freedom for the market mechanism. The most difficult of the countervailing arguments to answer is that which turns on the importance of being able clearly to demonstrate the cost of support. How decisive this is must be largely a political question. In an educated democracy it may be that the cost (which the consumer has to bear) of managing, *i.e.,* rigging, the market to the advantage of the domestic producer would not remain concealed for long. More amenable to economic reasoning is the related question of whether it is preferable that the burden should fall on the taxpayer or on the consumer. But this again cannot be decided in the abstract. The balance of the argument will depend not only on the level of the subsidy (or on the managed price) but also on the degree of prosperity of the country, its income distribution, and the general balance of direct and indirect taxation. In some circumstances, a shift of taxation to indirect from direct (and, concomitantly, a support system for agriculture that operates through the market rather than by direct subsidies) could be less regressive than appears at first sight.

The emphasis on retaining a world free-market price as a yardstick for efficient production and low cost loses some of its force in those instances where conditions of production or marketing falsify in one way or another the true competitive position. Agriculture has for so long and so intensively been the subject of special arrangements, very often and very largely backed by the State, that it is not difficult to question the existence of a true free-market price that conforms to the requirements of economic theory. Nor is it entirely beyond doubt that a system of agricultural support that results in keeping food prices lower to the consumer than they would otherwise be is necessarily beneficial from the point of view of keeping industrial wage costs down, and thereby maintaining competitive prices for industrial products—particularly when allowance has been made for the additional burden of taxation.

Thus it will be seen that from the point of view of the producing country, there is no clear balance of advantage or disadvantage on a priori grounds. What can be said with greater assurance is that a change from one system to another—as, for example, that which would be involved if Britain joined the Common Market—would produce considerable problems of short-term adjustment.

In the case of food-exporting countries, it is again difficult to be categorical about the relative attractiveness of one or another system. In principle, exporters are bound to dislike any system of agricultural support in importing countries since, by definition, it reduces the demand for foreign agricultural products. Nevertheless, they are often said to prefer the system of direct subsidies which implies free access to the market on the ground that the finance minister of the importing country thus becomes their best ally in resisting excessive support for the domestic producer. On the other hand, since price formation in a free world-market is apt to be distorted by export subsidies, by dumping, by artificial freight rates, and by other devices, free access may be regarded by some of the exporting countries as a mixed blessing, since it does not provide any guarantee against unduly depressed prices.

As far as the farmer is concerned, preference depends on the particular circumstances of the time, the state of the economy in general, political considerations, and historical background. From his point of view the ideal system might be that which existed in Britain during the war emergency, namely of fixed (annually negotiated) prices at which the whole of his annual output was bought. Of course, this system operated in a period of shortage when all that the farmer could possibly produce was needed by the community and was bought, allocated, and rationed by the Government; and when, moreover, the whole of the economy was carefully regulated so that the prices negotiated for the output of the "national farm" were geared into the general pattern of prices and incomes determined by the overall economic strategy of the war. This system of total purchase at fixed prices is, therefore, not one which one can reasonably expect to be acceptable in normal times.

It is noteworthy, however, that the negotiated price system was not abandoned after the war without some resistance on the part of the farmer. Similarly, once the British industrial producer had got used to the new system of "standard prices" and deficiency payments to bring the average of returns realized in a free market up to guaranteed levels, he would naturally be inclined to regard it as suiting his interest better than any other, unaccustomed, device. The annual negotiation of standard, as opposed to fixed, prices has acquired some continuity and this gives the farmer some feeling of security by providing farm organization leaders direct access to the government and the means for exerting pressure on it.

The Blending Process

Agricultural support policy everywhere results from a multiplicity of pressures by different economic interests applied through domestic and international political channels; it tends to become a mixture in which different basic systems coalesce, even while retaining central characteristics of one or another.

This has been the experience in recent years in Europe, in Britain, and in the EEC. The British system, though characteristically one of deficiency payments, displays features of those that impose the cost of agricultural support on the consumer rather than the taxpayer. There have been other admixtures, such as acreage limitations dictated by the nature of a particular commodity.

In general, pressure applied by farmers, along with that of overseas suppliers, has had the net effect of considerably diluting the purity of the British system and making it more akin to the continental. Low market prices have not pleased the farmer (who naturally feared the consequences of his increasing dependence on budgetary support) nor the exporting country, which, within or without the Commonwealth, saw its returns dwindling even though it continued to have access to the market and could perhaps count on maintaining its share. Minimum import price agreements, therefore, have been resorted to, flanked by the introduction of "standard quantities" for the domestic producer, that is to say, limitations on the amount of his output that could benefit from the full price guarantee. Sometimes, in the case of butter, for example, a quota regime has also been instituted. But once minimum import prices exist, there is no longer the same gulf, either in principle or in practice, between such a system and one that employs target prices, import levies, and the other essential features of the Common Agricultural Policy of the EEC.

But on the EEC side, too, there has been a tendency toward some practical modifications of the original concept. Direct subsidies to German farmers, for example, have been allowed for a transitional period (ironically one of the points on which there was the greatest resistance by EEC to any concession at the time of the British negotiations). Various other departures, some regarded as temporary, have had to be made in the process of negotiating agreement among the members. Leaving aside influences arising from the Community's relations with other countries, there are enough unresolved problems within the EEC to make it unlikely that we now have before us the final pattern of the new European agricultural system. Further critical negotiations are going to be necessary as a result of linking the Community's trade regime to structural reforms of its members' domestic agriculture through the mechanism which provides levies to finance those reforms. This continued resort to a variety of methods, old and new, makes it likely that the emerging support system will be more variegated than uniform for some time.

I have not dealt here with the United States, which has a long and complicated history of agricultural support. Over the years, American farm-support policy has had recourse to practically every method and device that can be thought of; and while for some periods, as during the New Deal, some system such as parity payments predominated and seemed to give the policy a characteristic appearance, variety has always quickly returned. Direct subsidies, support buying, sterilization of surpluses by Government storage, tariffs, and quotas—even specially designed health regulations—all these have been used at one time or another, and have spread to or been imported from the rest of the world. Through it all, American agriculture, technologically, has been one of the most progressive in the world and, like the British, has shown remarkable increases in productivity, thus providing a powerful argument against those who were ideologically disposed to attack the system of agricultural support on the ground that in reducing the impact of competition it would stagnate the farm economy.

In the most recent years, American farm policy has shown a tendency toward a greater degree of uniformity in the methods used. Support levels, in general, have tended to decline, and direct payments, originally confined to wool and sugar, have gradually been applied to other major crops as a means of supplementing the farmer's income from the market. This is, for the time being at least, the most important and characteristic form of farm support in the United States, and with its development has come some slight easing in the protection against imports of food from abroad which American agriculture has traditionally enjoyed.

The great problem that all countries have been, are, and will be facing in developing agricultural policy is to accomplish a most difficult balancing act tolerable to the various interests that have to be reconciled. There is an obvious conflict between the desires of the farmer, rightly or wrongly regarded as a powerful political factor, and the consumer, whose interests are the most ubiquitous in the entire population. If the consumer's food prices go up he will, as a wage earner, press for higher pay. Costs may then rise and domestic industry suffer a loss of competitive position in foreign trade. A balance also has to be struck between domestic agriculture and the general foreign trade interests of the country, which may be adversely affected by retaliatory action by food exporters among the country's trading partners. In one way or another all the developed countries of the world have to achieve such a reconciliation.

Notwithstanding the qualifications made earlier, in principle a system that combines considerable freedom of access to the domestic market by foreign exporters, relatively low or nonexistent tariffs, and a virtually automatic means of supplementing the farmer's income, while still maintaining incentives for increased efficiency—in short the basic British or the evolving American system—provides the most flexible mechanism for achieving as smooth a reconciliation as is possible among these various objectives. By the same token, the system which is being developed in the EEC—largely based on the wartime and immediate postwar Dutch experience—suffers from lack of flexibility, runs the risk of an excessively high level of protection, and does not guarantee adequate spontaneous pressure for improving agricultural productivity. In practice, current and future negotiations will determine which system, or which features of each, predominate in the next twenty years or so.

Currently, and for the early future, the agricultural negotiations that have taken place in the framework of GATT's "Kennedy round" may have some influence on future developments. So will the terms of settlement of the relationship between Britain, and other countries with a highly developed agriculture, and the EEC. The chances are that for the short term the present continental European pattern will prevail. In the long term, however, this is far from certain.

The Longer Term

In the longer run the answer may be very different. A number of countries are technically far ahead of the EEC in key sectors of agriculture. Britain is a more efficient and lower cost producer of cereals than any EEC member. Denmark is at least as efficient a producer of certain livestock products as the best in EEC. The natural economic advantages of a country like Argentina in cereal and beef production can only be negated by very high levels of protection in Europe. Within the Commonwealth, New Zealand is an extremely low-cost producer of all that depends on grass: sheep and dairy products. And there is the United States with its highly mechanized "farm factories" still making startling progress in efficiency and productivity.

There are highly important and difficult questions of international specialization involved here, the answers to which in the long run could have quite dramatic consequences on the worldwide distribution of production, of populations, and of relative standards of living. A pattern which emerges for obvious and very understandable reasons out of the balance of advantages in the internal negotiations of the European Six and to benefit, for example, Dutch livestock products or French cereals or horticulture, may nevertheless become a source of tension when set in this wider context. It must not be thought, however, that an answer could or should be found in reestablishment of the patterns of the 19th and early 20th centuries—that is, of Europe as a whole assuming the role once played by Britain as the workshop of the world, relying on overseas granaries for her food. Britain's own wartime and postwar development consigns this notion to limbo; this onetime world workshop now produces a considerably higher proportion of her food requirements, and maintains a larger and better-fed population than she ever did before. The proportion of her population engaged in agriculture, moreover, is lower than ever and still declining.

It is clear, therefore, that technical progress in agriculture has made any simple pattern of agricultural/industrial geographical specialization obsolete. Rapid increases in population and in urbanization have been accompanied by revolutionary changes in food preparation and marketing; these have already blurred the old lines of division between agriculture and industry and will continue to do so. A simple answer in the traditional terms of the doctrine of comparative costs has little relevance as a guide to practical action.

The picture is further complicated by political changes, such as the division of Germany; by rapid industrialization in countries like China and the Soviet Union which have become very important importers of foodstuffs, particularly cereals; and by the increase and refinement of demand for food which must be expected to result from the industrialization, increased population, and improved living standards in the underdeveloped countries.

For some years these factors should provide some room for maneuvers which will help ease the pressures between developed countries that traditionally have been food exporters and those that have been importers. But tensions will continue since it is highly unlikely that there will be an even rate of progress for the various developments involved: growing demand for food in underdeveloped countries; economic growth and continued decline in rural employment in the developed countries; and better external and internal commercial arrangements. There will, thus, continue to be a great need for positive international action to minimize conflict and to maximize the cohesion of the one-world concept. Among these arrangements, commodity agreements, designed to even out short-term price fluctuations and to introduce some measure of international production planning, will play a vital part for basic commodities such as cereals and sugar. There is also urgent need for a greater degree of international cooperation in development programs in less advanced countries to link food production and import policies, aid and technical assistance, and the commercial policies of the advanced countries into a more consistent whole. We shall return to these issues when we have considered the general question of the future of the less developed countries, with their special problems of tropical agriculture.

Chapter 12   The Less Developed Countries

THE END of the colonial era came with a rush in the years after World War II, and its legacy is one of the most dynamic elements in the world economic order, a source of tension and of vital political/social/economic issues that may not be wholly resolved for generations to come. The problems of the less developed countries have had wider recognition and more publicity than any other in the field of contemporary political economy. They provide a most fashionable subject for international discussion with a popularity that apparently cannot be impaired by continuous repetition. Some of the most sophisticated commentators on world affairs now rate "the North/South problem" as much more important than "the East/West problem." We hear a great deal about the relation between the "haves" and the "have nots"—a distinction that had a very different meaning in the Twenties and Thirties, when it was used to refer to the conflict between colonial powers and countries that had no colonies. Hazards of prediction are brought sharply to mind by this ironic reminder of the very different preoccupation of little more than a generation ago.

The vast literature on the less developed countries is matched by the concentration of governments and intergovernmental organizations on the issues they pose. We are, for example, in the middle of the United Nations' "development decade" which is intended to produce economic growth in these countries at a minimum average rate of 5 percent per annum. Great pressure is being exerted on advanced countries to commit to an annual aid program a contribution equivalent to at least 1 percent of their gross national product. In striking contrast to the abortive world trade conference held nearly twenty years earlier in Havana, 120 countries participated in the United Nations Conference on Trade and Development in 1964 which resulted in the establishment of certain permanent institutions.

Two sets of causes seem to be responsible for this surging interest. First, a series of political developments have thrust the economic position and prospects of the less developed parts of the world to the fore. The emancipation of these areas from colonial rule was the basic factor; independence gave them representation in the United Nations and voice in international negotiations. The "one man, one vote" rule of the UN made it certain that in a relatively short

133

time the numerical preponderance of the newly independent (virtually synonymous with underdeveloped) countries would gain considerable weight in world councils. And for these countries the rate of economic growth was bound to be a subject of great internal importance; political stability, which is not automatically the accompaniment of independence, was often primarily dependent on prosperity and material advance. To secure these objectives becomes a most important aim of any regime that wishes to stay in power; and to press for it in international arenas, where the striking gap between the rich and the poor nations can be most effectively demonstrated, inevitably becomes a major activity.

The postwar split between the East and the West had an important bearing on the way in which relations between developed and less developed countries have changed. The struggle for the political independence of colonial territories often was identified with Communism, which was assumed, justifiably or not, to have an affinity with all those seeking national liberation. Thus, in some ways, the competition between East and West was extended to include ideological supremacy in the newly independent, less developed countries. "A struggle for their soul" or for "the minds of men," as it was sometimes put, tended, at least in the earlier phase, to be an adjunct to, and even a motive for, efforts to accelerate the economic development of the former colonies.

But economic factors also played a major part in intensifying great power interest in these problems. The dislocations of war and independence, and the postwar economic problems of the advanced industrial countries, were inevitably reflected in the economic position of the overseas territories. Many found their income rapidly increased as the result of sharp rises in the prices of their primary products and, at the end of the war, many had accumulated substantial credit balances in foreign exchange. At the same time, intense competition for their products on the part of the belligerents, and their attendant inability to supply the manufactured goods needed by the primary producing countries, led to a loosening of long-established commercial ties and the creation of new trade patterns. Political independence accelerated the process. New relationships were established not only between an overseas country and a number of industrialized countries, but between less developed overseas countries themselves.

This is not to say that the connections forged in the colonial era completely disappeared. The British and French, the largest of the old colonial empires, have maintained a Sterling Area and a Franc Area, indicating that to a high degree the old financial patterns were preserved. But these are no longer exclusive; and tendencies are evident which will make them less and less so. In the case of the Franc Area, for example, forces are set in motion by association of former French overseas territories with EEC that are bound to loosen the special financial and commercial ties between France and these countries. More generally, as the problem of the trade of the less developed countries is dealt with in a broader context, a more variegated pattern of commercial and financial relations is bound to emerge.

The preoccupation of the less developed countries with their trade problems is broadened in the process; and, for their part, the former colonial powers are able to spread responsibility for the economic well-being of these countries. More general discussion and analysis of their problems is stimulated, especially as it bears on the connection between their trade and their growth performance, and between the aid they receive from the richer countries and those countries' commercial policy toward them. Interest in these problems so far has grown at a cumulative rate.

The impact of these changes on the practical activities of governments has produced a new direction of theoretical preoccupation and activity. The theory of growth that in the last twenty-five years has developed importantly in the purely analytical and descriptive/historical fields provided a useful background. Examination of the historical process of economic development in different sets of circumstances led to conclusions on policy desiderata for countries on the threshold of development. At the same time, these studies seemed to throw doubt on certain established principles of economic theory, particularly the doctrine of comparative advantage insofar as it relates to advantages for growth to be derived from international specialization. Both aid and trade policy vis-à-vis the less developed countries was given a new intellectual stimulus.

Thus, political pressures, economic changes, and intellectual advance combined to make everyone conscious of the problem of less developed countries in a fashion reminiscent of the way in which 19th-century opinion in the more advanced countries became generally aware of the poor in their own midst.

Elements of the Problem

It is not difficult to determine the fundamental nature of that problem. The President of the World Bank has itemized the striking contrast between the rich and poor countries: Some twenty industrialized countries in North America, Western Europe, and the Western Pacific, with one-fifth of the world's population, now account for more than half the world's wealth; the developing countries that are members of the World Bank have one-half of the world's population but account for only one-sixth of the world's product. In per capita income, the range is from the United States, with a figure of about $3,200, to Indonesia, with less than $50.

Admittedly, these comparisons are not precise, since comparative data are of very uneven reliability. The very concept of per capita income may give a misleading impression because of wide disparities in the distribution of income around the average. Nevertheless, the differences between countries are so striking that these qualifications cannot substantially affect the impression the figures convey. For example, of about eighty countries for whom statistics are usually available, the lower two-thirds in the list have annual per capita incomes that are only one-quarter of the average of the top twenty (which themselves show a range between $1,000 and more than $3,000). More than half of the lower two-thirds reach a figure of only about $200 and a quarter only $100 per annum. In other words, after the top twenty the figures fall away very sharply indeed.

In most cases low per capita income reflects both a small national product in absolute terms and a large population. Moreover, without significant exception, the rate of increase in population is exceptionally large in the developing countries. In the last five years some 200 million people have been added to the existing total in these countries—the equivalent of the population of the United States or the Soviet Union.

These few figures are enough to demonstrate how the world is divided between rich and poor nations. Such a state of affairs "cannot endure permanently," as Abraham Lincoln said of another deep cleavage in human affairs a hundred years ago. It is true that in some underdeveloped countries economic growth is not held in high regard and that many people, particularly among the ruling classes, are committed to maintaining the status quo. This, of course, is equivalent to maintaining a high degree of privilege against efforts at democratization, and it is becoming increasingly difficult. It is, therefore, impossible to believe that in the longer term any government can remain in power in any underdeveloped country unless it can be seen to be making strenuous efforts to better the lot of its people—and to be succeeding in the task. Moreover, the maintenance of amicable relations between nations now bound together by formal ties of world organization is clearly incompatible with the persistence of such gross inequality between nations as exists today.

Theories of Development

What, then, is being, and should be, done about it? First, a few words about diagnosis and the general theory of therapy appropriate to this case. First, there is the vexatious question whether a special theory of the development of the poorer countries is necessary. This is a highly contentious subject among economic theorists and economic historians as well as social scientists in general. There is much diversity of opinion on the extent of the resemblance between the current situation and future prospects of the developing countries and the earlier phases of development of the more advanced industrial countries. Are the former going to repeat the history of the latter? Is there a general theory of economic growth or development, applicable to all countries regardless of the level of development at which they find themselves? Are there clearly distinguishable stages of economic growth through which all countries must pass sooner or later? These are some of the questions that are being strenuously debated today. Beyond lie even more far-reaching questions concerning the general relationship of developed and underdeveloped countries. Here the questions range from fairly specific ones susceptible to analysis by the tools of modern economic theory (for example, the long-term trend of the terms of trade between manufactures—exporting and primary product—exporting countries) to the wider theories of capital accumulation, and the role that overseas investments plays in regard to the trend of the rate of profits in industrial countries, of which the theory of imperialism enunciated by Marx and elaborated by Lenin is the most comprehensive.

We cannot go into the details of these arguments here. So far as the relation of developed to underdeveloped countries is concerned, the Marxian thesis of imperialism can hardly be capable of surviving the progress of political emancipation of the former colonial areas and the tremendous upsurge of economic growth (much less impeded in the last twenty years than in the past by the trade cycle) in the developed countries. A theory which relies on the search for "super profits" through colonial investment does not seem to have much relevance at a time when one of the great difficulties of the world arises from the inadequacy of capital formation in general and, therefore, from a special shortage of funds for investment in underdeveloped countries. It is, nevertheless, true, though not necessarily related to the Marxian theory, that in a larger sense economic growth provokes a constant search for new markets which tends to draw new areas into the orbit of technologically advanced countries with a sophisticated commercial and financial structure. It is, however, the general drive of the innovator rather than any impersonal force such as the "rising organic composition of capital" that is responsible for this process. In regard to the likely future trends of development in relations between developed and underdeveloped countries, these simple yet all-embracing theories that rely on one general principle of explanation have little to offer.

More important for our purpose, therefore, is the theoretical debate over the question of the relevance of past industrial history in the West to the future pattern of the development of the poorer countries. Two difficulties confront the "pattern-makers" in economic history, be they Marxians, who regard the class struggle as the dynamic force; followers of Weber and Tawney, who see the motive of economic change in ideological, particularly religious, transformations; or the more modern, pragmatic economists such as Walt Rostow, who endeavour to identify and distinguish past "stages" of economic history without committing themselves to a view of the causes of the transition from one to the other. In the first place, they have to demonstrate their thesis convincingly in relation to the past; in the second, they have to prove the validity of the postulated pattern for the future.

The first is by no means easy, as the never-ending debate proves. In the end the choice is among one or the other of the unilinear explanations, or a descriptive pattern (such as Rostowian "stages"), or a more eclectic multilinear view. What is important from our point of view is how much each can contribute to a meaningful analysis of an existing situation in an underdeveloped country; to the identification of significant sources of tension and dynamism within it; and, thus, to some indication of the directions in which policy must move if it is to bring about or accelerate the achievement of a higher level of economic development. In this light, I find it difficult to escape the conclusion that while each of the more dramatic theories has something to contribute, none alone can provide an effective guide to policy.

I consider that the history of Western industrial societies does not provide an adequate guide to the future path of economic progress of the developing countries. The single most important reason for this is that broadly speaking the growth of modern industry in the West was a spontaneous, unplanned process, the political element being until relatively recent times only on very rare occasions directly focused on economic objectives. This view, of course, rejects the Marxian view of the state, and properly so, I contend, since we can now see that the consequences in terms of economic growth by no means coincide with what, on other grounds, Marx predicted. The relative separation of the political factor from all the other influences that went to the making of economic progress in the West immediately provides a striking contrast with the current situation in the developing countries. Here the political factor is dominant, and future development in which governments do not play a major part are not thinkable.

As I have mentioned earlier, there is hardly a developing country that does not have an elaborate economic plan stretching over a period of years. This is so notwithstanding the fact that the great majority have predominantly free-enterprise economies, though this is not so much a matter of ideology as it is a reflection of the vital role of agriculture in the economy. Indeed, the poorer the country, the greater seems to be the proportion of agriculture in its national production and, therefore, the extent to which "private" enterprise predominates. The situation is not much different in rudimentary or semi-developed branches of manufacture dominated by small craftsmen, or in the commerce of small traders, which tend to resist collectivization. To change this situation, to accelerate the movement toward more advanced forms of agriculture and food production, and toward more sophisticated industry, requires changes in the economic structure that can only be accomplished with the aid of a considerable measure of state intervention.

Another factor is that technological advance has made it possible, and perhaps mandatory, to skip many of the "stages" through which Western countries have passed; these can now be telescoped, but this presents a corresponding need to telescope phases of economic and political change which evolved over extended periods. This, too, requires a high degree of central management of the economy that only governments can provide. Again, development in this stepped-up manner is clearly impossible without reliance in one way or another—for funds, technical assistance, or trade concessions—on more developed countries; and this necessarily calls for centralized means for conducting international relations and negotiations.

Finally, general theories of past development are difficult to apply to the developing countries because they are not only very different in social and cultural background from the prototypes of industrial development in Western Europe and North America but also differ widely among themselves. Thus, the problems of economic growth display a considerable variety of special and unique features in Latin America, Africa, and Southeast Asia, even though all these areas undoubtedly have many features in common.

The Common Objectives

If the applicability of theories of historical development to the developing countries is limited, we may usefully look at the objectives these countries appear to have set for themselves (or are likely to be motivated by); examine the means being employed to move toward them; and speculate on future trends in both respects. Of course it is not possible to separate entirely the objectives and the means for their attainment. For example, a higher degree of economic equality can be both an objective of development and a means of stimulating it. The same may be true of policy aimed at ending exclusive reliance on a single crop. Behind the question of objective and means there is the deeper philosophical question of the kind of society and the quality of life the developing countries are seeking.

Modern technology and methods of organization have made it theoretically possible to reproduce almost anywhere on the globe the complex of material living conditions developed in the most advanced countries, and the social and economic relations that are appropriate to them. The ancient barriers of climate and soil and water supply have not disappeared, but their significance is far less that it was in the era of colonization, which imposed the contemporary pattern on much of the world. If a West European or North American industrial community now is accepted as a model, it could, with more or less difficulty over a varying period of time, be created in many other areas of the world. This is not the place to consider whether this is a sensible objective in the light of the sharp questioning of the values of the urbanized and industrialized mode of living always endemic and now virtually epidemic in the intellectual circles of Western countries. The determining fact seems to be that as of now the material conditions of Western society are widely regarded as desirable objectives and that, almost regardless of political structure and ideological bent, all policy is devoted to their achievement. I leave it to others to explain why this should be so.

The economic objective of the developing countries, then, can be stated quite simply: it is the achievement of the highest possible rate of economic growth, as that term is understood and measured by the advanced countries. Of course, there are other aspects of development of a political or social nature which vary from country to country. Also, as in Western communities, not all the results of national economic activity are measurable, and it is precisely these imponderables which confer on the pattern of life in each country its special flavour. But the general trend is quite plain; and considering the appallingly low standards of food, clothing, shelter, and health in the less developed areas, and their concomitants in deprivation, illness, and early death, it can be argued that deep philosophical speculation about the true quality of misery or happiness as related to material conditions is simply irrelevant.

What are the obstacles to the achievement of the objective of rapid growth? The choice of the order in which one lists these is naturally a matter for argument, since it will to some extent influence, if not determine, the hierarchy of means or intermediate objectives which are then prescribed. But whatever order is chosen, there can be no dispute about the major factors which must appear in any list. These are the tremendous rate of increase of population; excessive reliance on a few crops, or in some cases only one; the lack of an adequate political administrative, social, and economic infrastructure; and a very low level of food supply. Each presents a major difficulty to be overcome, and each also reinforces the others, thus creating a vicious circle which has to be broken at a number of points simultaneously.

The "population explosion" is the most spectacular feature of recent developments, or at least the one that has attracted most attention. It has been particularly marked in the last twenty-five years: the increase in world population during that period, from about 2.5 billion to about 3.4 billion, is greater than the total population of the world 150 years ago. At the same rate the next hundred years would see at least a sixfold increase of the total, even more if the accelerating rate of the next few decades is maintained. The less developed countries have made a disproportionate contribution to this rapid rate of increase; in the last thirty years or so, their populations have grown twice as fast as those of the industrialized countries; and the projections for the future show this trend to be continuing. One consequence is that the less developed countries have a much larger proportion of children to adults as compared with the developed countries, and this compounds the difficulty of achieving a rapid growth rate.

The root causes of population growth, and its relation to levels of development and standards of living, have been much debated and involve a number of disciplines. It is generally agreed that in the less developed countries there are now being repeated elements in the history of the developed countries in which economic advance, industrialization, and a declining death rate were accompanied by rapid increase in population. But there is a significant difference: none of the industrialized countries ever achieved at any time anything comparable to the rate of increase that has been experienced by many of the developing countries in recent years. The chief factor seems to have been the very sharp fall in the death rate, due to a combination of economic improvement, with its generally beneficial effect on health, and to the direct impact of medical progress, particularly of broad public-health measures.

The result of this population increase—whatever its analogous effect may have been in the 19th century—is certainly to complicate growth problems in the developing countries today. This is undoubtedly a question of scale, and no general "law" can be deduced. For most of the countries, however, it can be said that at the current rate at which people are multiplying in the less developed countries, and at the rate at which it is possible to push industrialization and the advance of agricultural technique, there is bound to be constant adverse pressure on the per capita national product. Improvement is, therefore, impossible without an attempt at restraining the rate of population increase.

Monoculture, the dependence on one crop or on a very few, is the usual characteristic of those underdeveloped countries which already have been drawn to some extent into the circle of international trade. It is not relevant here how this came about, and there is no point in reviewing the still-lively arguments over the extent to which former colonial powers were responsible for directing the development of primitive tribal communities from subsistence farming to plantation crops or large-scale mineral extraction required by the industrial communities of the West. The fact is that history has created a major obstacle to attainment of the desired goal of growth now that the desiderata of economics have become associated with political emancipation.

Monoculture in the long run is not compatible with the development of an economy based on an industrial foundation, which alone can give assurance of a high and sustained rate of further economic growth. It is true that even in the advanced countries one or other economic sector may from time to time be predominant, and in some this may still include agriculture. Denmark is an example, although even there recent trends have eroded the predominant position of agricultural exports. (New Zealand might be cited as a country maintaining a very high standard of living while still largely dependent on agriculture, but for this purpose she is more to be regarded as a specialized region of a more variegated economy, that of Britain.) In any case in all these countries there is a certain ebb and flow in the fortunes of the different sectors, which is itself one of the concomitants of economic progress.

Monoculture also presents difficulties in the short run. Many primary commodities are exceptionally subject to marked fluctuations in price. Thus to be heavily dependent on a single crop or mineral for export earnings puts the whole economy of the country on a very precarious basis. It jeopardizes economic development to a substantial degree, since financing must, to some extent at least, depend on the earnings from exports.

The Missing Infrastructure

There is no single prescription of any significance for the betterment of the economic performance of these countries which does not rely to a considerable extent on government policy for its efficacy. This means that there must be administrative machinery able to cope with the detailed consequences of policy decisions. In relation to general macroeconomic measures, such as taxation, or those in the realm of direct intervention, such as the measures of trade policy instituted from time to time, the government bureaucracy is called upon to perform a number of tasks that require a rather advanced stage of development. For these countries this can be achieved only through an educational effort devoted to creating highly trained manpower capable of performing skilled administrative tasks, and thereafter of channeling it into the right occupation. This is, clearly, a long process; and it is complicated by the strong demands for such talent in other sectors, particularly business management.

The political and social infrastructure, then, must be recast in a form appropriate to a modern economic society. A suitable educational system, the institution of a modern health service, provision for leisure activities, and a general broadening of the usually restrictive cultural framework are examples of the sort of transformation that must accompany economic development. It is, of course, true that the two processes mutually reinforce each other. But this does not necessarily make it any less difficult to achieve a pace which corresponds to the desired rate of economic advance; this generally involves painful and sometimes revolutionary changes that arouse strong resistance rooted in traditional modes of thought and practice, and compounded by the necessity of telescoping change into a very short span of years.

The political structure in most developing countries is the result of a slow historical evolution, and it is rarely adapted to the demands of a more highly developed and complex economy. The apparatus of government, therefore, must make a drastic departure from the traditional mode if it is to cope with the new relations between the organs in whom political power resides, the developing administrative machine, the growing business community, and the foreign governments and international organizations who control aid and trade relations. Beyond these practical issues there are far-reaching ideological problems which also have an immediate structural relationship to government. In the industrialized countries, differences of view over the political organization of society have become relatively stabilized, and in the same manner relations between countries with different political regimes have tended toward a reasonably stable pattern despite their unresolved differences. I have expressed the view earlier that as a result of developments in the economy and in the techniques of economic management, similarities in practice have gained in prominence while the deeper ideological debate has tended to sink into the background. In the less developed countries, however, the old, basic dispute is, understandably, very much alive. It colours internal power struggles and often retards the development of those political and social institutions which are essential for economic growth.

So far as the economic infrastructure is concerned, there are certain obvious requirements: an adequate transport system; the development of rivers and harbours; the provision of sources of energy. These are themselves constituents of economic growth, even as they are also the indispensable foundation for further growth. In nearly all the developing countries these elements are either not present at all or exist only in a most rudimentary form when the deficiencies are measured against need. Less tangible, but equally important, are certain types of more complex economic relations. The development of an "internal market," the importance of which Walt Rostow has rightly stressed, is an example of the hen-and-egg difficulty found here. The absence of a market system greatly limits the availability of consumer goods, and the scarcity of consumer goods precludes a market. In these circumstances it is difficult to provide the necessary stimulus for greater agricultural output, its more effective marketing, and indeed the organizational framework in which the necessary developments can take place. A suitable environment of commercial and banking services, of insurance, of legal advice and practice, and of logistic support for new forms of organization for enterprise is rarely far enough advanced to sustain, let alone foster, economic growth.

I have also mentioned inadequacy of food supply as one of the barriers to economic advance. The standard of nutrition is generally deplorably low in level and variety, too low to foster receptivity to complex educational demands, or to sustain the energy modern industry requires. Often, therefore, improvement of food production must have a first priority, even at the cost of forgoing foreign exchange earnings that might be derived from crops or minerals suitable for export. Gifts of food from other countries have been used to ease the situation, but they do carry with them the danger that they may retard necessary development of indigenous agriculture by encouraging premature concentration on industrialization.

Recital of the few statistics of national income I have given, together with the brief catalog of obstacles to growth, should be enough to show why a worldwide problem of development exists. To complete the picture it must also be pointed out that the problem is very different from that which European industrialized countries overcame, and even from that which other, newer areas faced as they emerged from colonial status in the modern period. The opening-up of North America or of Australia, for example, has no parallel in the case of the developing countries. Aside from the perhaps critical question of climate and its effect on the possibilities of agriculture, the settlement of large temperate areas with sparse populations enabled the settlers to duplicate the essential factors in the process that had already taken place in the industrialized countries of Europe. The present developing countries are, as it were, entering the race when the handicap is greater, the distance to be run longer, and the speed of the established competitors far in excess of their own. Moreover, the means available a hundred years ago were different; hand in hand with European settlement went the export of large amounts of European capital, beginning in the colonial and continuing into the post-colonial era. Private overseas investment was available to bear the brunt of the cost of the initial development of the North American continent, the provision of the transport and other infrastructure, the development of extractive industries, and the early stages of manufacturing industry until domestic capital formation could take over.

For a number of reasons the part comparable international capital movements can play in promoting and sustaining development is now more limited. In the immediate postwar years private investment was discouraged by the excessive nationalism which often followed political independence, producing a series of expropriations and severe restrictions on the manner in which foreign capital might be employed. While this factor has less importance today, the accelerating pace of technological change in the developed countries is enlarging the demand for capital on the home market, where there is often the possibility of higher rates of return as well as greater security.

Help from Without

Thus, the contemporary problem of development must be tackled in ways different from any known before. It requires the active help of the rich countries; this was recognized in the creation of the World Bank and its affiliated institutions, and in the principles of the Havana Charter; and it visibly has been demonstrated by the very large amounts of aid which have been flowing bilaterally or through international agencies from the developed nations. In the last five years alone $30 billion of "official net capital flows" have gone out from members of the OECD, most of this sum representing net aid after allowing for the costs of servicing past debts in interest and repayment. This, on the face of it, is a large sum, but it is small when measured against the need of the recipients, or against the capacity of the donors.

The needs of the developing countries have been variously estimated (the margin of error in such estimates is bound to be large) with the annual total expected to lie between $8 billion and $20 billion by the end of the present "development decade," after allowing for export earnings and debt service. This is based on the assumption of 5 percent growth per annum, which would only allow a little over 2½ percent increase in per capita income. Even if the lower figure is accepted, the task is formidable, particularly when it is recalled that the service of debt is an increasing burden (it has more than doubled in the last five years) and is now offsetting about one-half of the development funds made available to the poorer countries.

It may be questioned whether any estimate based on an arbitrary growth rate has much meaning, given the structural obstacles to growth in the developing countries. But figures lying toward the lower end of the "gap" estimates cited above are supported by the President of the World Bank himself. The Bank's periodic review of the capacities of the developing countries to make effective use of development finance is based on detailed studies and includes estimates of capacity "to save and export, to follow acceptable economic policies, and to plan and carry out high-priority development." On this basis the Bank President estimated that they could absorb $3–4 billion more per annum than they are now receiving.

There is no doubt that the lot of the poorer countries can be ameliorated by financial and by commercial means, or that these depend upon relations with the outside world. The former include aid and loans—private or official—as well as special arrangements to help with the burden of past indebtedness. In the financial sphere measures can be taken within the international monetary system that will help the developing countries cope with the short-term balance-of-payments difficulties that have a particularly disruptive effect on their development plans. Special trade policies and arrangements can be designed to help the developing countries maintain and increase their earnings of foreign exchange.

The question of aid can be regarded under a number of headings. There is, first, the amount, measured globally and as between different donor countries. There is the form it takes: as a loan on more or less commercial terms; as a "soft" loan, *i.e.*, one in which the interest and repayments terms are especially favourable; or as an outright gift. Aid can be in fully convertible currency with no strings attached, or it can be limited as to use, both in respect to the area in which, and the goods on which, it can be spent. It can be wholly "tied" to the exports of the donor country, or it can wholly or partially be in kind. It can be given bilaterally or it can be channeled through the World Bank or other international institutions, so that a developing country is relieved of direct ties with a particular donor country.

So far as the total flow of aid is concerned, enough has already been said to show that it is inadequate; against this it is being frequently pointed out that the global total still accounts for only a very small, and declining, fraction of the donor countries' national product—that is to say, their capacity to help is growing while the aid they actually supply remains virtually stationary; the contribution now probably amounts to only about 0.6 percent of their collective national income. Also, there has been a relative increase in the amount of loans as against grants in the total flow of funds, the proportion of the former having doubled in the last few years, thus increasing the future burden of debt service. The American national product alone in one year has been seven or more times the total amount of net Western aid; it is, therefore, hard to maintain that the industrial countries are not in a position to increase their aid at least to the level of the 1 percent of their annual income that has been suggested as a target.

It is true that the United States, far the biggest supplier of aid, and the United Kingdom, which is among the biggest, are currently suffering balance-of-payments difficulties; and it is true that as the international payments mechanism is now constituted they can claim that an increase in aid would aggravate that problem. But lend-lease, the Marshall Plan, and the whole postwar experience of the Western world's management of their internal economies have shown that the limits to the expansion of production (while they still exist and if exceeded can give rise to severe problems of inflationary gap) are not determined in the way that the economics of the Thirties postulated. Both the countries mentioned are constrained also—and perhaps primarily—by the burdens of very heavy defense expenditure and, in the absence of improvements in the international payments system, by the need to safeguard the reserve function of their currencies. Here the problem abuts on that of international liquidity which I shall discuss in the next chapter.

The Forms of Aid

As for the forms aid may take, there is little doubt that, in principle, the most beneficial form from the recipients' point of view is that it should be "untied" and made available in convertible currency. It is also clearly preferable, from this point of view, that aid should not have to be related to specific projects; that there should be no bar, in principle, to general assistance to the balance of payments, as well as to the use of aid to finance some measure of local expenditure where domestic budgetary possibilities are limited. However, in practice, there is good reason to qualify these broad desiderata, sometimes heavily. It is no reflection on a recipient country to say that sometimes complete freedom in the form in which aid is used can lead to its being applied to less than maximum advantage. Aid in kind, *e.g.,* food, where used to "prime the pump" but not to retard agricultural improvement; "tied" aid in goods that can help a particular capital project and that would not otherwise be forthcoming; some pressure to improve the domestic fiscal system so as to enable local expenditure to be met from local sources—all these can be helpful to the local government, on occasion more helpful than a completely free contribution.

Nor is it possible to be categorical on the question of whether bilateral or multilateral aid is to be preferred. Some bilateral aid is, in any case, inevitable, given the close links that still exist between some developing countries and some industrial countries. Political considerations, of course, often intrude; but where they result in aid being provided where otherwise it would not, they are, on balance, beneficial. Moreover, where the relationship between donor and recipient is an old established one, there is likely to be available special knowledge of the conditions in the developing country that can make aid more effective.

Nevertheless, as a general proposition, multilateral aid would seem to be more fruitful; and the tendency over the next few years, in the absence of major political changes, is likely to be in that direction. On the simple level of effectiveness of administration, the international agencies must in the long run be able to provide a better service. They can recruit specially suitable personnel, and provide unique training and wide experience. Their services are bound, therefore, in the end to cover a much wider range than any national administration is likely to be able to cover. Certainly, to judge by the excellence of the staff work of the World Bank, this point is already well established.

In general, the framework of an international organization is likely to be a better one for the coordination of aid programs to their most efficient ends. Coordination there clearly must be, since in most cases—India is a leading example—a large number of aid-giving countries are involved, and uncoordinated programs might lead to chaos. The Development Assistance Committee of the OECD was created precisely as a forum for the coordination of aid policies. Multilateral aid through the World Bank or the International Development Association (IDA) also makes coordination very much easier, if not automatic. It is much easier to evolve generally acceptable principles of policy, and criteria for evaluating programs and policies, and to apply these with a reasonable degree of uniformity when the management of aid is centralized. These are the practical factors that contribute to the trend toward extension of the proportion of multilateral aid.

Possibly most important of all is the fact that special economic links between a single developing and a single developed country may well be regarded by one party, or both, as politically disadvantageous. International institutions can more readily maintain a neutral political attitude; at least it is not as easy to accuse them of the opposite. It is often highly desirable, and at times vital, that the benefit of the practical experience of the advanced countries regarding management of the economy and the optimum use of aid funds be made available to a developing country; an international organization is almost always in a better position to have such views listened to and seriously taken into consideration.

The flow of international capital from private sources into the developing countries does not appear likely to play a very much increased part in the near future. In many developing countries political and economic conditions are not yet at a point where substantial foreign private capital funds are likely to be diverted from the more attractive domestic investment opportunities I have cited. Nevertheless, for the longer term this source of help to development must not be underrated. In the measure in which official aid programs achieve their objective of creating the infrastructure necessary for economic growth, private capital flows will grow. The process is cumulative.

An extremely important aspect of the financial problem, to which reference has already been made, is that of the growing burden of debt. This is beginning to be increasingly recognized, and some countries, with Britain in the lead, have taken steps to ease their loan terms. Unfortunately, others, the United States and Germany among them, have recently moved the other way. There can be no doubt that this will be one of the critical problems in relations between the rich and the poor in the next decade or so, and the World Bank and the IMF are fully aware of it. It is not at all an easy issue to tackle because of repercussions on domestic financial policy and practice as well as on the prospect of future private as well as official capital flows. Nevertheless, some radical rethinking will soon be necessary and it is hard to believe that major refunding operations will not take place in the next few years.

I have mentioned the International Monetary Fund in connection with the question of debt burden. The Fund is not formally concerned with development aid programs. Nevertheless, it is vitally involved in the changing economic situation and prospects of the developing countries which constitute the great bulk of its membership. These countries are faced with a heavy pressure of demand for imports to sustain their development programs. For reasons which have already been mentioned, their foreign exchange earnings fluctuate and are, in any case, unlikely to grow as fast as their foreign exchange needs. Balance-of-payments deficits, often very severe, could almost be called a normal phenomenon. This means that as a group the developing countries are constantly pressing on their foreign exchange reserves. For example, if the special case of the oil-producing countries is left out, the reserves of the developing countries, taken together, have fallen markedly in the last decade or so.

This meant that these countries have had to have recourse to the credit facilities available in the Fund to an extent that constituted the bulk of the total drawings from the Fund. To take account of this special situation, the Fund has evolved an arrangement which allows special additional assistance to be afforded to a developing country suffering from a shortfall in its export earnings when the Fund is satisfied that this shortage is of a temporary character. The general increase in quotas in the Fund in 1965 also helped the developing countries. But the adequacy of international arrangements for providing liquid resources remains critical, not only for the immediate needs of the developing countries but because, as lack of liquidity hampers the growth of the developed countries, it impairs their ability to provide aid and loans to the developing world.

The Impact of Trade

The commercial problems of the developing countries are linked to their inevitably precarious balance-of-payments position. This is another important area where the policy of developed countries can have great effect. A case can be made that trade measures necessary to help the poorer countries may in the short run be adverse to some vested interests in the industrial countries, but in the long run they will assist economic growth in those countries. Continual review of the protection granted to agricultural products of the temperate zone that compete with those of the tropical areas, such as fats and sugar, is one such example. Others are the removal of tariffs, quantitative restrictions, and internal taxes and revenue duties on tropical and other primary products imported from the developing countries. Over and above this it is necessary to move faster in the reduction of tariffs on imports from developing countries than on those from other industrialized countries, *i.e.,* by the granting of preferences to developing countries.

The whole process ought to be designed to encourage the developing countries themselves to move toward more liberal regimes in trade with each other. Of particular importance is a trade structure that encourages exports of semi-processed and processed products from the developing countries, the products, that is, of their early progress in manufacturing industry. Finally, agreements for the stabilization of primary commodity prices should be strengthened and extended to more commodities.

All these suggestions in the field of trade policy were made by Britain at the United Nations Conference on Trade and Employment in 1964, and they are a general summary of the more forward-looking ideas expressed there and elsewhere by some of the more developed nations. In practice much remains to be done on each. Every one of the Western developed nations has something to be less than proud of; and the developing nations themselves are not always without blame; in their relations among themselves they sometimes tend to reproduce the worst features of the protectionist history of earlier industrial development. Again, this is an area where the European Economic Community in its relations with its own associated territories has set up tendencies that will require careful adaptation to a wider framework if they are not to frustrate the general progress toward a sensible trade policy for development.

In the field of commodity agreements, too, responsibility for lack of progress cannot always be laid at the door of the importing (generally the industrialized) countries. Exporters, also, like to be protected when prices move against them, while remaining free to exploit the situation when it turns in their favour. This attitude adds to the inherent difficulties faced by many primary commodities, particularly tropical crops, in which the production cycle, the price (and sometimes income) elasticities of demand and supply are such as to create an unstable situation with attendant violent fluctuations of price. Much work has been done on the theory of commodity agreements, and there have been many practical experiments. A number of such agreements have come into being, using devices such as export quotas, minimum price provisions, buffer stocks, or a combination of them. But their existence is precarious, and one of the main tasks of the next few years is to strengthen and extend them not only in the interest of the less developed countries but for the sake of the stability and growth of world trade in general.

Other policies must be considered in the general area of relations between the developed and the developing world. Migration is clearly one of them, though its scope cannot be very great at this stage. The import of manpower would be helpful in relieving the shortage that is endemic in a number of industrialized countries, but it would also take high ability to deal effectively with the extremely difficult social and cultural problems it entails. In any case, migration is not likely again to be great enough to make much of an impact on the population problem, which must be tackled at the point at which it is most acute: the rapid increase in births. Much more promising is the kind of reverse operation deliberately designed to transfer labour-intensive industries from advanced to developing countries, a process that takes account of the special difficulties of both. This, of course, is closely bound up with the question of capital investment in developing countries. One development that could be helpful in this regard would be the establishment of a collective institutionalized method of safeguarding foreign investors and of standardizing the rules governing their treatment by the developing countries. The World Bank is, in fact, endeavouring to produce a broadly agreed convention to this effect.

Technical Assistance

A very large area of help to developing countries is covered by what is generally known as technical assistance. The details of this effort, often the most satisfactory to both donors and recipients in aid programs, are not of relevance here. An extension of these efforts to increase assistance with economic policy-making and execution might well become a new and useful feature. This is a very difficult area, as attempts within the Commonwealth or between the EEC and its overseas associates have shown. Governments in the developed countries are understandably hesitant to go very far in this direction because they are anxious to avoid being involved in politically embarrassing consequences that might arise from their intervention in the internal affairs of the developing countries. The line of demarcation easily becomes blurred between coordinated planning and commitment to policies designed to ensure the achievement of certain planned objectives that may involve considerable burdens. The wider the framework within which such attempts at coordination are made and the more clearly the discussion is kept separate from specific obligations in aid or trade policy, the more they are likely to have a beneficial educational effect.

This does, however, depend a good deal on the stage of development reached by the developing country, and leads to a consideration of the efforts it must make itself to accelerate its economic development. I have already referred to a number of major obstacles, particularly the creation of an adequate administrative and political infrastructure. Here the responsibility of the developing country is naturally paramount. Consultation with experts from other countries or from international organizations is appropriate and usually essential in drawing up a suitable development program. Too often, this has not been done adequately. Emphasis may be placed on prestige projects; or some theory demanding excessive emphasis on the fostering of one particular industry may dominate; or there may be lack of balance in the development of the educational system; or improvement in domestic food production may be neglected; or insufficient attention may be paid to ensuring that the benefits of aid and development programs are spread in a manner that arouses neither internal nor external political criticism—all of these defects have been conspicuous at one time or another and in one developing country or another.

Some of these faults can be remedied or avoided by wise and effective internal administration and by close cooperation with other countries and organizations that provide aid and technical assistance. But some certainly must be attributed to the inherent difficulties of guiding economic development, or, to put it in another way, of knowing what is the appropriate size and structure of a development program. The theory is not yet in a state when unequivocal answers can be given to specific questions of this kind, particularly as they reflect the disagreement between, broadly, the "free-market forces" approach (including reliance on the doctrines of comparative advantage) and the "balanced growth" approach.

For the time being, then, it seems clear that there is no panacea for the problems of the developing world. From a practical point of view, all the means I have discussed—and, no doubt, others—will have to be used to the fullest possible extent, whether they depend primarily on the contribution of the advanced countries or on the efforts of the developing countries themselves, or, as in most cases, on the closest possible cooperation between them.

On the theoretical front the present tendency seems to be for a fairly eclectic approach, which combines elements of market economics with the balanced-growth propositions, to take the place of the more dramatic theories of "take-off" points and "development stages." I would venture the opinion that this is not likely to change during the next few decades. All-embracing theories of the developmental path of the underdeveloped countries rely on a historicist view, and this has been generally eclipsed by the rush of recent events. This view, moreover, tends to ignore the great variety of conditions prevailing in different underdeveloped countries.

I would expect considerable progress to be made in the more detailed consideration of what constitutes appropriate development for different types of developing countries; that is, through an approach in which descriptive, empirical, and analytical elements can be combined. The great experience being gained by academic economists in the administration of aid programs and through service in drawing up and executing development plans should be particularly helpful—paralleling the increasing use of economists in the internal administrations in the more advanced countries.

A final word may be offered here on the future prospects of the developing countries: one of the most important contributions the developed countries can make is to manage their own economies in such a way that they can maintain their own high and steady rate of economic growth—and the intellectual and material resources upon which the world still depends.

Chapter 13   The International Monetary System

IN DISCUSSING the international monetary system, I do not have in mind the institutions and practices that exist in the private commercial and financial sphere that provide a network of international payments to serve those who have occasion to meet monetary claims across national boundaries. I am concerned here with the official intergovernmental arrangements that govern these private transactions, since they control or at least influence the type and volume of international transfers and the price (that is, the rate of exchange between national currencies) at which these take place. In describing the postwar institutions set up at Bretton Woods I have already given a brief account of the main principles on which these arrangements were to be based. I have also indicated that today these arrangements are increasingly called in question. Indeed, next to the problem of the developing countries, what economists label "international liquidity" has been the most fully and frequently debated issue in the last five years.

In order to understand the reasons for this dissatisfaction, and to comprehend the various remedies proposed for the defects that are thought to exist, it is necessary to look again at the system as it developed during the last twenty years on the foundation laid by the establishment of the International Monetary Fund, buttressed by GATT, the World Bank, and by development policies in general, and by numerous specific bilateral and multilateral commercial and financial arrangements. Briefly, the present system is based on general acceptance of the view that trade unrestricted so far as possible and currencies convertible at fixed rates provide the best basis for economic relations between nations. Departures from these principles had to be for carefully defined reasons and under some sort of multilateral supervision. They also had to be accompanied by carefully worked-out plans for returning to the original concept and to a new position of equilibrium. The Fund was to provide the main source of finance enabling countries to sustain balance-of-payments disequilibria without undue resort to measures that ran counter to the basic principles of international economic conduct. In the meantime the "adjustment process" (the new name for the classical "mechanism") would be at work.

In fact, the Fund arrangements, though central, were not the most active of those in operation during, say, the first decade of their existence. Up to about 1952 the scene was dominated by international loans, primarily made by the U.S.; by Marshall Plan aid; by the early operations of the World Bank; by the arrangements made by the European countries, through the European Payments Union, to provide a kind of miniature, regional monetary fund to make available temporary credits as well as to ensure currency transferability; and by various *ad hoc* arrangements between governments. At the same time, a measure of cooperation between central banks began to be restored. Indeed, while Marshall Plan aid was flowing into Western European countries, the Fund deliberately and explicitly restricted the availability of dollar drawings from its own resources to "exceptional" cases among the recipient countries.

During the next five years, roughly from the end of the first phase of recovery until about 1956, the process of gradually increasing cooperation among the world's monetary authorities continued, but the main emphasis shifted. With the achievement of the immediate objective of restoring the European industrial and commercial structure and some, albeit precarious, balance in international payments, increasing stress was being laid on progress toward the wider aims of the Bretton Woods world: widespread convertibility of currencies and the maintenance of fixed exchange rates together with accompanying domestic disciplines—containment of inflationary pressures, budgetary equilibrium, etc.—without which it was thought that the international system could not be preserved. This emphasis inevitably meant that there was still hesitation and delay in the use of the IMF's facilities to help countries in difficulty, though now for different reasons: namely, insistence on fairly stringent criteria to be observed by the countries seeking such assistance, these criteria being derived from the basic principles to which I referred earlier.

Nevertheless, the machinery of the Fund was being improved in a variety of ways and was in a state of readiness for an increased range and scope of operations when a more active phase began in the latter part of the Fifties. The Fund's activities generally increased *pari passu* with the achievement of convertibility of the major currencies and with the gradual disappearance of most barriers to trade, other than tariffs. Although some years were less active than others, the upward trend was unmistakable and led in 1960 to a decision to place greater resources at the Fund's disposal. There was a general increase of 50 percent in the Fund's quotas and several special increases for particular countries, reflecting their enhanced economic strength.

A Clash of Trends

At the same time, the Fund's position as an international forum for discussion of economic and financial problems grew markedly during these years, in sharp contrast to the earlier period. In the process, it developed certain characteristics which reflected the different trends of economic thought at work at the time of its foundation. It is not possible to go into these in detail here from a historical point of view, but it is worthwhile saying a word about them, because they have come to the fore again recently in a somewhat different and wider context.

In the mind of Keynes, the original concept of IMF was that of an international central bank: an automatic lender of last resort. It would be the central institution of an international clearing union "based on international bank-money" (which Keynes called "bancor"), which would be fixed, though not unalterably, in terms of gold, and would be accepted by all the members of the Union as the equivalent of gold. When Keynes, in the speech in the House of Lords, to which I have already referred, spoke of the reconciliation that had been effected between the desiderata of domestic policy and the new international system, he may perhaps have been thinking more of his own original proposal than of the arrangements which actually emerged at Bretton Woods. For the American conception was rather different; and given the great gap in economic strength that separated the United States from the other countries, and its reflection at the time in the ubiquitous and severe dollar shortage, that conception carried weight.

In the American view the fund should make credit available to members for strictly temporary accommodation and on the basis of explicit conditions both of repayment and of conduct of policy. This was, if not as farsighted as the Keynesian concept, at any rate more in line with existing economic and political realities. Up to about 1960 the Fund developed those inherent potentialities that reflected the latter conception and for this purpose it certainly became an increasingly effective instrument. Given that progress was also being made in internal financial stability, currency convertibility, and multilateral trade, the return to "normalcy" seemed reasonably well assured. A more restricted view of the Fund's function seemed, therefore, appropriate to the general climate of accepted opinion of the time.

But this trend was based on a deceptively optimistic view of the actual development in the international financial world. I would specially single out two aspects of these developments as being responsible for the change that came over the general direction of thought from about 1960. The first of these is the awareness of the position of the balance of payments of the United States. It almost appears that recognition of the U.S. position spread quite suddenly. The world had become so used to the "dollar shortage," and there had been so much preoccupation both of analysis and of policy on both sides of the Atlantic with measures to alleviate and remove it, that it took some time and an acceleration of an existing trend for everyone to become aware that the United States was running a substantial and increasing deficit on the balance of payments. The other factor was that while the economic and financial arrangements seemed to be approximating more to the ideal pattern, the trend was in fact often interrupted by recurrent crises in a number of countries, including Britain, whose currency had for so long fulfilled the major trading and reserve function, a role which it was now sharing with the dollar. The nature of these periodic convulsions can, I think, be best summed up by saying that they consisted in a sharp clash between policies designed to further domestic desiderata and those designed to help the evolution of the international monetary and trading system toward the goal set up at Bretton Woods.

To cope with this clash, to bring about again the reconciliation between domestic and international objectives which Keynes thought had been effectively completed at Bretton Woods, various new devices were introduced. These, however, neither changed the main character of the system nor guaranteed it from recurrence of similar critical situations. I propose to say a few more words about the U.S. balance of payments; about the periodic payments crises of other countries, particularly Britain; and about the changes made in recent years that have resulted in the present shape of the "gold exchange standard." We can then go on to consider the current debate over international monetary reform and to speculate about its probable outcome.

U.S. Payments Balance

The U.S. balance of payments, however defined, has been in overall deficit for many years. Since the launching of the Marshall Plan, there have been only two years when the net balance on account of goods and services has not been in surplus, and usually in substantial surplus; but no year when this surplus has not been more than exhausted by a net deficit due to long-term private capital outflow, government loans, and aid. When allowance is made for short-term capital and similar movements there was a very small surplus in one year only. The causes of this position and the consequences for the strength of the dollar are matters that have been the subject of much study and analysis under official and private auspices. They cannot be pursued in any detail here. The important fact is that the U.S. deficit has persisted for a very long time and that, insofar as any one item or set of items in the balance sheet can be said to be responsible, this has resulted from the sum total of capital transactions, that is to say, U.S. government aid and loans and private overseas investment. A caveat must, of course, at once be entered to the effect that these items cannot in the ultimate analysis be separated from the merchandise and services balance. For practical issues of policy, however, the distinction is useful.

Despite this situation, the position of the United States as the world's principal banker, and of the dollar as the world's principal reserve and trading currency, continued during the whole of this period and was consolidated. The reasons are not far to seek. The part played by the United States in world trade was very large and growing. The market in dollars had continued for a long time to be entirely free from restrictions, a position not enjoyed by any other important currency during the postwar period. The United States held for a long time the vast bulk of the world's gold, still the ultimate basis for currency and credit. The United States had developed to a considerable degree what it had lacked even in the immediate prewar days, namely, a large and highly diversified credit and banking mechanism. Finally, the United States throughout the postwar period was the only substantial source not only for governmental capital flows (Marshall Plan and other forms of aid) but also for private capital for overseas investment.

For a long time, indeed a surprisingly long time, the beneficial effects of the United States deficit for the rest of the world were readily accepted and no question was raised about the strength of the dollar. It was only toward the end of the Fifties that the U.S. balance-of-payments deficit and the position of the dollar emerged as matters of concern to the U.S. government and became a matter of international discussion. The change occurred for a number of reasons. In the first place, with the exception of one year in which it was substantial as a result of the Korean war, the deficits for about ten years had been running at a relatively modest annual figure. From 1958, however, they showed a sharp increase. Furthermore, although the replenishment of reserves held by other countries in the form of gold or dollars (the counterpart of U.S. deficits) had been regarded in earlier years as a necessary part of postwar reconstruction, that process now was considered to have been substantially completed; by 1959 U.S. gold holdings had fallen from $24.4 billion (at the end of 1948) to $19.5 billion, whereas short-term claims on dollars (and, ultimately, gold) held by foreign countries had risen from $6.1 billion to $17.7 billion.

Against this background, a sudden jump of annual deficits to levels of around $3 billion was a natural cause for concern. Again, while for political and economic reasons the importance of the maintenance of the U.S. aid program was widely recognized, its significance for the maintenance of U.S. exports was not so generally appreciated; and the continued flow of aid tended, therefore, to be regarded as a source of continuing weakness in the balance of payments and the dollar. Finally, the financing of the deficit in this latter phase tended to be done increasingly through the use of gold, thus both reflecting and contributing to the growing concern.

From the early Sixties, the U.S. administration began to regard the remedying of the balance-of-payments deficit as a major objective of policy. At the same time, the difficulty of achieving this by traditional means was soon recognized, particularly since the Administration was also embarking on a domestic expansion program designed to produce a substantial rise in the gross national product by making fuller use of unemployed resources. The then Secretary of the Treasury, C. Douglas Dillon, pointed out that the U.S. could not "either prudently or effectively utilize many of the simpler and more direct types of action by which other countries have sometimes dealt with their payments deficits." These measures, he noted, included devaluation, import restrictions, and "substantial restriction of credit designed to raise interest rates and reduce domestic consumption." The reasons for the inhibitions were: security considerations that required the maintenance of military aid programs; the need for reducing unemployment and promoting rapid growth at home, which precluded deflationary policies; the obligation imposed by America's wealth to continue to help developing countries; and the desire to maintain a high level of international trade, which militated against restrictive trade policies that could call forth retaliation. It is interesting to note the similarities in this catalog of desiderata, so far as the relation between international payments and domestic policy are concerned, and that laid down in Keynes's House of Lords speech.

The precise methods adopted by the U.S. to deal with the situation and the subsequent course of developments do not directly concern us here. However, the series of U.S. deficits and the subsequent attempts to remedy them are related to the functioning of the world's monetary system and to the current debate on this subject. But before I deal with this factor it is necessary to say something more about the balance-of-payments situation of other countries, particularly of Britain, the manager of the world's other reserve currency. In this way, we shall be able to see more clearly the state of the monetary system and to appraise the criticisms and plans for reform to which it has given rise.

European Counterbalance

In many ways, the monetary experience of the European countries during the postwar period is a mirror image of that of the United States. I have already referred to the replenishment of reserves, both in gold and hard currency, that took place in the Fifties. Throughout that period, through direct aid to Europe, through its vast program of aid to the developing countries, and through its overseas investment which played a most important part in supplying European industry with capital and know-how, the United States was helping to strengthen the European countries' international payments position.

The extent to which the European countries benefited varied from country to country and from time to time. To analyze the causes that produced these differences would require one to trace in detail the economic and financial history of the countries concerned, including their domestic economic policies, the ups and downs in their competitive position, their trading policies, their participation in aid programs and overseas investment, the course of their defense programs, particularly insofar as it involved a burden of overseas expenditure: in short, the whole complex of their economic relations with each other, with the United States, and with the rest of the world. This would go far beyond the scope of this chapter. A few important relationships may, however, be mentioned not only because they were important historically but because they constitute the dynamic factors that may operate to determine future patterns.

Among the important considerations in regard to any one country to be borne in mind, I would like to cite particularly: defense and aid; the progress of productivity of domestic industry; the pattern of domestic resource allocation; and the level of development of the domestic capital market and the basic policy decisions on the monetary front taken in the immediate postwar period, in particular the level of exchange parity at which the country's currency was stabilized. To these factors must be added, particularly in the most recent past, the country's basic attitude to the existing international monetary mechanism and, therefore, its policies in regard to reserves management. Much if not all the variations in individual countries' experience can be explained in terms of these factors.

Two countries, for example, whose experience has been almost exactly the opposite of that of the United States, France and (at least until very recently) Germany, have carried relatively smaller defense programs than those of the United States and Britain; neither, moreover, was involved in substantial foreign expenditure. Germany has only in recent years become a major contributor to aid programs; France, though high up in the "league table" of donors, makes her aid available primarily within the Franc Area, and through an elaborate network of trade and price agreements that makes it very difficult to assess the true foreign-exchange burden of the program. Both these factors were, therefore, favourable in terms of securing and maintaining a strong balance-of-payments position and of building up reserves. It is sometimes argued that the exchange-rate policy of the two countries also worked in the same direction. In the case of France a series of devaluations, particularly that of 1958—in the case of Germany a relatively low postwar parity, not sufficiently revalued later—conferred on both a competitive advantage in foreign markets which helped to create a general export orientation of industry.

Even if these considerations constitute some explanation for the fact that both France and Germany have in recent years shown a strong tendency toward balance-of-payments surpluses, they are not, by themselves, sufficient to explain more than the existence of a generally favourable climate. Other factors must be invoked to show how they were able to take advantage of this situation. So far as Germany is concerned, a rapid rate of increase in productivity combined with a relatively less rapid increase in home demand (especially in the earlier part of the period under review) is primarily responsible. It appears that the experience of hyper-inflation before the war, of destruction during the war, and of an occupation regime for some years after had the effect of shattering long-established patterns of resource allocation and retarding the growth of claims of private consumption (including leisure) compared with investment and exports. The availability of an important source of additional manpower from Eastern Germany also helped sustain continued economic expansion without the emergence of an inflationary gap.

This factor was also operative in France, partly from the attraction of immigrants from neighbouring countries and partly from the domestic manpower reservoir in agriculture, which, during this period, was beginning to experience the first wave of technological revolution. The prospect, and from 1958 onward the reality, of the Common Market also stimulated the productivity of French industry, its greater readiness to face competition and its increased interest in export markets. Nor were Germany and France big capital exporters; a good deal of the capital exported from the United States found its way into financing the development of their industries. How far, in both countries, a rigorous application of domestic policies directed toward the containment of inflationary pressures and the maintenance of a balance (or surplus) in international payments may take credit for the results is a controversial issue. What is certain is that France in particular has in recent years professed to regard these matters as important and has urged her trading partners to accept this view. This has been accompanied by an attitude in regard to the whole character of the international payments system, and especially to the role of gold in it, that constitutes a major strand in the present controversy on the subject.

The problems Britain has had to face in the same period have had similarity both with those of France and Germany and with those of the United States. Like the other two European countries, Britain had to rebuild her industry on a new technological basis, after redeploying it from wartime uses. She had to face up to newly established and still-changing trade patterns, which meant that she could not rely on traditional markets or goods for the foreign exchange earnings needed to provide food for her people and raw materials for her industry. In addition she was burdened with obligations for defense and overseas development which, though reduced compared with her traditional role, were nevertheless heavier than those of any other European power. In this latter respect she resembled the United States rather than France and Germany. And above all, she shared with the United States, albeit in less degree, the task of managing a trading and reserve currency, a problem neither of her European industrial competitors had to cope with.

The British problem was further complicated by developments during the war and in the early postwar phase to which some reference has already been made. Her war effort had been financed by a massive liquidation of foreign investments built up over many decades, and by the creation of a heavy burden of debt. This consisted not only of the large North American loans which were, of course, funded over a long period but also of very substantial sums held on short, or relatively short, term as sterling balances by Commonwealth and other countries. It is possible to argue—and often is argued—that the settlement of Britain's wartime indebtedness, which has taken the form of these sterling balances, was done on unduly generous terms to the lenders, taking due account not only of the size of Britain's war effort but also of her postwar commitments in foreign and defense policy and, above all, of her role as a banker, all of which, past and present, redounded and would redound to the benefit of the creditors. A tougher attitude on the part of Britain's negotiators, and a more farsighted one on the part of her creditors, would, it is contended, have been in the interests of both. This sort of argument cannot, of course, be settled decisively. The fact remains that while the unfavourable consequences of the heavy sterling balances are sometimes exaggerated, their existence has undoubtedly constituted a restraint on British economic and financial policy.

Another factor which, at the least, retarded Britain's recovery in the financial sphere was the premature attempt at convertibility in 1947, to which I have already referred in connection with the American loan. The rapid abandonment of this attempt and, two years later, the devaluation of sterling, although they were both inevitable and in the short run helpful to the economy, also revealed certain weaknesses and therefore may have helped to make the subsequent recovery of sterling as a reserve currency less easy, and Britain's role as a world banker less secure.

From 1950 onward Britain was next only to the United States in the relative burden on total resources devoted to the defense program. Apart from the overall effect, a sizable proportion of this spending was foreign exchange expenditure and was, thus, a direct burden on the balance of payments. Furthermore, much of it imposed a direct load on metal-using industries and on advanced research, development, and technology. It, therefore, competed sharply for scarce resources against the claims of industrial regeneration and of exports, both of which had an outstanding role to play in the total economic reconstruction effort.

More controversial is the role to be assigned to Britain's relation with the European integration movement. As an outsider she lacked the immediate inducement that membership of the Common Market gave to French and German industry to modernize and compete. For a time, and to some extent, the creation of EFTA served to open up a wider market. For a time, too, the 1961–63 negotiations in Brussels held out the hope of early British membership in EEC and encouraged a number of British companies to plan for a wider European market. In any event, some British companies whose operations are large and widespread enough and who have ready access to capital have gone in for European-wide planning of production and marketing. However, in terms of relative rate of productivity advance or export orientation it is difficult to escape the conclusion that her continental competitors have, during this period, had a more powerful incentive than Britain.

The impact of domestic policy is even more difficult to assess. The early postwar period witnessed a major change in attitudes not only to the relation of government policy to the level of employment (which was virtually ubiquitous) but also to certain social priorities that tended to raise the whole level of expected public and private consumption. This shows up sharply in contrast with other claims on the national product and, more important, in comparisons with some continental countries, particularly Germany, where the historical background and the political climate were different. It has been argued that given the magnitude of the tasks Britain had to face, coupled with a relatively slower population growth unrelieved by a large agricultural or other manpower reservoir, the conflict between domestic policy desiderata and those of international balance was bound to be more sharply felt than elsewhere. The dangers of inflationary pressures accompanying economic expansion and showing up in balance-of-payments deficits, or the dangers of the pursuit of payments balance and, a fortiori, of surpluses involving deflationary pressure, would be particularly acute in Britain.

This reasoning is to some extent borne out by Britain's economic history since the immediate postwar recovery phase. The period has been marked by fairly regular and quite substantial alternations of high and low activity, of balance-of-payments disequilibria, and by an endemic tendency to deficit. It would be extremely misleading, however, to look upon these features of Britain's postwar experience in isolation and to ignore the very remarkable achievements that also occurred. For example, there has been a striking revolution in the relative importance of major industries, with many of the traditional leaders being replaced by some of the newest enterprises relying on advanced technology. The extent to which exports cover the financing of imports is vastly greater than before the war. Yet, at the same time, and particularly in the most recent years, Britain, like the United States, has sustained a steady and large outflow of foreign investments that now constitute a volume of assets greater than her total liabilities.

Despite these achievements, however, if we take on one side all the objectives of policy, domestic and international, and, on the other, the rate of advance of productivity and the strength and resilience of the financial framework, the problem of reconciliation in Britain could be described in much the terms I have quoted from C. Douglas Dillon as applying to the United States— only with greater emphasis!

Needs for Liquidity

I have not dwelt on the British case for its own sake (nor even only because sterling is a world currency), but because it has important bearing on the general debate over a proper monetary system. Even a very brief account of the main issues in the postwar financial history of a few of the leading countries makes it clear that the international financial arrangements entered into immediately after the war, flexible and varied though these were, could not have coped with the problems of German and French surpluses or British and American deficits without considerable additions and amendments. I have already mentioned the greater activity of the Fund that began toward the end of the Fifties. This was accompanied by two major quota increases, and these provided an important new source of credit facilities. A further strengthening of the Fund's ability to provide short-term credit facilities took place with the establishment in 1962 of what were formally designated General Arrangements to Borrow, through which ten countries undertook to provide the Fund, under certain conditions, up to $6 billion in their currencies. This reinforcement not only made it possible to provide funds when needed but, perhaps more importantly, provided visible, massive defenses available to currencies to discourage foreign exchange speculation.

In addition to this basic strengthening of the system and on this foundation, other devices were introduced. Cooperation between central banks has grown very considerably in scope and intensity. The periodic meetings of governors at the Bank for International Settlements in Basel have provided a useful opportunity for collective discussion of mutual problems and for making arrangements for practical mutual assistance in informal circumstances attended by very little publicity. Bilateral and multilateral "swap" arrangements of currencies have frequently been resorted to, not surprisingly those between the Bank of England and the Federal Reserve Bank of New York (the managers of the two reserve currencies) being the most considerable and active.

The general development of the system during the period is perhaps best illustrated by the composition of total monetary reserves and their distribution among countries. These reserves of governments and central banks consisting of gold, dollars, sterling, other currencies, and IMF gold tranches have increased since the late 1950s by about 25 percent (or by about 50 percent in the two decades since the end of World War II). While this is substantial, it was much less than the increase in trade, as measured by the total exports of the non-Communist countries. This grew by over 50 percent in the comparable shorter period and by 200 percent in the longer period. Another significant fact is that the increase in gold supplies, mainly from freshly mined gold and gold sales of the Soviet Union, has been relatively modest, so that the proportion of gold in the total has declined. The bulk of the increase (about twice as much as that of gold) has come from increased holdings of dollars and, to a minor degree, sterling. This development is also reflected in the relative position of the two reserve centres. The net reserve losses of the U.S. and Britain (measured in the loss of gold and in the rise in their net overseas liabilities to monetary authorities) have, in fact, accounted for well over three-quarters of the gains in the reserves of other countries.

In combination these formal and *ad hoc* monetary devices, plus the steady outflow of American funds, short- and long-term, have met the needs of world trade. The increase in liquid resources of central monetary authorities to meet balance-of-payments fluctuations has been adequate to a substantial, though not to a proportionate, degree. Many official spokesmen regard this record as a testimonial to the strength, resilience, and adaptability of the existing monetary system. But it is dangerously optimistic to regard it also as a guarantee of adequate performance in the future. Recent developments have already provided considerable strains and have led to much argument about the continued viability of the system without major reforms.

There is serious criticism of the fact that the needs for increased liquidity now must be met through the continuing balance-of-payments deficit of the country that manages the world's premier reserve currency—the United States. Objections have come from both sides of the controversy on world liquidity: those who are concerned about the dangers of a shortfall of monetary reserves and those who consider that an excess of liquidity is the greater threat. Coalescence of these two extreme views into common acceptance of the proposition that a continuation of American deficits on the scale of recent years cannot be tolerated has led to two important developments. On the one hand, it has stimulated the search for new methods of adding to international liquidity; on the other, it has intensified the study of the relation between balance-of-payments fluctuations and domestic policy—the adjustment process—and has led to a great deal of formalized international discussion of the changing situation in individual countries, with special emphasis on that of Britain and the United States.

Area of Debate

Formally, the main forum for the first set of discussions is the International Monetary Fund; for the other, the OECD, in particular its Economic Policy Committee. In practice, they are joined together in two separate groupings, with largely similar membership: the Group of Ten (consisting of the "deputies" of the Ministers of Finance and Central Bank Governors of ten of the most industrialized countries) and the Working Party Three of the OECD's Economic Policy Committee.

I mention this institutional arrangement as an interesting sidelight on the machinery for resolving important and far-reaching differences of views between countries without which no account of how the gold-exchange standard works at present would be complete. Working Party Three is primarily concerned with what has come to be known as "multilateral surveillance," a process evolved in the postwar period first in the Marshall Plan, and later extended to many other fields of international cooperation. This provides that a country's actions (and the data and forecasts on which these are based) are periodically examined by its "peers." In the activities of Working Party Three, this procedure is applied to the "adjustment process" and pursued with a rather higher degree of severity than has been known in OECD circles since the examination of import programs that underlay the division of Marshall Plan aid.

Not surprisingly, the divisions of view that appear from time to time in this forum reflect different attitudes on the proper relationship between domestic monetary and fiscal management, the balance of payments and economic growth, and so forth. These are issues that grow out of the conflict between stability and growth. They are further complicated by the fact that when they involve the two reserve currency countries they also reflect differing views (based not only on differing economic analysis but tinged by general political considerations) on the proper organization of the world's monetary system.

It is at this point that the activities of Working Party Three abut on those of the Group of Ten, with whom, as I have said, it substantially shares membership. A recent report of the Working Party Three on "The Balance of Payments Adjustment Process" notes that the study is "complementary to the studies in the Group of Ten concerning international liquidity." Since these groups came into prominence in the early Sixties their work has dominated official discussion of this subject (which has also been very active in academic and quasi-academic circles). Their influence on current affairs has, however, been different. The Group of Ten, concerned as it is with the future, has only indirectly affected contemporary events, possibly only to the extent to which rumours of its discussions, well- or ill-founded, may have affected speculative trends. Working Party Three, on the other hand, must be accounted a part of the existing international monetary mechanism, as much a part of the reality as central bank cooperation, "swap" arrangements, etc., without which the gold-exchange standard might not be working as it is. The "flexibility" and resilience of the present arrangements have had as their counterpart the development of the system of "multilateral surveillance" of which Working Party Three constitutes the most important formalized institutional expression.

It can be assumed that the pressure for examining possible improvements in international liquidity would exist in any event, varying in degree according to the extent of dissatisfaction with the present mechanism. The current deliberations add to this an acute sense of the degree to which domestic policy and payments equilibrium may conflict, and of the extent to which the availability of remedies for short-term balance-of-payments troubles may be linked, with a sharpening of international restraints on domestic freedom of action. Rightly or wrongly, an improvement of the international monetary system may then be thought of by some as a means of alleviating this problem—while, by the same token, others may be confirmed in their belief that the existing system would work satisfactorily if domestic policies were appropriately managed.

Let us, then, consider the basic positions at opposite ends of the spectrum of opinion concerning the general adequacy of the present system. When the subject is shorn of its technical complications, a single point of importance emerges as the one around which differences cluster: the extent to which countries may be willing to hold foreign exchange balances, particularly dollars, alongside gold in their ultimate central currency reserves. A closely related point is the extent to which credit facilities, additional to reserves, are available to tide countries over balance-of-payments deficits and thus mitigate the sharpness of the "adjustment process." The relationship between these aspects of what is essentially one problem arises from the fact that they both turn on the elusive factor of "confidence," that is to say, on the willingness of governments and central banks to "extend credit"—whether this be to the currency, or to the policies behind the currency, of another country.

There is general agreement that the annual accretion to the world's monetary gold holdings would, by itself, be inadequate to sustain the growth of world trade. There is also agreement that an adequate growth of liquidity in recent years has depended on increasing resort to various means of creating credit (recited earlier) and that the continuing United States deficit (which has meant both a redistribution of U.S. gold reserves and a growth of dollar balances held by a number of countries) has been the major factor in this process. There is further agreement that the United States deficit cannot continue at a high level indefinitely. At this point the agreement ceases to be of the same degree of generality, and there are those who believe that a bolder policy on the part of the United States, including even a refusal to buy gold at a fixed price, would soon change the attitude of other countries. This is in some ways an attractive view, but it seems unlikely at present to be destined to have a major influence on the debate.

Some believe the United States will itself be unable, or at least unwilling, to suffer the continuing loss in gold reserves to which such a persistent deficit must give rise. Others will take this view because they dislike the domestic effects of a continuing influx of U.S. funds, though the remedy—reversal of their own balance-of-payments surplus position—is in their own hands. Still others are particularly concerned with the outflow of United States long-term capital that they fear will lead to economic penetration and the eventual domination of their own industries by American enterprises.

But whatever the reasons, if the U.S. deficit is eliminated or at least substantially reduced, one important source of world liquidity is also put out of action. Thus, whether as a result of America's own concern over her balance of payments, or because of increasing unwillingness of others to "hold" more dollars, the problem becomes one of finding a new source of increased reserves to replace those hitherto provided by the outflow of U.S. funds. In the short term, much of the discussion will, if only for tactical reasons, continue to be concerned with U.S. economic policy and its effect on the U.S. balance of payments and the resulting position of the dollar. In the longer run, however—that is to say over the period ahead with which I have been concerned in this study— it is safe to predict that a more general approach to the problem of the proper organization of the world's monetary system will prevail.

Directions of Reform

What are likely to be the limits within which this discussion will take place? I put the question in this way, because there presently exists a number of plans for reform, often differing from each other only in their highly complex technical details. It is inappropriate to consider these here, where the purpose must be to distinguish the possible pattern of international monetary reform according to broad criteria. One such criterion is the role assigned in any new system to gold. Another is whether it includes the creation of a new form of reserve asset, additional to (or even in replacement of) gold, and whether such an asset is to replace or merely to supplement foreign exchange holdings. The basis of distribution of any new reserve asset, its institutional management, and its relation to the needs of developing countries present unresolved issues, as do the related questions of the place of the short-term balance-of-payments adjustment process and the longer-term relationship of currency values to each other. Running through these main problems in all the reform plans is the fundamental question of the degree to which the international monetary system is to constitute a determining factor for domestic economic policy—that is, the extent to which national sovereignty can, should, or must inevitably be subordinated to the constraints arising out of membership of an international economic community.

I believe that the last-named criterion is the most fruitful to employ, not only in the light of various other reflections on the international economic order that have gone before but also because it brings out most sharply the specific differences of various reform plans. At one extreme, then, is the view that domestic economic policy should be completely unhampered by the existence of surpluses or deficits in the balance of payments; or, putting it in another way, that the "adjustment process" should be turned on its head and applied to the balance-of-payments situation rather than to the character of the domestic economic policy being pursued. This would be achieved by a regime of completely flexible exchange rates.

There are few serious economists who would advocate the complete absence of any intervention in exchange markets and absolute disregard of reserve holdings on the part of the monetary authorities, that is, the wholly free market in foreign exchange that unimpeded fluctuations in rates would require. Nor would such a system in the long run provide that genuine autonomy of the domestic economic system by freeing it of fluctuations originating outside, which on the face of it seems to be its primary characteristic. Complete flexibility of exchange rates does not mean that an economy is independent of others: so long as it maintains trade and some freedom of factor (capital and labour) movements with the outside world, there will be "terms of trade," *i.e.,* terms on which its products and services exchange for those of other countries; and the degree of influence of these terms of trade on its domestic economic structure will depend on the relative weight of foreign trade in its gross national product. What exchange-rate flexibility does mean is that the reaction of domestic economic factors to outside movements is slowed down, since it is no longer the result of deliberate acts of economic policy immediately triggered off by declining reserves, pressure on exchange rates, and so on.

Flexible exchange rates are, therefore, hardly to be thought of as, in themselves, a new and substitute system of international economic relations, but rather as a possible ingredient in such a system. The apparent advantages—in terms of freedom to pursue policies of growth and full employment without the threat of a sudden reversal caused by balance-of-payments considerations—do not need any elaboration. The disadvantages cited by the critics lie partly in the very absence of restraint, which, it is claimed, may give rise to excessive domestic inflation that eventually would have to be the more sharply restrained precisely because the monetary early warning signals have been dismantled. There is little, if anything, in past experience to provide decisive evidence one way or another on the likelihood of political action in this regard.

Possibly more significant are the effects of such a system on international trade; here both advocates and critics of flexible exchange rates have something to say. The former fear that the clash of domestic policy and balance-of-payments restraints in a system of fixed exchange rates may become so severe as to create an irresistible temptation for the introduction of direct controls on trade and payments. Critics of flexible rates (who, as one might expect, would simply say that governments must show the necessary strength to defeat these illiberal impulses) point to the destructive effects on trade and capital movements that continually fluctuating exchange rates must have. Here, again, it is difficult to be confident about the nature of the political decisions that are likely to be taken in one or another set of circumstances. Examples, however, of the trade-destroying effects of violent exchange fluctuations are not difficult to find.

Even this necessarily brief account of the two opposing schools will show that the argument, though it may affect the way in which the international monetary system is to be organized in the future, goes far beyond the narrower question of the nature and distribution of reserves on which that system is to be based. Is it likely that in the next twenty-five years or so this wider question will be explicitly tackled in the context of international economic action? In a sense, as I shall show presently, this will depend on the solution that is found for the narrower question of the monetary mechanism, and to that I now turn.

The Monetary Mechanism

The first issue is that of the future place of gold in the system. Among the most distinguished economists working in this field are a number who, deriving much of their inspiration from Keynes, regard continued reliance on gold as a barbarous relic. They point to the tenuous link between gold production and reserve stocks and the need for, and even the actual availability of, reserves and credit in present-day international finance. Those who admit that some mechanism is necessary that regulates the total volume of domestic credit by linking it to an international system through intercurrency values and international reserve fluctuations still contend that such a mechanism ought to be deliberately created to reflect current knowledge of international trade and finance and to be less capricious in its working than the anachronistic reliance on gold. Schemes to meet these criteria call for creating a new ultimate standard to which exchange rates may be fixed (even though their value may be revised from time to time) and in which international reserves (whether balances of actual currencies or newly created "units") may be expressed. Most of these schemes, which have a respectable intellectual ancestry, make use of index numbers—usually of a large number of internationally traded commodities— with various embellishments to reflect long-term changes in basic international economic data.

At the other end are those who believe that any ultimate international standard for valuing currencies and determining reserve fluctuations must be subject to a considerable element of arbitrary choice: thus they argue that it is not self-evident that a link to, say, a commodity index number would be more satisfactory than one to a single commodity, gold. Even if the special attributes that originally gave it its peculiar place in human affairs have ceased to be important, gold, it is claimed, still has tradition and custom on its side. Indeed, some of those who take this view wish to return to a more exclusive reliance on gold than has been customary for many decades now: in the extreme, the complete abolition of the gold-exchange standard and the general acceptance of gold as the sole currency reserve of central banks. So drastic a change from the present position in which dollar (and sterling) balances play a vital part in central reserves could not be brought about unless some means could be found not only to eliminate these balances but to replace them in the reserve holdings. Thus the "gold school" is led to join at this point an argument frequently advanced by those who take quite the opposite view of the relation between reserves and domestic policy. This is that the price of gold in terms of the dollar (and, therefore, of all other currencies) should be raised, generally, it is argued, to at least twice its present level. The purpose of such a move, as far as the "non-gold" school is concerned, would be to increase (double) the value of existing gold reserves as well as that of future annual accretions to the world's supply of gold. (It would also delay and possibly reverse a declining trend in gold production and, perhaps, discourage dishoarding.) Thus, a large additional margin for domestic expansion unhampered by the threat of reserve losses would be created at one stroke, or future moves in that direction at least would be less hampered, or both these results would be secured.

The "gold school" does not, of course, share this objective. On the contrary, as has already been made clear, its advocacy of a more complete acceptance of gold stems from a desire to see the freedom of domestic action more, rather than less, circumscribed. It accepts, nevertheless, the idea of a sharp increase in the price of gold as a means of providing the wherewithal for eliminating the dollar and sterling balances that form part of the reserves of a number of countries, as they form part of the short-term external liabilities of the U.S. and Britain. It is not quite clear whether in the view of the "gold school" this raising of the price of gold must be a once-for-all operation, or whether it could be repeated if the increased value of the annual accretion of monetary gold proved to be inadequate as measured by a tendency for balances of some currencies to start accumulating again, thereby acquiring the character of reserves.

Before I proceed any further, we might consider whether either of the two extreme schools has any real prospect of prevailing. This is probably the most difficult of all the pertinent questions in this field. This is now a very hotly debated subject, and pressure for action in one direction or the other appears to be increasing. Changes in the area of currency and international monetary arrangements, however, are usually slow and take place as a result of minute alterations whose total import can only be assessed after a long period of time. Nevertheless, some predictions seem possible.

It is, I think, completely out of the question that the world will return to the kind of gold standard the "gold school" has in mind. The history of monetary arrangements in the last few centuries has shown a steady tendency to superimpose increasingly elaborate mechanisms making for a very complex "gearing" between gold and the availability of credit, domestic and international. The emergence of sterling or of the dollar as "reserve" currency is not the result of the adoption, in solemn constitutional assembly, of some authoritative economic report by the trading nations of the world; on the contrary, these developments came about through an involved mixture of historical occurrences. Indeed, the very change in the relative positions of sterling and the dollar in recent decades is an example of the impossibility of "willing" a particular result rather than having to wait for it to occur over a space of years.

In important respects the argument of the gold school runs counter to the facts of the geographical occurrence of gold, the distribution of existing reserves, the position of the developing countries, the hoarding propensities in some parts of the world, as well as current political relationships. But even if these formidable barriers could be overcome, and the changeover "lubricated" by a sharp increase in the gold price and the elimination thereby of existing balances, some new budding reserve currency would soon emerge. A deliberate policy of periodically repeating the process would hardly seem feasible, if only because it is doubtful whether the prospect of repeated increases in the price of gold would be compatible with the high degree of fixity of exchange rates this school also advocates.

On the other hand, while I expect the world to be moving, though not necessarily steadily, in the opposite direction toward continuing restriction of the role of gold, I am not confident that a new "index-number" or "commodity" standard will emerge in the next twenty-five years or so. The theoretical difficulties of achieving such a standard are still very considerable. The choice of the commodities to be included is no simple matter given rapid changes brought on by technological advances in the relative significance of different materials, and the changing pattern of trade that must be expected to result, *inter alia,* from the advance of industrialization of the less developed regions of the world. There also are major practical political difficulties associated with the manner in which the index-number is to be constructed or managed over time, and it is difficult to believe that these will be any less acute than those aroused by differing national interests as reflected in countries' attitudes to gold. Subject to what is said below, I would, therefore, expect progress toward a more contrived and intellectually based standard to be slow.

The Mixture as Before

It is, I believe, more reasonable to suppose that changes will be of the same general order as those which have already transformed the international monetary mechanism in the last thirty years. The practical possibilities for the immediate future seem to lie in combined development on a number of fronts, on each of which a certain amount of international action or at least discussion is already taking place. These include further development of the facilities of the International Monetary Fund, through further quota increases (though these are not so likely in the immediate future) and through the creation of reserve assets by one of a number of devices such as investments, active credit, and open-market policies, or even a return to the original Keynesian concept of "bancor."

Perhaps even more likely in the short term is the creation of a composite reserve unit by the richer countries of the world, distributed in a manner that would reflect their current position in regard to gold, more than is desirable in the long run and taking only limited account of the needs of the developing countries. On the other hand, it is highly unlikely that the outcome of current discussions (jointly between the IMF and the Group of Ten) would be to significantly impair the continued use of the two reserve currencies, rather than to supplement them. Reserve currencies cannot be "made" by fiat; though their use for reserve (or trading) purposes can, in time, be eliminated, it is almost equally difficult to unmake them at one stroke.

There is, however, the question of how far the relatively modest and slow improvement of the monetary system I have postulated for the near future will also include some strengthening of the reserve currencies themselves, so that even though they will be increasingly supplemented by other reserve assets, they can continue to fulfill their own function more satisfactorily. This question is bound up with the progress of the British and American balance of payments, a subject of more topical concern than can appropriately be discussed in the light of the time scale here relevant. Nevertheless, it is reasonable to suppose that if the modestly optimistic evolution here suggested does take place, that is, if no major clash occurs, some solution for those weaknesses in the reserve currencies that are not wholly due to a country's own current economic policies may also be expected. In particular, the next few years may well see some arrangement that would reduce the weight of British short-term debt as a factor that intensifies the impact of current balance-of-payments disequilibria. Similarly, some new arrangements are likely in due course in regard to dollar holdings: the regulation of American short- and long-term capital outflows, and the policies other countries pursue in regard to the conversion of dollar balances into gold. Nor is an agreement to change the price of gold as part of a combined and concerted series of measures to be excluded, though it is hardly likely to take place while the present, sharp differences of view between countries persist. In this connection mention also should be made of the impact on monetary matters which an enlargement of the European Economic Community to include Britain might have. I think that on the whole the result would be to promote and to hasten the favourable developments I have outlined here. At the moment of writing, the French Government's views on most of these matters resemble more what I have described as the gold school than do those of her partners in the EEC. It is hardly conceivable that a British Government would adopt these views. One must, therefore, suppose that a change in the French position would be a corollary—or consequence—of British entry into the EEC.

To sum up, I would expect (though this expectation does partake somewhat of hope) that in the next five to ten years perceptible progress will have been made toward the developments I have described above. If, but only if, this degree of international cooperation can be secured, then the way might be open to more substantial reforms thereafter. At this point the larger question which I have mentioned earlier obtrudes again, namely, what view of the proper relation between domestic policies and the international monetary order should underlie, or be an integral part of, the mechanics of that order? If a major clash can be avoided in the monetary sphere (and this is bound up with the preservation of a high degree of international cooperation in economic matters generally in the next few years), further progress on this crucial question might then become possible. But at this point, money, reserves, exchange-rate, and gold policies, as well as "multilateral surveillance" and all the other fancy theories of recent years, become involved with the more general and far-reaching issue of the proper organization of the international economy as a whole. This question may be put in another way: what degree (or purpose) of national sovereignty in economic matters is likely to be possible and appropriate when the end of the century looms near?

Chapter 14　Agenda for the International Economic Order

THE INTERNATIONAL PROBLEMS that have emerged in this study clearly are of great scope and urgency. The basic structure of economic, financial, and industrial relations between countries was elaborated some twenty years ago; it has been shown to be less effective than it was planned to be, and to have required much patching up to make it even moderately serviceable. This has raised particular issues of major direct significance. One is the tendency toward regional grouping, particularly in Europe. No less critical is the pace of development the less developed, *i.e.,* poorer, countries and regions of the world will be able to sustain in the future; related to this are their trading and financial relations with richer countries, which involve not only the international economy but the general organization of international relations. And, in many ways, all of these turn on the future manner, direction, and size of the scientific/technological revolution—and whether it makes possible movement of capital resources so they are generally available not only between rich and poor but also among the rich themselves. The monetary mechanism that both reflects and makes possible these international economic relations is in a state of reexamination. The results are still far from clear.

Are there any fundamental issues of an economic character that can be said to embrace all these particular problems? I believe they are reducible in the end to two main classes: the first, and more specifically economic, has to do with providing for sustained growth of the economy consistent with some degree of international financial stability. The summary question here is whether domestic growth can be harmonized between countries carrying on substantial economic relations to a degree which will ensure that major, sudden reversals of trend can be avoided. This may, at first sight, be thought to be primarily a problem affecting the advanced countries of the world. In fact, however, I believe that it cannot be tackled, let alone resolved, without involving the less developed countries as well.

The second class of questions involves political considerations related to the unresolved foreign policy and defense issues that at present plague the world. There are, of course, obvious and inevitable implications for economic affairs in the existence, or absence, of a reasonable prospect of peace. High on this list

174

in the light of modern economic thought is the impact of the size and specific character of resources devoted to defense on the problem of growth versus stability in its domestic and international aspects.

I have already described the question of growth and stability as the central one in general economic policy during the remainder of this century. The existence of this dichotomy was explicitly recognized in the international economic structure of the postwar world, which is based on the proposition that when countries trade their products and their services the further development of the economy of each is dependent in some measure on what is happening in the others.

If a country were a completely closed economy, it would still face the problem of the rate of growth it could maintain, but this would take on an entirely different form. Difficulties still could develop in respect of the technological, educational, and social factors that determine growth, or within economic components that develop at a different pace as growth proceeds. Inflationary and deflationary gaps might appear; and they might produce severe social and political strains if they resulted in violent changes in the distribution of the national product among different classes of the community.

Growth and Stability

In a developed international economy these strains are impounded in a wider series of variables and are thereby complicated and often aggravated. If domestic growth proceeds at a rate seriously incompatible with a relatively smooth domestic "adjustment process," that is, the maintenance of a reasonably harmonious relationship between productivity growth and factor incomes, this will be reflected in a change in the balance-of-payments situation. If this is substantial enough, it will trigger policy changes (primarily in the monetary and fiscal field) designed to accelerate the adjustment process. Changes in the balance-of-payments situation also may be produced by movements whose origins lie outside the country but which produce relative price or monetary movements which also call forth policy responses with consequences for the adjustment process. Thus, the existence of international economic ties adds another dimension to the concept of "stability" with which growth has to be harmonized.

It is easy to see how this factor may completely transform the way in which the problem of compatibility between growth and stability will present itself to the citizens concerned. Any process of substantial adjustment in the major economic aggregates involves unwelcome changes in the position of some classes of the community, in absolute terms or relative to the position of other classes. It does not matter how clearly the implications of these changes are perceived by those affected by them. Whether the damage is real or imaginary, whether it is short-lived and obviously necessitated by conditions for improvement in the longer term or not, resistance is sure to be forthcoming: the resultant clash of interests and opinions must be resolved in the political arena.

When the need for change is intensified, or caused, or, at least, made obvious by international considerations, the political reactions will be different. While general understanding of the implications of belonging to an international economy has grown greatly in recent decades, the force of nationalism is still strong enough to make it unlikely that any country faced with a severe adjustment problem as shown by balance-of-payments difficulties will not try to moderate it by some interference with the free functioning of its international economic relations. This has been recognized, as we have seen, in all the arrangements of recent years designed to make the international economy run freely and smoothly. Departures from the normal pattern have been allowed in a number of respects; quotas can be imposed on imports; other current transactions can be limited; exchange parities can be altered; capital transfers can be restricted; and short-term monetary movements can be made subject to certain conditions. But all these limitations on the free flow of trade in all its aspects are possible only in carefully defined circumstances; are subject to some degree of international supervision; and are permitted as temporary expedients only, to be reversed as soon as possible.

In critical moments, however, these permissible limits of departure from the accepted canons of international conduct tend to be strained, sometimes very severely. The theoretical basis for choosing the right course is by no means unambiguous. It is true that according to classical economic theory, complications in the harmonization of growth and stability arising from international trade are by no means to be regarded as an evil. International trade widens very substantially the possibilities for economic growth for all participating countries; this benefit cannot be had without some internal constraints; and recognition of this fact stands as a major achievement in human relations over the last two hundred years. In a number of important ways the area of autonomous national action has been restricted, the circumstances in which it still might be undertaken made the subject of international agreement, and devices introduced for reducing as far as possible any damaging consequences.

In principle, then, it is generally agreed that the solution for the problem of growth with stability in the international sphere precludes any reversion to more primitive forms of national autonomy in the economic organization among nations. It is also clear that there is enough dissatisfaction with the way in which the desiderata are currently reconciled to make untenable acceptance of present arrangements as the best of possible economic worlds. There is a considerable body of economic doctrine to show how, in a less than perfectly free world economy, economic benefit for an individual country may be had by resort to measures that would still further reduce the degree of freedom. But, on the whole, most economists are hostile to any drift to increasing control, which they believe could easily be engendered by measures that start out by providing only limited restrictions. Most economists, whatever their individual differences, maintain the classical internationalist tradition.

How, then, can the recurrent pressure for nationalist solutions, to which politicians of all countries are subject, be reconciled with the preservation, indeed the enlargement, of international economic relations? There are, of course, well-authenticated, historically proven, long-run benefits for all concerned in the resulting promotion of domestic growth. The present need is for methods that make it easier for those in charge of a country's affairs to resist restrictionist methods while at the same time taking into account the international effects of domestic policies. The provision of international credit facilities—liquidity—to meet temporary balance-of-payments difficulties and make the adjustment process less painful and more politically acceptable is of the utmost importance.

Given the amplitude of possible fluctuations, however, it is doubtful whether any improvement in this regard foreseeable for the near future would be adequate to remove the possibility of intolerable strains on domestic politico-economic objectives, which in all countries include maintenance of a high level of employment and of a respectable rate of growth. It is here, as we have already seen, that the advocates of exchange-rate flexibility deploy their strongest argument. In its most modest form it consists of widening the limits within which rates are allowed to fluctuate without calling forth intervention by the authorities. But most of those who are attracted by the advantages of greater flexibility would prefer the pegs to be removed entirely, although conceding that intervention from time to time by the authorities would still be necessary.

Both the provision of adequate liquidity to ease adjustments and the introduction of greater flexibility in exchange rates to the same end raise considerable problems of a political character. They are both designed to make the task of national authorities easier as they cope with the workings of an international system to permit them to respond to the pressures of those who vote for them and to the needs of those who do not. The question is whether this can be achieved under the kind of international political structure we have developed so far. Despite the relatively high degree of cooperation between sovereign governments that has been achieved and appears likely to continue, it is doubtful whether our institutions (in the complete sense, including organization, mechanism, procedure, and attitude) are yet adequate to the task without further restriction of national sovereignty.

There are, of course, those who would solve the problems of international relations by restricting the traditional scope of government intervention in economic matters; the task of reconciling national sovereignties, it is argued, would then be easier since the area over which sovereignty is exercised would itself have shrunk. In my view, this is not a probable course of development; I believe, therefore, that means must be found for conscious pooling of national sovereignties in areas we have hitherto left to informal cooperation.

The Common Approach

The problem of sovereignty also arises, perhaps even more acutely, in matters of international economic relations that go beyond the exchange of goods and services and the monetary mechanism required to sustain it. The movements of labour (and the planning of population developments that lie behind them); the flow of scientific and technological knowledge, the control and planning of its exploitation, and its relationship to the quality of human life; concerted, or at least harmonized, attitudes toward the growth of public as opposed to private consumption; the creation of some degree of a common approach to the international corporation as well as to international capital movements—all of these matters are rapidly assuming major importance, but they are still the subject of only haphazard and sporadic international consultation.

Much has been done in the field of aid to developing countries to enlarge and to formalize international cooperation. Yet here, too, the approach still largely opposes the developed countries to the underdeveloped, rather than providing a basis on which to evolve a common understanding of the problem of worldwide economic growth. Most people would readily agree that it is vital to maintain the momentum of world production and trade and that sustained growth in the developed and the developing countries mutually condition each other. It is now commonly understood that steady growth in the developed countries is essential to their ability to facilitate development in the poorer countries by trade and aid; and that bringing the underutilized resources of the poorer countries into the circle of world production and trade can help maintain growth in the developed countries without dangerous inflationary pressures. But the means for ensuring that this "virtuous circle" of aid is maintained are as yet extremely primitive and bedeviled on both sides by political complications.

Thus as one looks at the most pressing international economic problems one becomes increasingly conscious of the need for the massive development of a common approach. I repeat that it would be wrong to suppose that nothing significant has been done to this end. Indeed, in many ways the last two decades have seen a more determined attempt to intensify consultation and cooperation among nations than seemed remotely possible in the last few years before the war. Even in the difficult area of international monetary relations the network of arrangements developed around the Fund, the OECD, the Group of Ten, and so forth, covering long-term liquidity problems, short-term balance-of-payments support, and international supervision of domestic adjustment processes, stands as a monument to recognition of the essential interdependence of national economies.

There are, however, still many gaps, and the methods so far employed are still subject to severe limitations. In the end, the processes of intergovernmental negotiation can only carry matters forward to the limit of the understanding of governments of their true interests as they relate to the interests of others and to the political pressures under which, rightly or wrongly, they consider themselves to be labouring. Sometimes, this goes a very long way indeed. Interallied machinery during the war achieved a degree of combined action which made the existence of formal national sovereignty virtually irrelevant. The Marshall Plan operation was another example of most intimate cooperation without constitutional devices that required any formal abandonment of national sovereignty (although, in fact, a good deal of sovereignty was yielded in practice). But these examples are not a very good guide to the possibilities of that future when we must hopefully assume the absence of an overriding political factor in the accepted common objective of war or reconstruction.

Does this mean that we have to content ourselves with the slow pace of development that present methods of international cooperation seem likely to permit? When one considers the recrudescence of nationalist attitudes—often arising directly in the economic field and always reflected in it—and the deep-seated, historically based suspicion of supranational constructions, the answer would appear to be in the affirmative. Against this, however, is the actual experience of regional grouping, which is bound to produce a general impatience with nationalist economic restrictions. The European Economic Community, despite the buffetings it has suffered in the course of premature attempts to push integration into the quasi-political realm, represents a major rallying point for those who are pushing for the development of a common approach to the international economy and believe it can be accelerated and intensified by the use of novel devices. I have already committed myself to the view that EEC will survive and, in the long run, grow in strength.

Any regional grouping, of course, represents only partial progress; it is still subject to the pull of conflicting interests within that often militate against an enlightened view of wider problems; and in the case of EEC the effective reach is limited to Western Europe and a small part of it at that. Enlargement of the community to include Britain and other European countries would enhance its importance and its prospects—and this would be reflected in the great issues involving relations between Western and Eastern Europe, between the United States and Europe, and between the rich and poor countries. At present, progress on these more distant fronts is impeded by political considerations and by the economic consequences of heavy defense burdens to which these considerations give rise. We are left, then, with the truism that the evolution of integrated world economic order is indissolubly bound up with the reduction of political friction required for a peaceful world.

Conclusion

I HAVE PRESENTED in the preceding pages a selection of certain features of the economic order which I regard as of special importance in the evolution of that order during the rest of this century. Such a selection, as I conceded at the outset, inevitably reflects personal views and preferences. Much is necessarily left out. I have, for example, said nothing of substance about the impact of new methods of controlling various economic processes, made possible by the computer.

The results achieved by the application of computer techniques in the private economy, in the management of an individual firm or industry, are undoubtedly striking. This leads naturally to speculation on the early extension of similar methods to the national economy, with possibly startling results. Leaving aside projections that seem to border on the realm of science fiction (and their profound philosophical implications), one can readily envisage a considerable area of national decision-making facilitated by the computer. The storage of information and its retrieval is already making rapid progress in the sphere of governmental activity. The development of computerized command functions in stock control, or in determining cash balances versus investment decision, is advancing in private industry and will, no doubt, be applied to similar activities in the public sector.

I doubt, however, that in the next two or three decades problems in economic policy-making of the order of those I have been dealing with here are likely to become susceptible to solution by means of the new cybernetic science. I believe this to be so, even if one were to accept that development of inherent intelligence in the new machines, including even the capacity for self-improvement, were to make great strides in the phase immediately ahead.

Such developments may well make great improvements in the use of mathematical techniques of economic analysis by making it possible to speedily solve complicated mathematical problems that would otherwise require months or years of concentrated effort. More speculative is the effect of the use of these techniques in industrial production. There are those, already impressed by the

181

complexity of the modern process, who see in the growing role of the machine as controller of production and distribution further evidence of the subordination of individual human wants to the needs of a self-perpetuating, continually enlarging industrial process. A discussion of this view goes beyond the scope of this study. I would merely say that while I believe vigilance in regard to this aspect of growth to be doubtless necessary, I do not take a fundamentally pessimistic view of the ultimate relation between technological advance and the human personality.

Solutions to the fundamental economic problems I have tried to identify in the preceding pages involve considerations that go beyond the accepted limits of economic science. Therefore, they cannot be subjected exclusively to the methods currently available to economists, or likely to become available in the near future. It is to this wider problem of the relation between economics and economic policy that I must turn in concluding this essay.

A prerequisite to an understanding of this issue is a forecast of the framework of social organization in which economic problems will continue to appear and to be resolved.

If it could be supposed, for example, that through the continued growth of industrial units, or through the use of the regulatory powers of the state, or through some change in human attitudes, the element of competition in the economic order were to be seriously curtailed, or even eliminated, a most important "datum" of the whole socioeconomic process would be altered. Despite the evidence of organizational changes in industry that do, from time to time, seriously alter (and apparently impair) competition, I doubt whether there is any real evidence of a long-run tendency for the competitive drive as such to wane. The fact is that new forms of competition are constantly springing up; and if one is prepared to recognize these for what they are and not to suppose competition to be confined to the model of the elementary textbook, one can, I believe, safely assume that it will continue to be a powerful economic factor. Indeed there is evidence that the more centrally planned economies are evolving in a direction that, through emphasis on individual enterprises, is deliberately intended to strengthen the element of competition.

More difficult to evaluate are the sociopsychological data that the economist will find at the back of the economic process. It is quite possible that the acquisitive instinct, the attitude toward different types of work, and the desire for accumulation of a fortune to "leave behind" will undergo further changes in the next few decades as they have in the past. Taxation of incomes, capital gains, and inheritances have already brought about many changes, particularly in the United States and Britain. These will continue to have their effects not only on attitudes but also on organizations—the growth of philanthropic foundations, the changes in the structure of capital markets, and so on. Nevertheless, it is hard to see why these changes should, in the near future, fundamentally alter the character of the data that economists have to take into account. There is too much historical evidence of the very slow pace of change in these. matters (including such statistical tests as the great stability of the curve of personal income distribution) to lead one to expect revolutionary developments in three decades or so.

I would expect, then, the general framework to remain broadly the same— that is, of a "mixed economy," in which the line of demarcation between the public and the private sector of enterprise and between public and private consumption will be shifting from time to time. Shifts will not necessarily always be in the same direction, but I would expect the trend in the advanced countries to be toward an extension of public consumption and some greater concern with the relationship between private business and public authority in areas (for example, those requiring the application of highly advanced technology) in which the state is bound to play a dominant part. Given the observed trend toward greater concern for consumer choice and competitiveness of individual enterprises in the centrally planned economies, the distinguishing marks of the two systems will become more blurred, at least in the economic sphere.

If this broad picture is reasonably accurate, the problem of the relation between the economist and the policy maker will continue to be much as it is now. It is, therefore, important to be clear about the factors that enter into decision-making in economic policy and to recognize the limits of the contribution that the economic scientist can make to this process. I have said enough at earlier stages to show that I believe that contribution to have been very great indeed in the last twenty or thirty years; and there is no reason to think that this trend will not continue. The relative ease with which the transition from a war to a peace economy was accomplished twenty years ago, compared with the trials and tribulations after World War I; the attitudes revealed in the Marshall Plan and in the policies relating to the development of less advanced countries; the high level of monetary cooperation achieved in recent years—all of these developments are eloquent testimony to the achievements of the "New Economics" in the field of policy. One can be reasonably confident that never again shall we see masses of the workless and the hungry march on London or Washington; nor, despite some current discontents, is it likely that we shall suffer the hyperinflation that ravaged so much of Europe in the early Twenties. The credit for this will rightly go to Keynes and his followers.

Nevertheless, there are difficulties and dangers in excessive reliance on what can be achieved by fiscal and monetary management. I have cited some of these, and they are recognized—albeit implicitly—in the search for new policies to supplement the accepted macroeconomic concepts. The goal of reconciling the conflicting objectives of steady growth, high levels of employment, and domestic and international financial stability remains elusive and will require continual search for new policy devices.

To this end, means will have to be drawn from fields other than those susceptible to economic analysis. At many points there are "residues" behind economic reasoning; and the presence of value judgments, usually unspoken and often not even explicitly realized, inevitably determines the limits of policy. The path of wisdom surely lies not in attempting the impossible task of "automating" the process of economic analysis and management so that the prescriptions for policy can be read off on a dial, but rather in bringing into the open and subjecting to critical analysis the preconceptions and prejudices, the value postulates, and the romantic "illusions" that are the inevitable admixtures of economic reasoning.

This does not mean that pure economic analysis is to be regarded as at all times superior. An interesting example of its limits can be seen in current attitudes in Britain on membership in the European Economic Community. At the time of writing, it appears that a large majority of British economists are very dubious about the supposed economic benefits, if not wholly hostile to the proposition. Even if one discounts political considerations (which can hardly be eliminated in practice), there are certainly adequate grounds under the prevailing theory of international trade for reaching such a conclusion. However, an equally substantial majority of British industrialists appear to hold exactly the opposite view. Where is the choice to lie? Given the fact that we do not yet know nearly enough about the real determinants of the urge for innovation, of investment decisions, or of competitive drives, would it not be wiser to accept the verdict of those who actually operate the economy rather than of those who analyze it? I think so; though there is of course much history to prove that this is not always the right choice!

What then is the proper role of the economist as a theorist in practical affairs? This is perhaps the most difficult question of all to answer; it has plagued thinkers throughout the ages. The Platonic ideal of the Philosopher-King calls for a fusion of functions; in this instance it would be those of the economist and the politician. Yet there is much to be said for the other view, expressed by Kant, who held that it is neither to be expected nor desired that "kings should become philosophers or philosophers kings," since the possession of power inevitably corrupts the judgment of reason. A partnership, uneasy at times, is probably the best that can be achieved in the present state of our knowledge. This does not, however, mean that the economist should not have decided views—and express them—on the great issues of public policy. If he becomes a moral philosopher in the process, he should still try to keep the different considerations that are brought to bear on a problem sufficiently clear so as not to impair his role as an economist.

On one particular issue—the greatest that mankind faces in the next few decades—he must clearly speak out. In so doing, he will follow the example of the greatest of the economists of the past who long ago determined the precondition for the achievement of any of the worthwhile objectives of economic endeavour: the creation of a one-world economy.

It is highly unlikely that this great goal will be attained during the period here under review. The question is: "Will a real beginning have been made?"

Index

187